D1735257
ORIGAMI
Chic
A GUIDE TO
FOLDABLE FASHION
SOK SONG
Capstone Young Readers
a capstone imprint

Origami Chic is published by Capstone Young Readers
A Capstone Imprint
1710 Roe Crest Drive
North Mankato, Minnesota 56003
www.mycapstone.com

Library of Congress Cataloging-in-Publication Data is available on the Library of Congress website.

ISBN: 978-1-62370-771-2 (paperback)

Summary: Thirty original fashion origami models from origami master Sok Song, complete with written instructions and illustrated diagrams.

Editor: Alison Deering
Designer: Aruna Rangarajan

Image Credits: Photographs by Capstone Studio: Karon Dubke, Sarah Schuette, studio stylist; Marcy Morin, studio scheduler; Author photo by Alexandra Grablewski
Folding Papers Textures: Shutterstock: Alex Gontar, AlexTanya, Anastasiia Kucherenko, EvenEzer, Gorbash Varvara, Jut, Kumer Oksana, Love_Kay, maralova, Maria_Galybina, Mirinka, NataliaKo, OJardin, OKing, Ola-la, Olga Borisenko, Olga Lebedeva, Picksell, Prezoom.nl, Regina Jershova, SalomeNJ, Studio Lulu, Sunny Designs, surachet khamsuk, Svetolk, tukkki, TabitaZn, Transia Design, Vikpit, wacomka, WorkingPENS, Yudina Anna; Sok Song
Design Elements: Shutterstock: AlexTanya, Altana8, Baksiabat, BeatWalk, Gorbash Varvara, Iveta Angelova, Nadin3d, NataliaKo, OJardin, SalomeNJ, Regina Jershova, shorena, Svetlana Prikhnenko, Zubada

Printed and bound in China.
010015R

For my darling, beautiful, and fashionable nieces, Lexy and Evelyn! — Uncle Sok

TABLE OF CONTENTS

TOPS

BOTTOMS

DRESSES

SUMMERWEAR AND OUTERWEAR

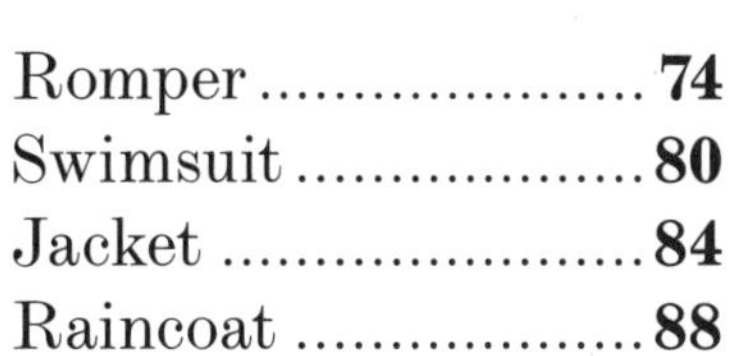

ACCESSORIES

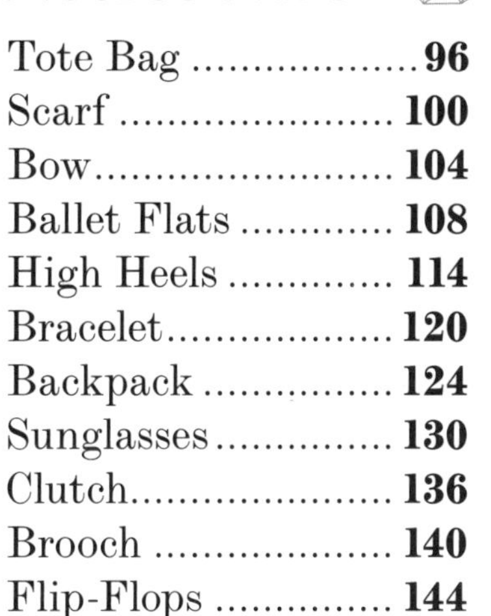

Making crisp, accurate creases is the key to a clean and polished origami model. Use these lines and symbols to help you and guide your creases. Don't worry if you've made a mistake or something seems confusing—just back up a couple of steps and try again.

LINES AND DASHES

VALLEY FOLD

MOUNTAIN FOLD

CREASE LINE

HIDDEN LINE

ACTION SYMBOLS

FOLD

FOLD AND UNFOLD

UNFOLD

FOLD BEHIND
(MOUNTAIN FOLD)

PLEAT

REPEAT

TURN OVER

SQUASH

MAGNIFIED VIEW

90° ROTATE

DISTANCE

FOCAL POINTS

DIFFICULTY LEVEL

EASY

MEDIUM

CHALLENGING

COMMON FOLDS

VALLEY FOLD

Fold the paper to the front so the crease is pointing away from you, like a valley.

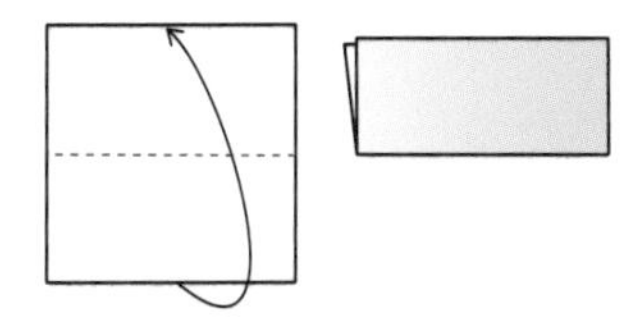

MOUNTAIN FOLD

Fold the paper to the back so the crease is pointing up at you, like a mountain.

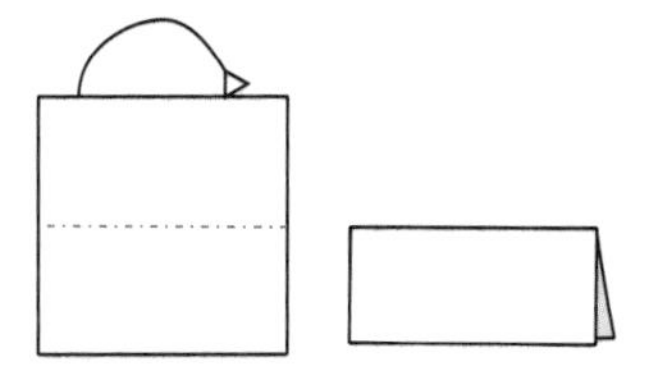

INSIDE REVERSE FOLD

Fold the flap or corner to the inside, reversing one of the creases.

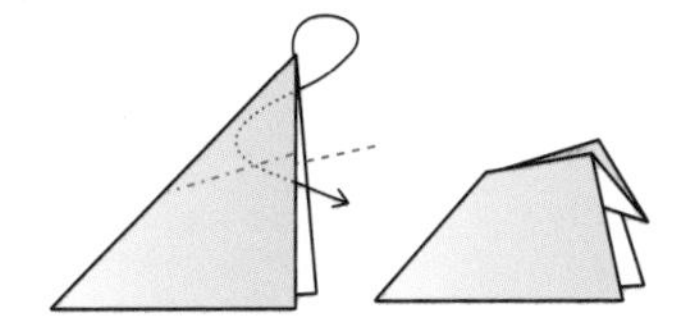

OUTSIDE REVERSE FOLD

Fold the flap or corner to the outside, reversing one of the creases.

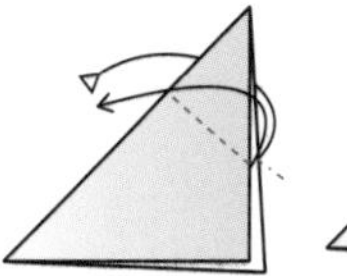

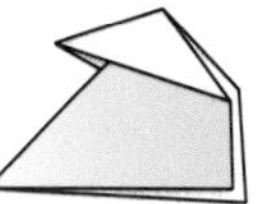

SQUASH FOLD

Open the pocket and squash down flat. Most often, this will be done on the existing pre-creases.

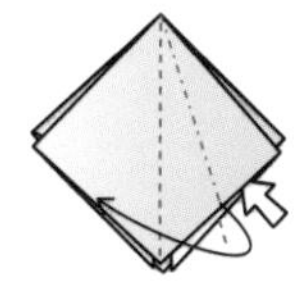

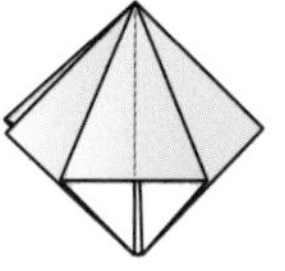

PLEAT FOLD

Fold the paper to create a pleat.

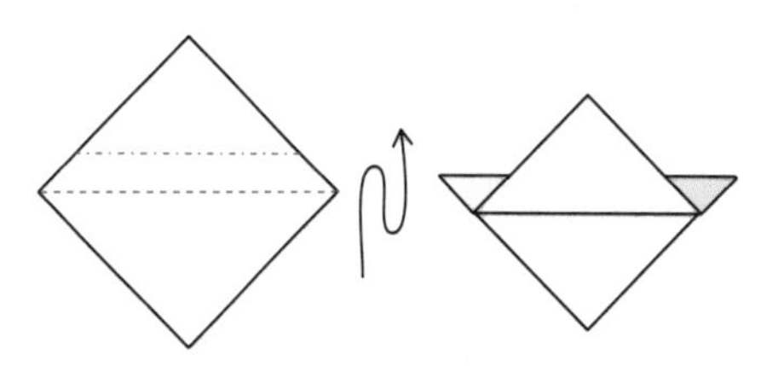

Tops

Sweater

A sweater can be a functional piece, keeping you warm and cozy in cooler weather, but it can also add a quick pop of color to any outfit. This simple paper cardigan uses both sides of the paper to create contrast. Try experimenting with the angle of the sleeves and the length of the collar/lapels to see what proportions you get in the finished product.

STYLE TIPS

- Toss a sweater over a T-shirt or blouse for a cool, layered look.
- Pair with jeans and flats for a casual outfit or a dress and heels for a fancier ensemble.

HOW TO FOLD

1

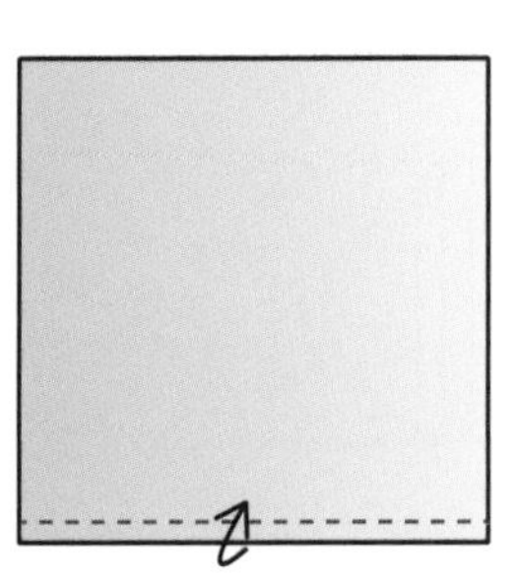

Fold a thin rectangle at the bottom of your paper to create a border for the lapels. (Note: The side facing up will become the outside of your sweater; the side facing down will be the lapels.)

2

Turn the paper over.

3

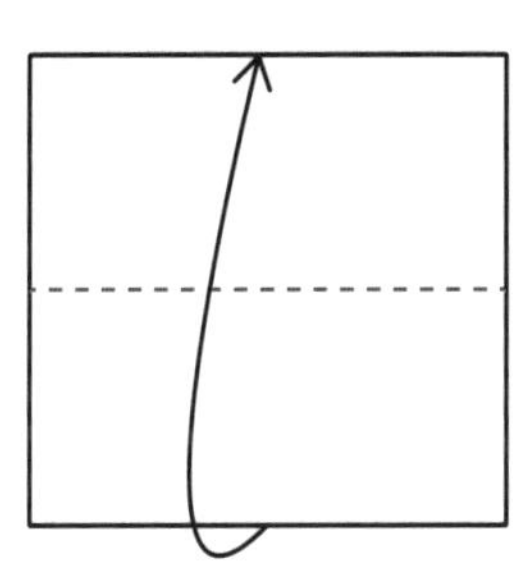

Fold the paper in half horizontally.

4

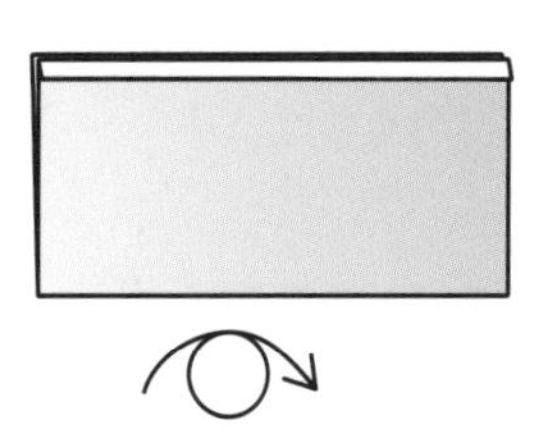

Turn the paper over.

5

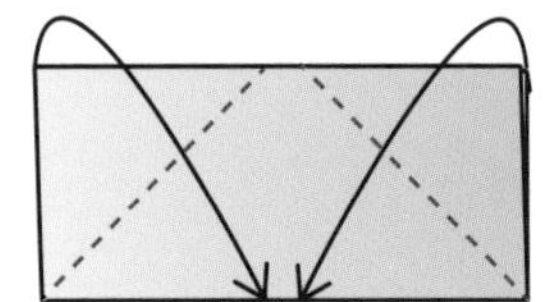

Fold the top corners down to the bottom, using both layers of paper. (Note: The corners will not meet in the center because of the border folded in step #1.)

6

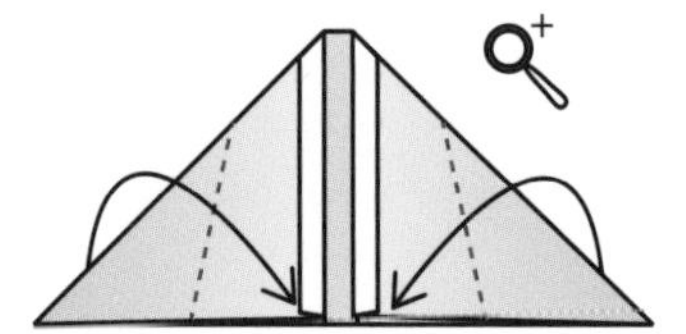

Fold the side corners in at an angle to create the sleeves. (Note: The next step is a magnified view.)

7

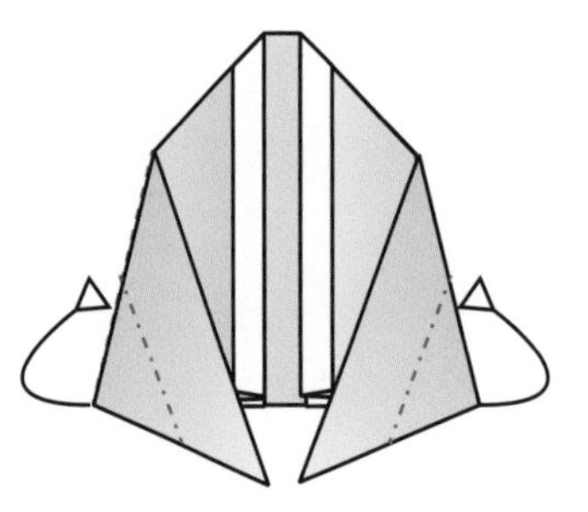

Mountain fold the side corners to the back to shape the sleeves. (See the next step for reference.)

8

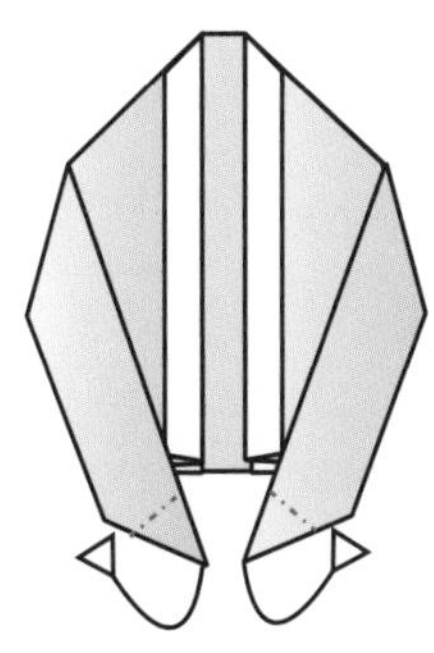

Blunt the tips of the sleeves by folding to the back, or tuck them in using an inside reverse fold.

9

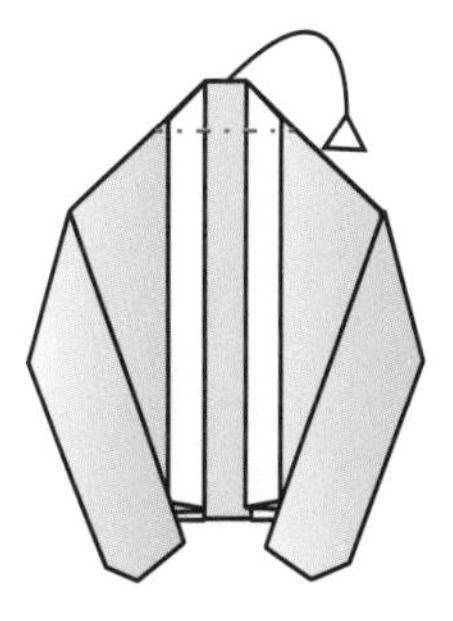

Optional: Fold the top section to the back to shape the collar, or leave it up depending on your preference.

Enjoy your finished sweater!

Blouses can come in many shapes and silhouettes, from sleek and fitted to loose and flowing. This paper version is accentuated by a contrasting collar and lapels, as well as modern, trendy cap sleeves and a peplum waist. You can play around with the size of the sleeves and collar by increasing or decreasing the size of the folds in steps #17 and #20. You can also eliminate the peplum by mountain folding the sides to the back on the finished model.

HOW TO USE:

- Use your blouse to decorate the front of a fashion-forward gift card.
- Let your paper blouse act as a stylish gift tag on a box or bag.

HOW TO FOLD

1

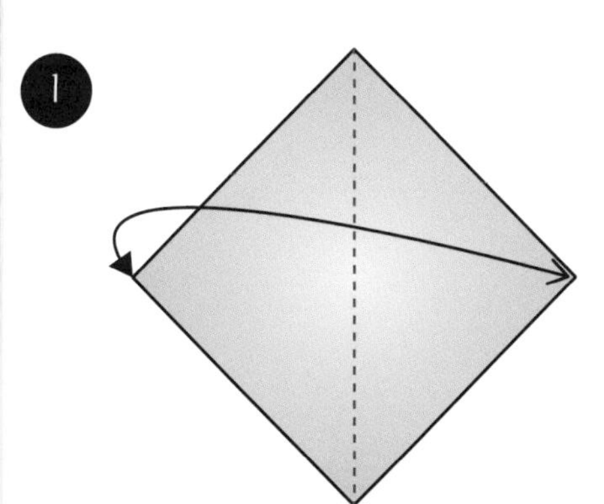

Fold the paper in half diagonally and then unfold. (Note: The side facing up will become the bulk of the blouse; the side facing down will become the collar and lapels.)

2

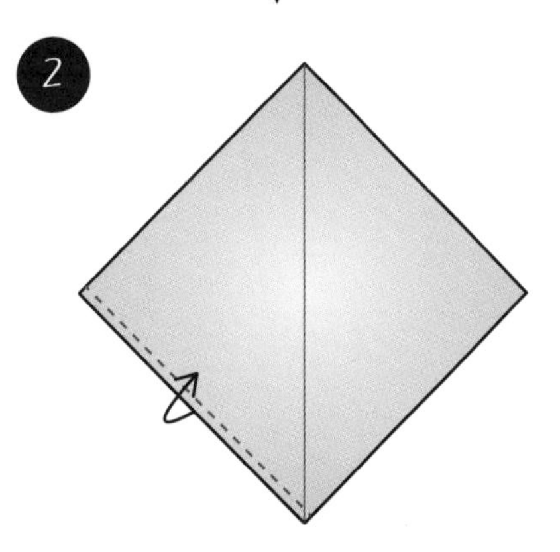

Fold a narrow rectangular flap on the bottom left side.

3

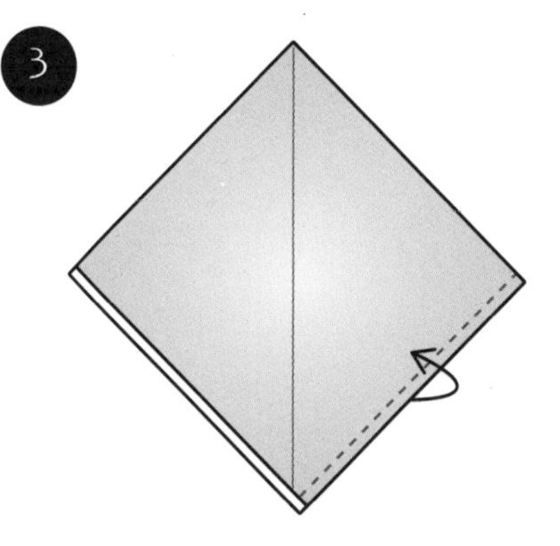

Fold an equally narrow rectangle on the bottom right side.

4

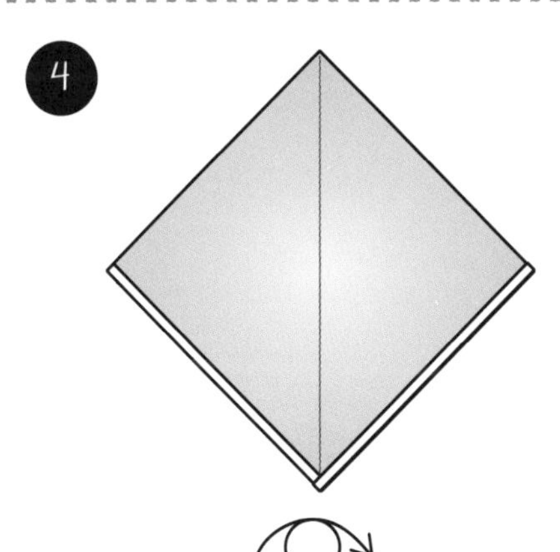

Turn the paper over.

5

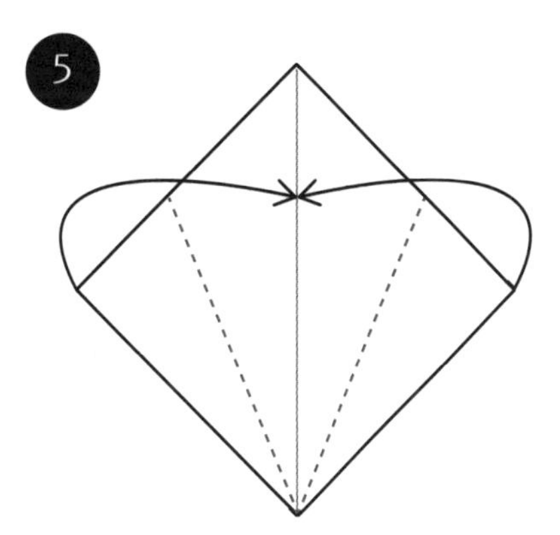

Fold the sides into the center crease. (Note: There will be a small, loose flap on the tip at the back. This will be folded inside later.)

6

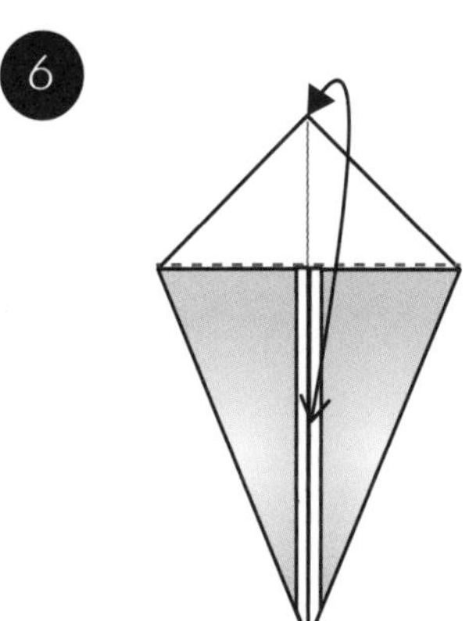

Valley fold the top triangle down and then unfold.

7

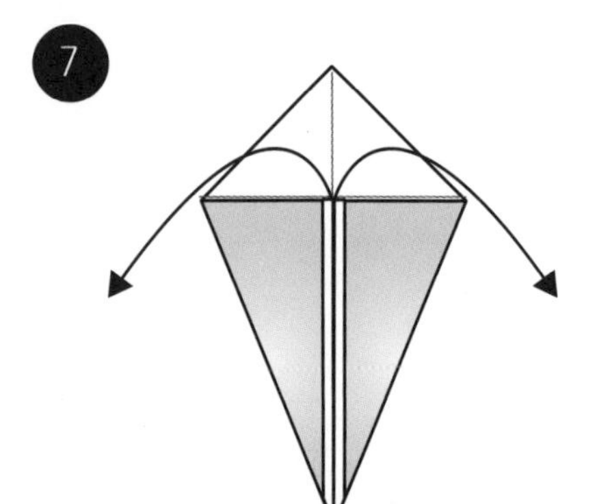

Unfold the side flaps.

8

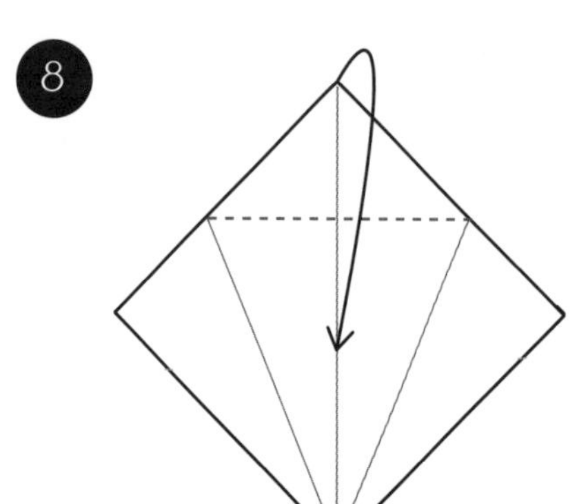

Fold the top triangle down on the existing pre-crease.

9

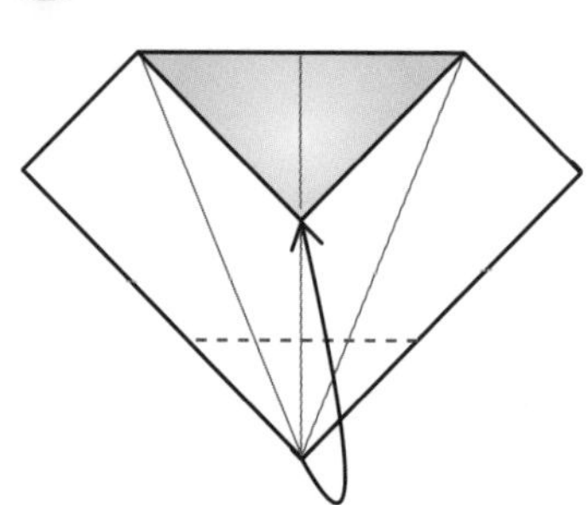

Fold the bottom point up to meet the tip of the top triangle.

10

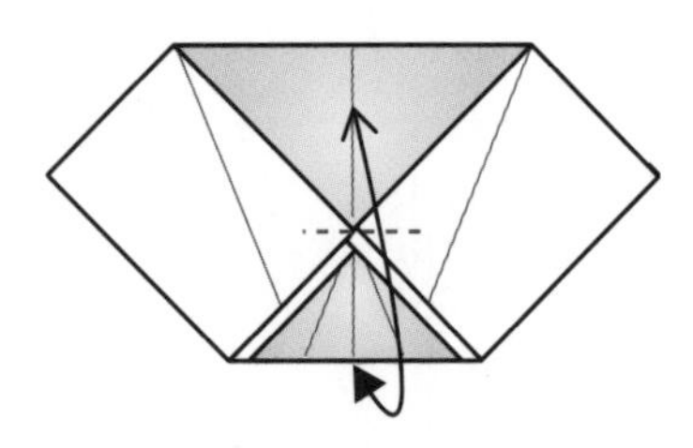

Pinch fold a narrow landmark crease where the two tips meet and then unfold.

11

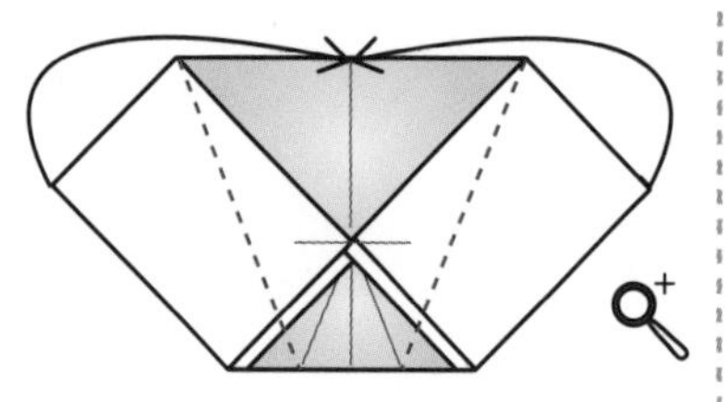

Fold the sides into the center on existing pre-creases. (Note: The next step is a magnified view.)

12

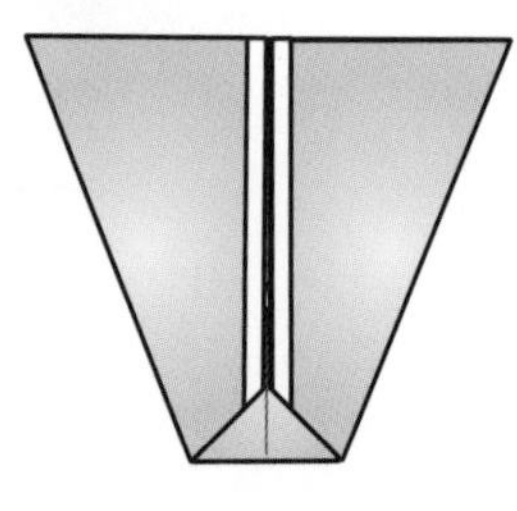

Turn the paper over.

13

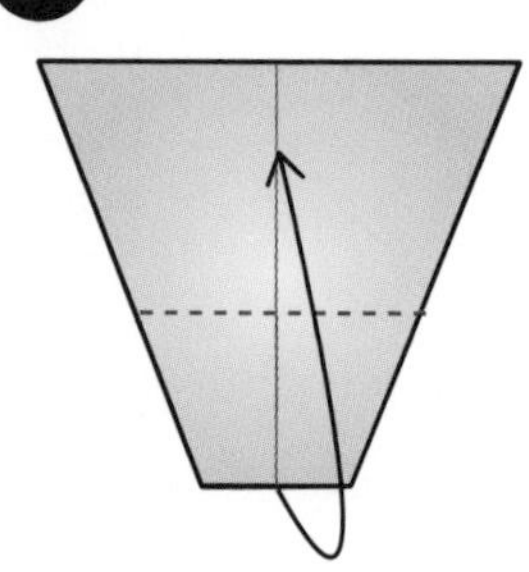

Valley fold the bottom edge up using the landmark crease made in step #10 as a reference.

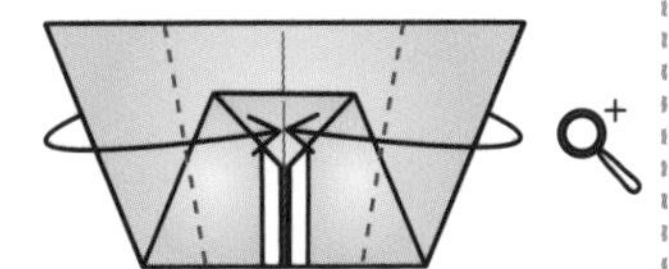

Fold the side edges into the center. (Note: The next step is a magnified view.)

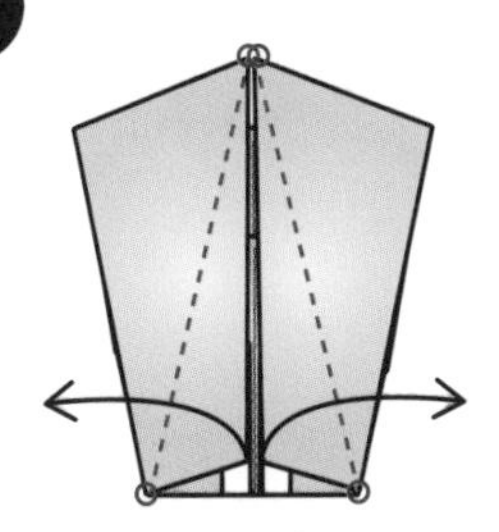

Fold the top flaps out on a diagonal. (Note: Fold from the outside bottom corner to the upper inside corner.)

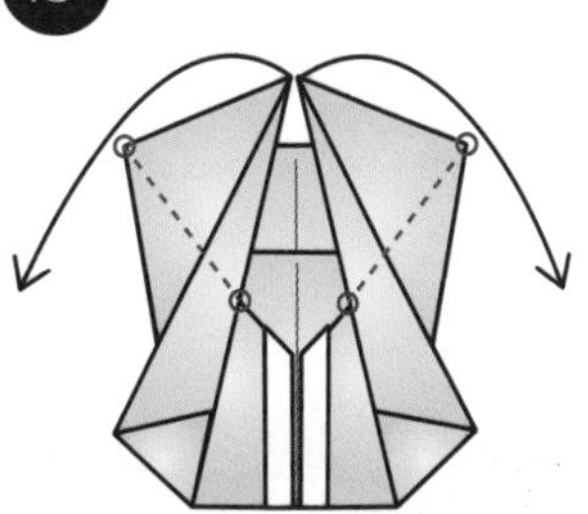

Fold the top corner flaps down to form the sleeves. Use both the corners and the circled point for reference.

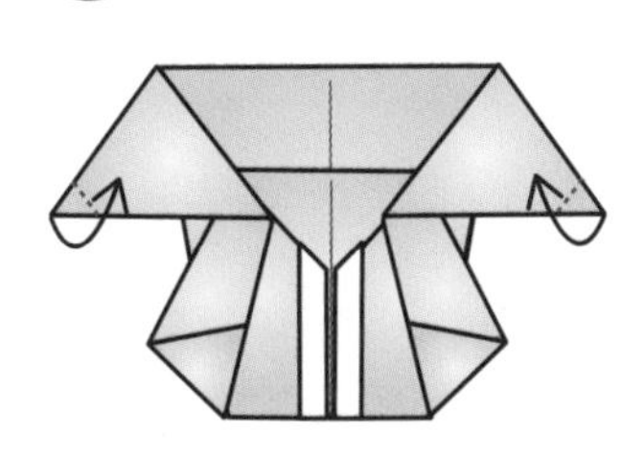

Fold in and blunt the tips on each side to shape the sleeves.

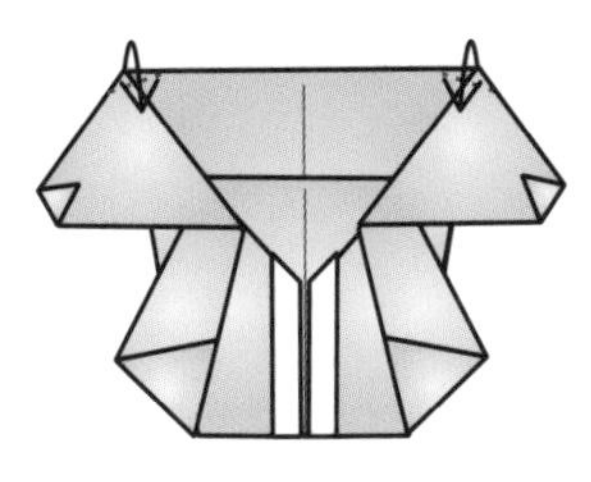

Fold in and blunt the top corners to shape the shoulders.

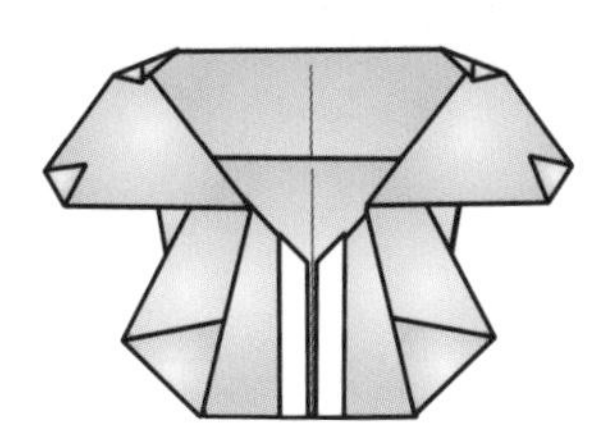

Turn the paper over.

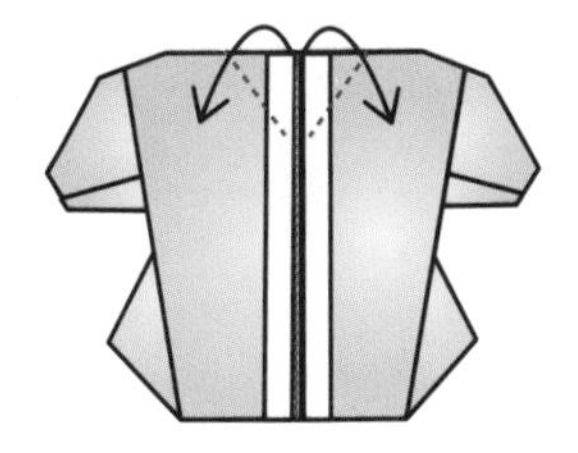

Valley fold the top center corners down to make the contrasting collar.

Enjoy your finished blouse!

Crop Top

Crop tops are a trend that keeps coming back. A crop top is a great, versatile garment because it can be either dressy or casual. This paper version has fun color-change sections for the midriff and lapels. Try folding in a variety of papers and patterns to reflect a dressier or more casual style.

STYLE TIPS

- Pair your crop top with shorts, a skirt, or high-waisted pants.
- Layer it over another top or blouse.

HOW TO FOLD

1

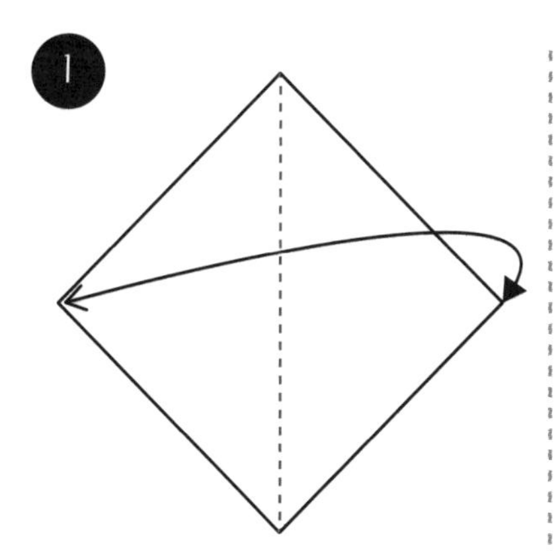

Fold the paper in half diagonally and then unfold. (Note: The side facing down will become the bulk of the crop top; the side facing up will be the contrasting sections.)

2

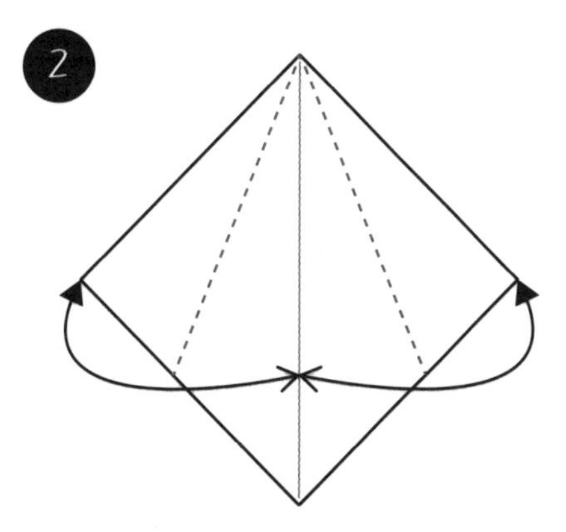

Fold the side edges into the center crease and then unfold.

3

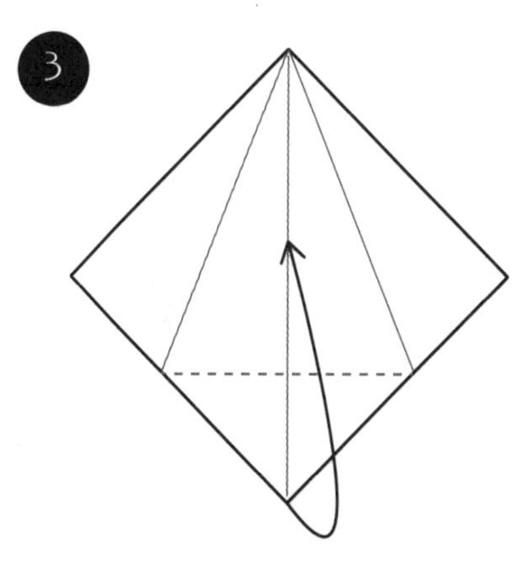

Fold the bottom triangle up at the bottom of the side creases.

4

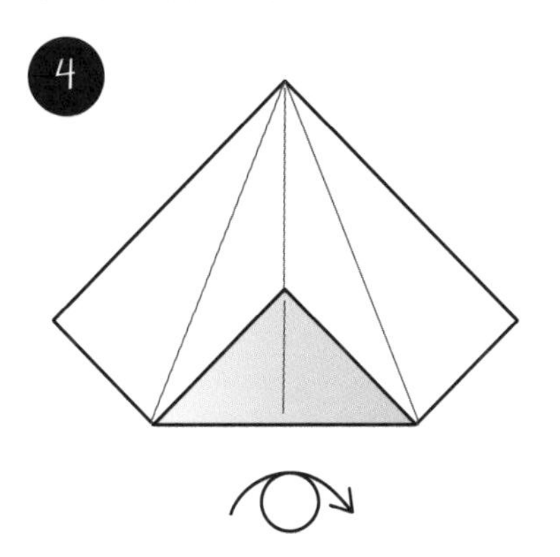

Turn the paper over.

5

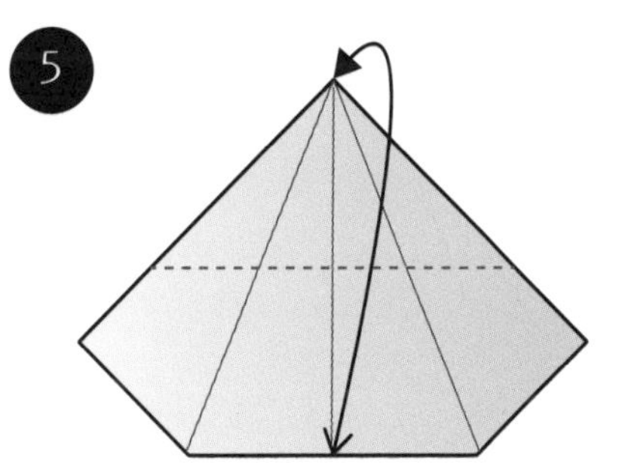

Fold the top corner down to the bottom edge and then unfold.

6

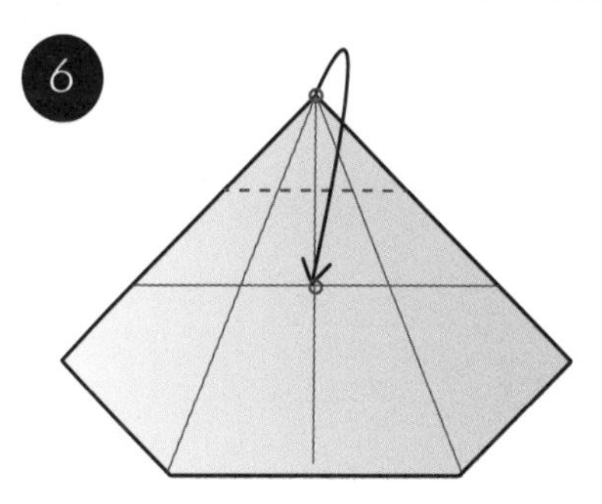

Fold the top corner down to the crease made in the previous step.

7

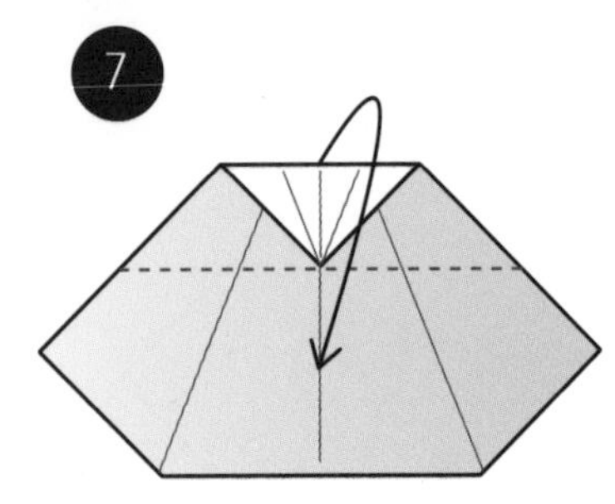

Fold the top section down on the existing pre-crease.

8

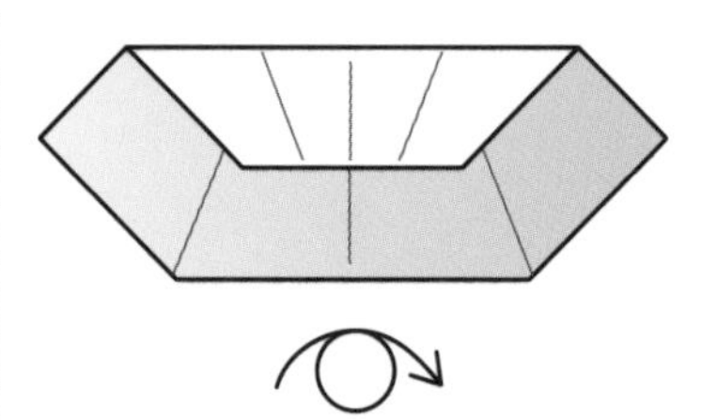

Turn the paper over.

9

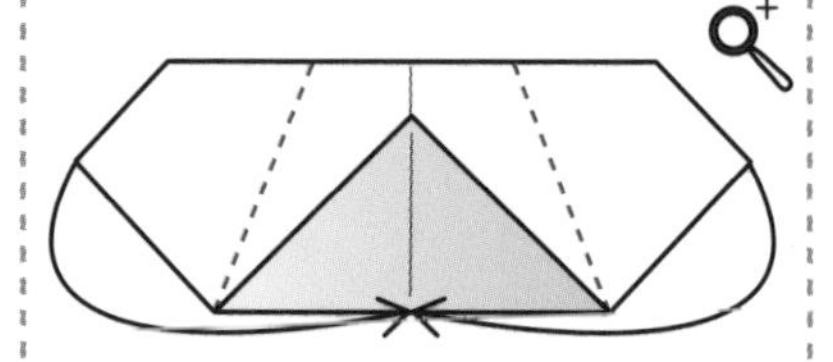

Fold both sides into the center on the existing pre-creases. (Note: The next step is a magnified view.)

10

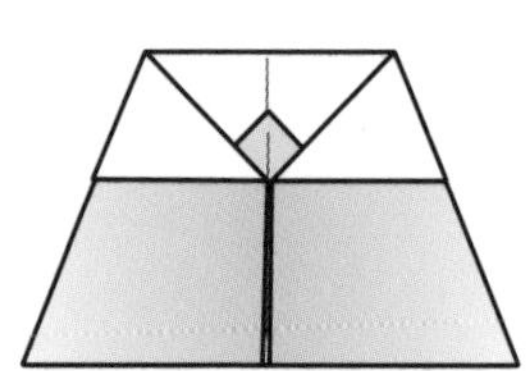

Rotate the paper 180°.

11

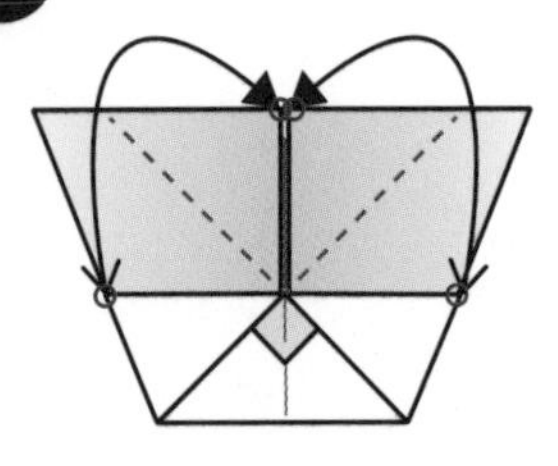

Using just the top layer of paper, fold the center corners down and out and then unfold. (Use the circled points for reference.)

12

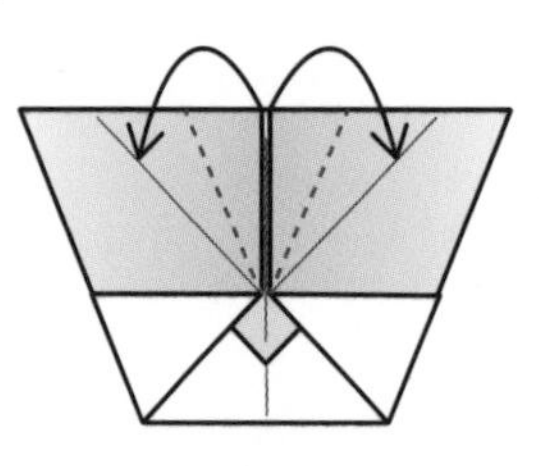

Fold the center corners out to the creases made in the previous step.

13

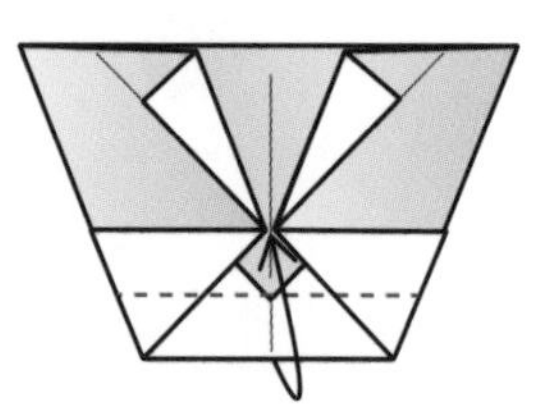

Fold the bottom edge up to where the paper changes color.

14

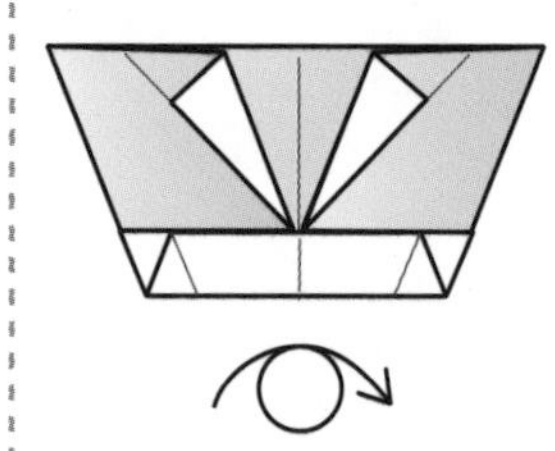

Turn the paper over.

15

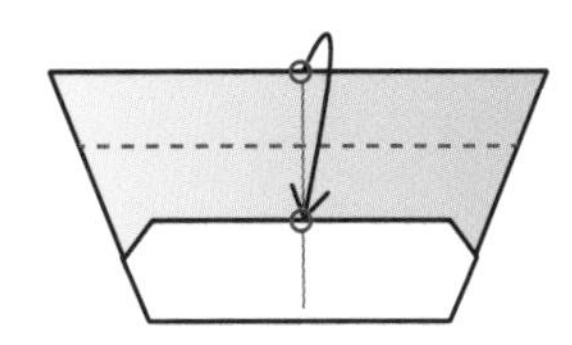

Fold the top edge down (through all layers of paper) to where the paper changes color.

16

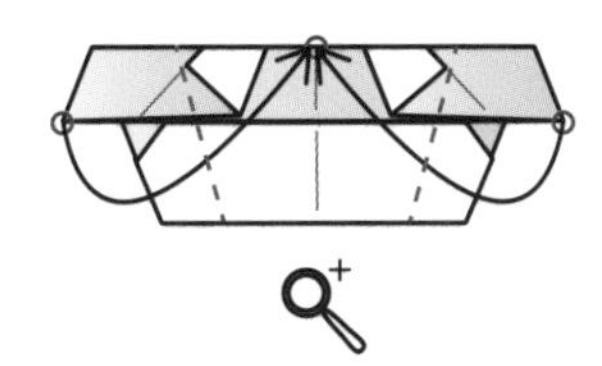

Fold the side corners in so they meet in the center at the top edge. (Note: The next step is a magnified view.)

17

Fold the triangle points back along the folded edge and then unfold.

18

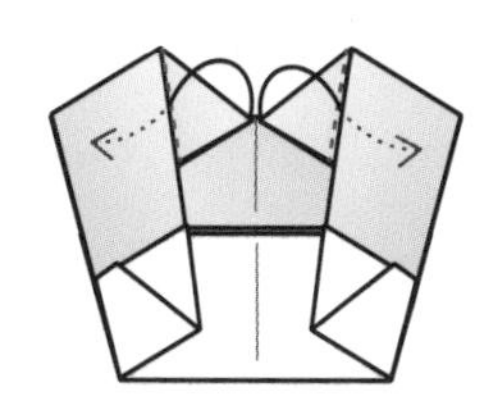

Tuck the triangle points inside the upper layer of paper. (Note: This is not an inside reverse—just tuck them under.)

19

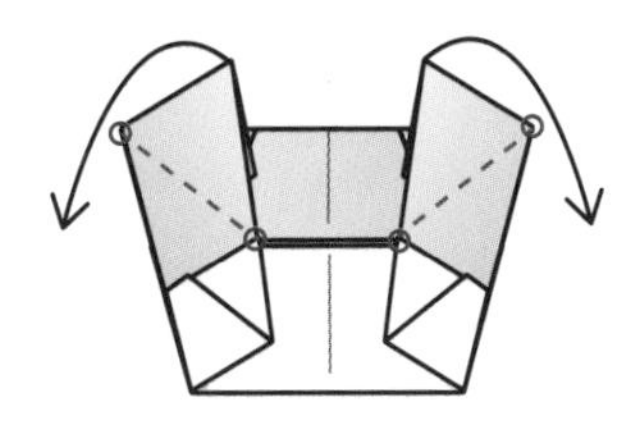

Fold the corners out along the indicated points to create the sleeves.

20

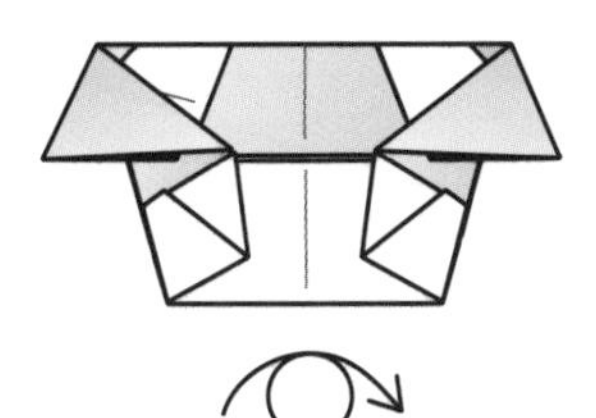

Turn the paper over.

21

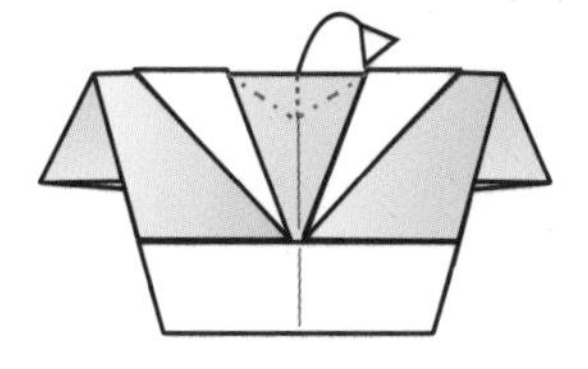

Optional: Shape the bodice with a V-shaped mountain fold.

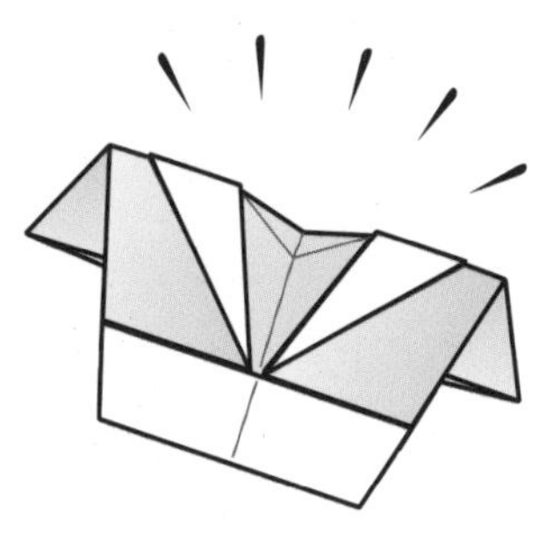

Enjoy your finished crop top!

T-shirt

T-shirts are one piece of clothing that never seems to go out of style. From basic cotton tees to luxurious silk styles, T-shirts can be worn in an endless number of ways. This paper version features an edgy pattern and a contrasting collar, but you can also try folding it in a floral paper for a sweeter style. Try several different patterns to make it your own!

STYLE TIPS

- Shorts or jeans pair perfectly with a T-shirt for a casual, relaxed outfit.
- Tuck your T-shirt into a high-waisted skirt for a fashionable, but still comfortable, look.
- Use your T-shirt as a layering piece; toss a sweater over the top to stay warm!

HOW TO FOLD

1

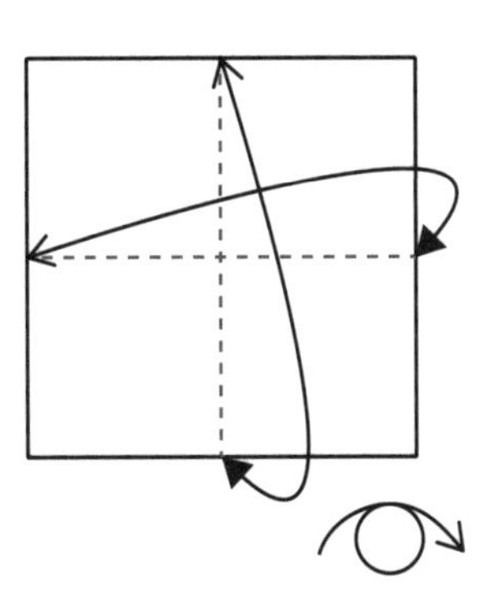

Fold the paper in half in both directions and then unfold. Turn the paper over. (Note: The side facing down will become the outside of your T-shirt.)

2

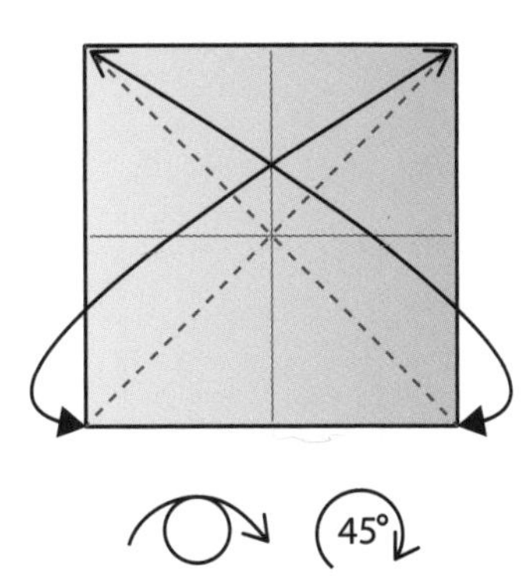

Fold the paper in half diagonally in both directions and then unfold. Turn the paper back over, and rotate it 45°.

3

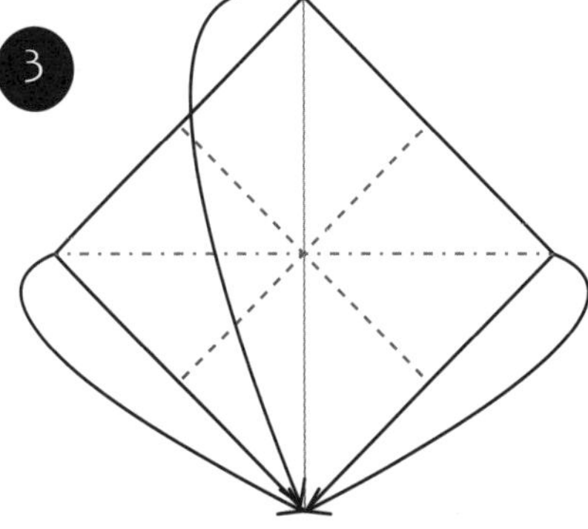

Collapse the model by bringing the top, left, and right corners together at the bottom using the existing pre-creases.

4

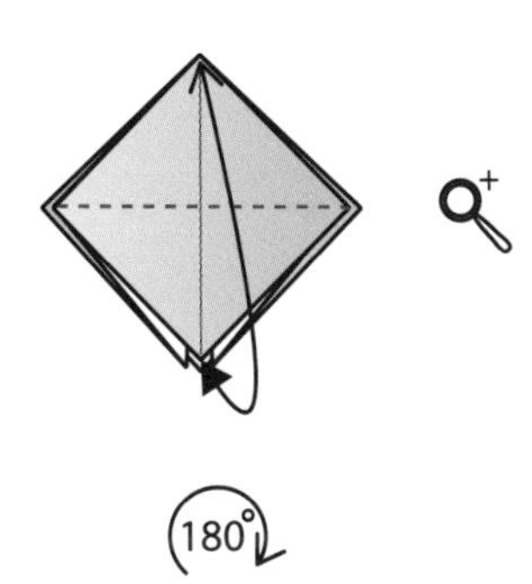

Fold the bottom corner up to the top and then unfold. Rotate the model 180° so the open section is at the top. (Note: The next step is a magnified view.)

5

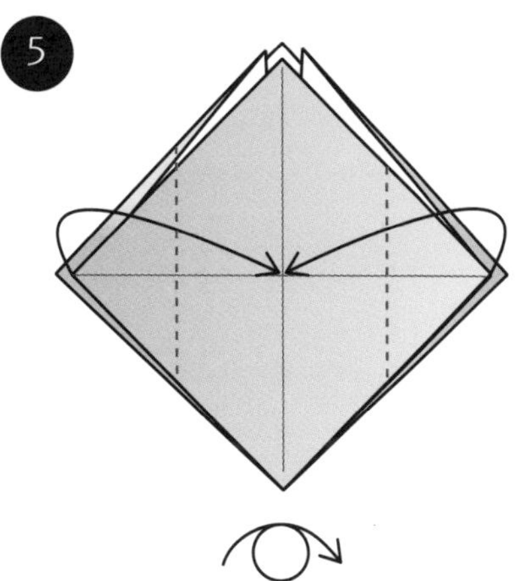

Using just the top two layers of paper, fold the side corners into the center crease. Turn the paper over.

6

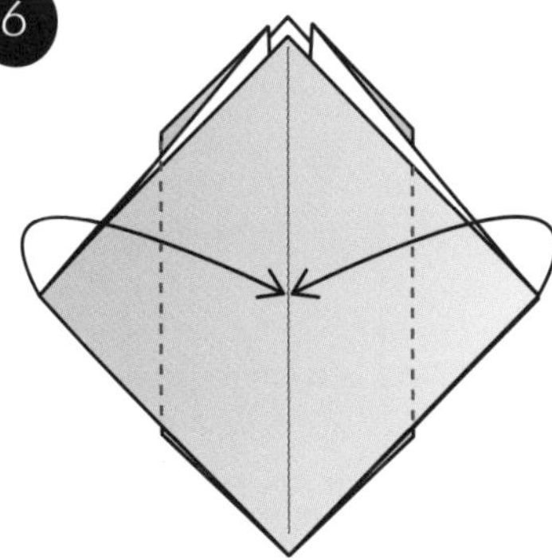

Fold the side corners into the center crease on this side, again using just the top two layers of paper.

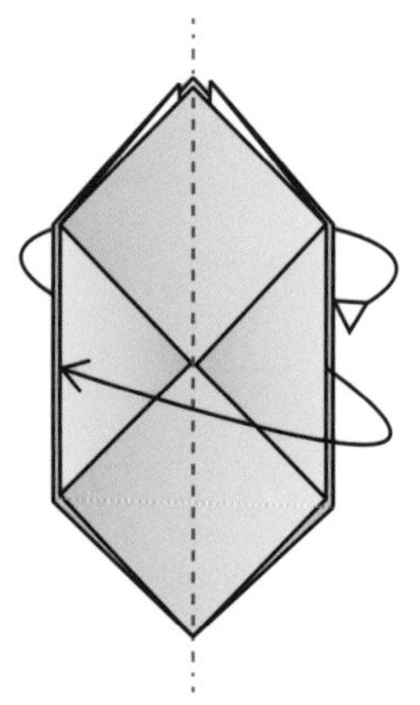

Rearrange the layers so the corners folded in the previous steps are hidden in between the layers. (See the next step for reference.)

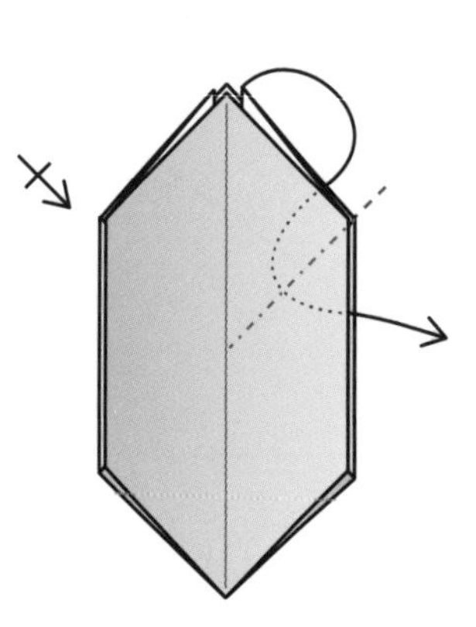

Pull the top, innermost corner out and down as far as you can. Use the folded triangles on the inside as a guide. Repeat on the opposite side.

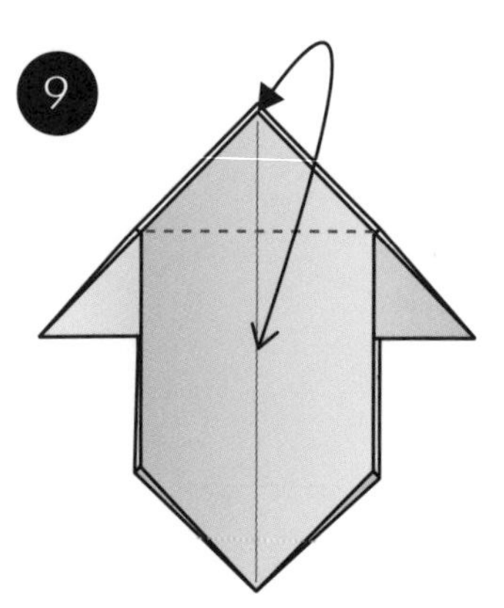

Fold the top triangles down (in both the front and back) and then unfold.

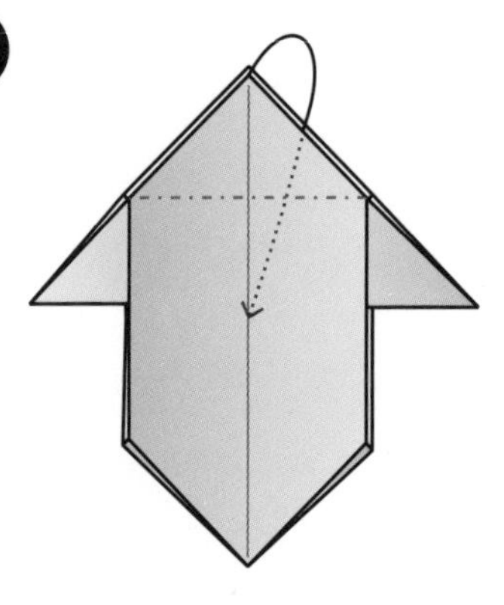

Mountain fold and tuck in the front layer so it is hidden inside.

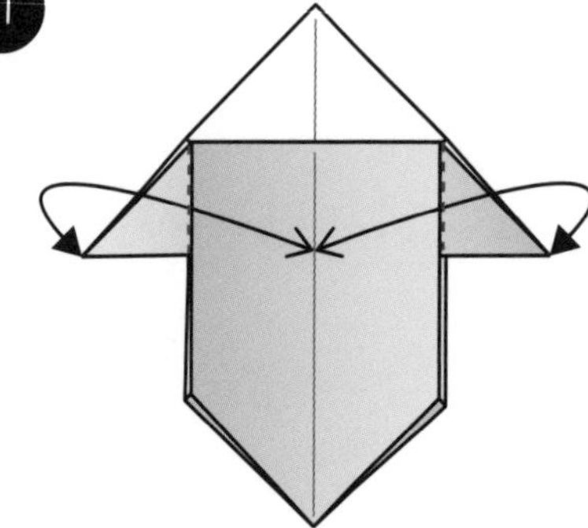

Fold the side corners in and then unfold.

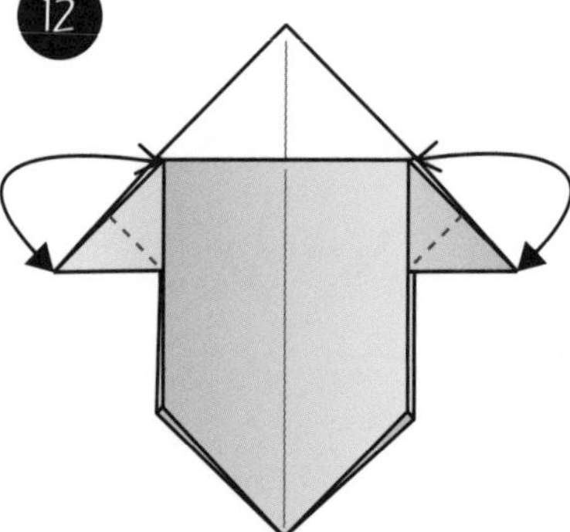

Fold the corners up, creasing the triangles in half, and then unfold.

13

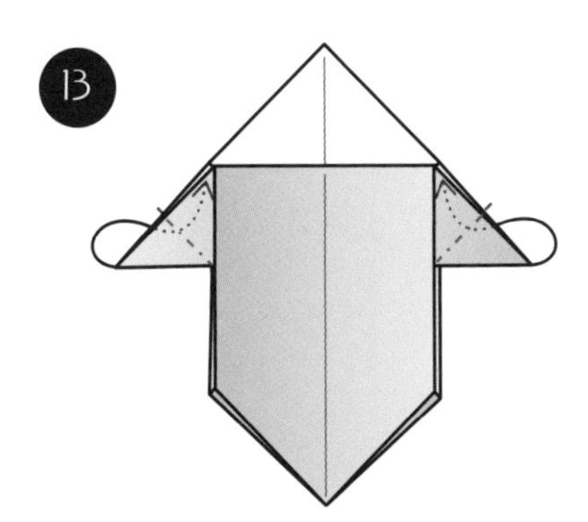

Open and then inside reverse the sides using the pre-creases, tucking the inner corners of the square inside. (Note: Just hide half of the square so a small triangle still sticks out.)

14

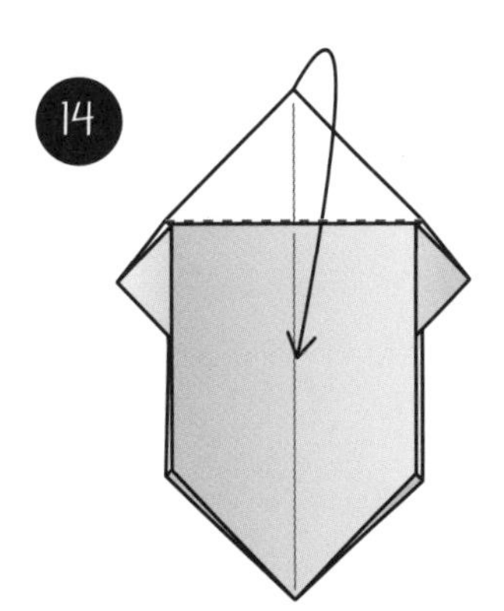

Fold the top triangle down over the front on the existing crease.

15

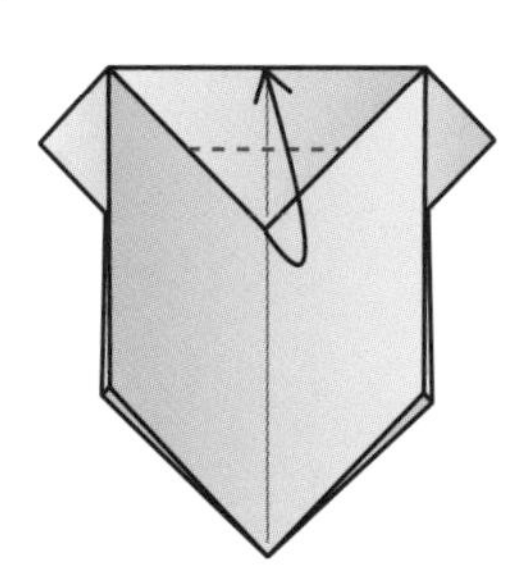

Fold the tip of the triangle back up to the top.

16

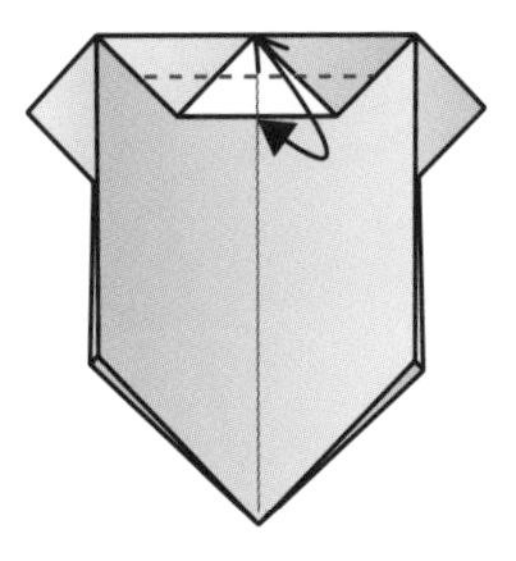

Fold the top layer in half through both layers of paper. Unfold the triangle back down to the bottom.

17

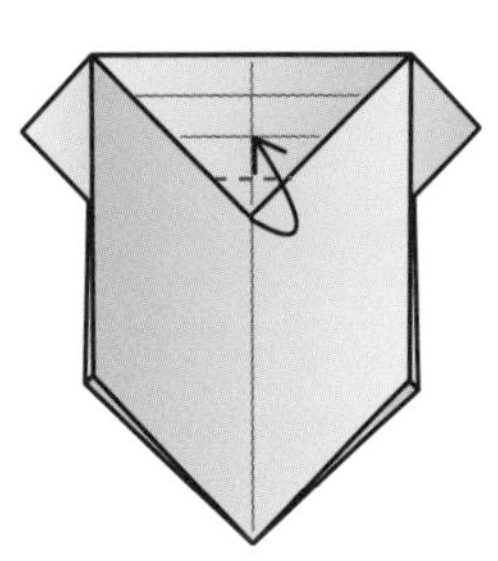

Fold the tip up on the first crease.

18

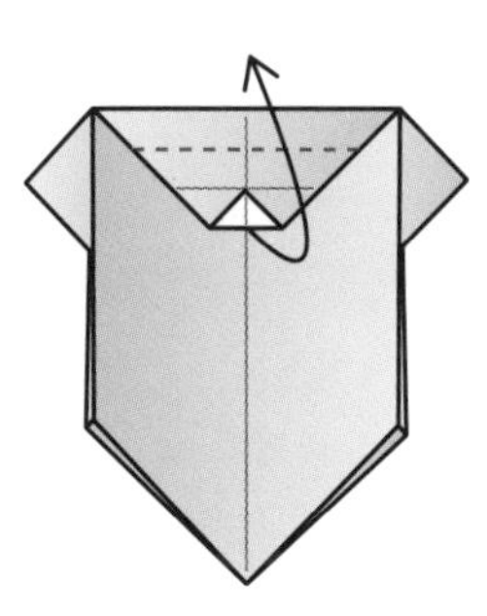

Fold the paper up on the crease closest to the top so that the top section sticks out and up. (See the next step for reference.)

T-SHIRT — ALMOST DONE!

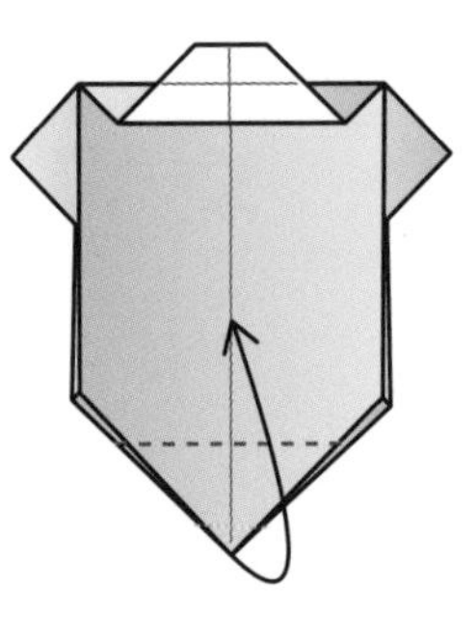

Fold up the bottom corner, making sure to leave a little bit of an angle on the sides.

20

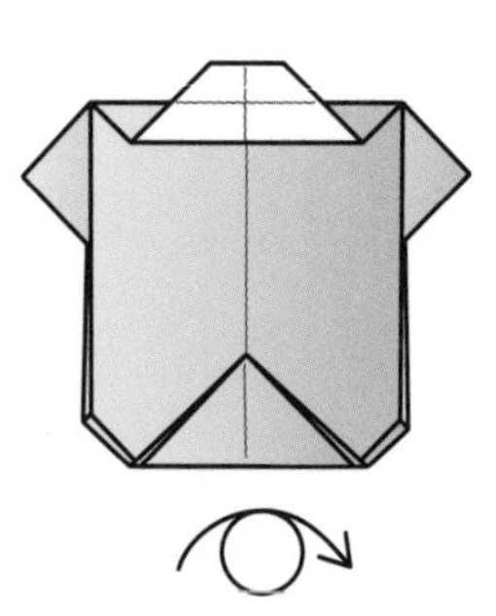

Turn the paper over.

21

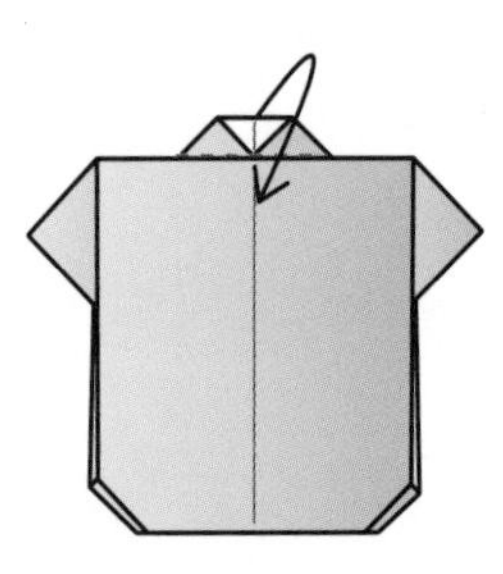

Fold the top trapezoid section down to form the collar/neckline.

Enjoy your finished T-shirt!

Bottoms

Miniskirt

Anyone can pull off a **miniskirt** with the right attitude! An A-line miniskirt (like this paper version, which flares away from the body) tends to be the most flattering on all body types. Since miniskirts show off a lot of leg, it's important to balance that with a top that offers more coverage. It's also important to wear the right shoes—flats will give your miniskirt a sweeter, more feminine look while boots will offer a tougher edge.

STYLE TIPS

- To balance the shorter skirt, opt for a full-coverage top, such as a long-sleeved blouse, T-shirt, or jacket.
- Pair your miniskirt with tights or leggings to make it through cooler weather.

HOW TO FOLD

1

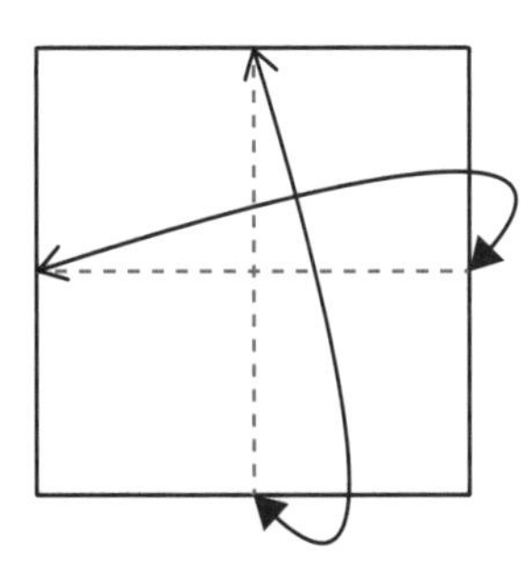

Fold the paper in half in both directions and then unfold. (Note: The side facing down will become the outside of the miniskirt.)

2

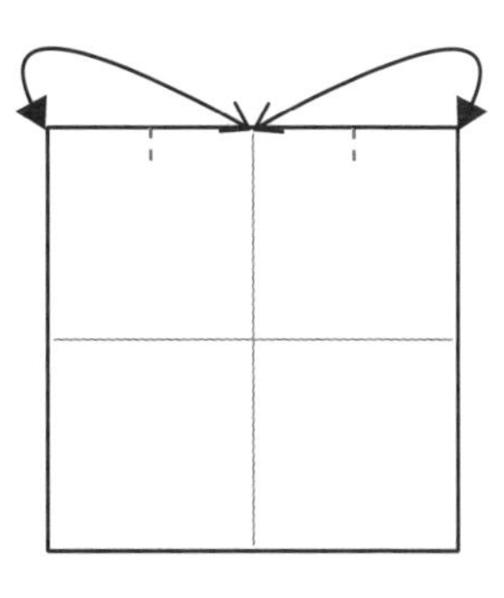

Bring the outside edges to the center crease and pinch a crease on only the top edge on both sides.

3

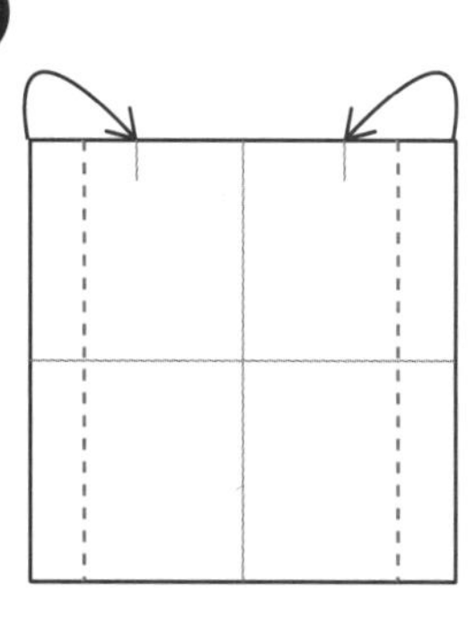

Fold the side edges into the pinch creases made in the previous step.

4

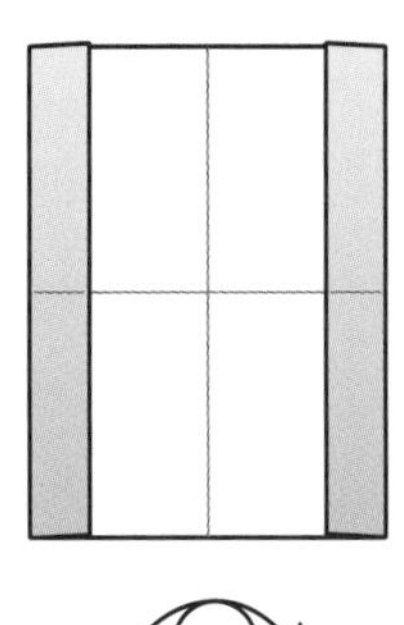

Turn the paper over.

5

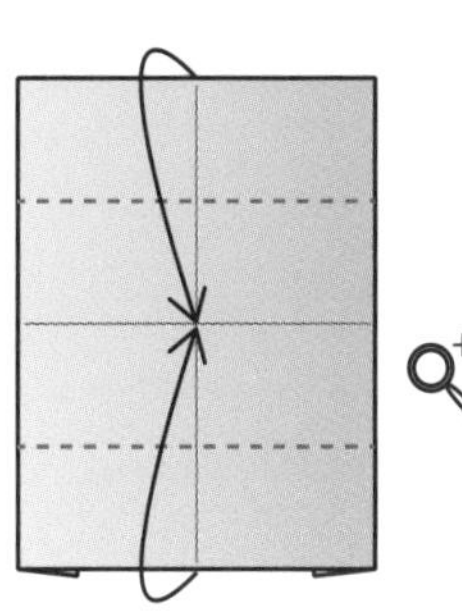

Fold the top and bottom sections into the center crease. (Note: The next step is a magnified view.)

6

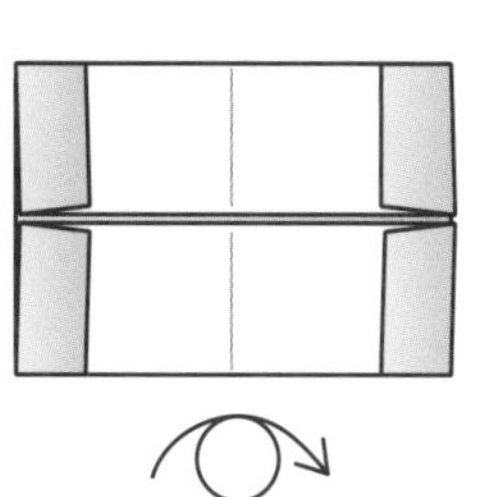

Turn the paper over.

7

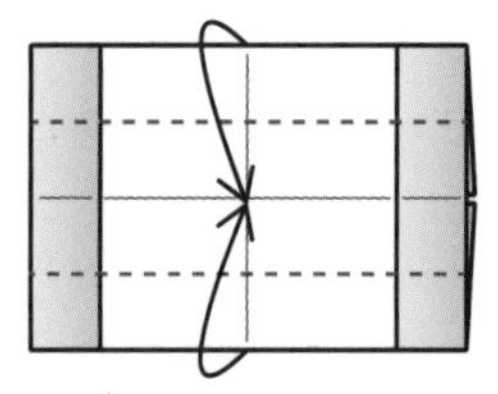

Fold the top and bottom edges, through all layers, into the center crease.

8

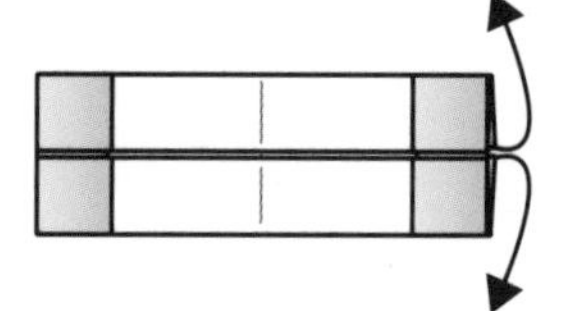

Gently pull out the bottom layers underneath and make the paper flat. (See the next step for reference.)

9

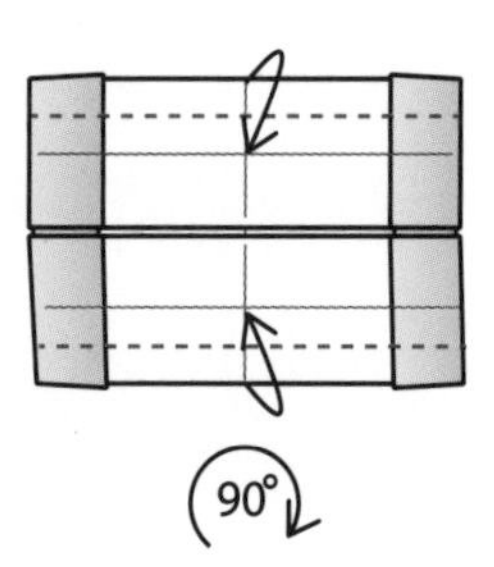

Fold the top and bottom edges to the upper and lower existing creases. Rotate the model 90°.

10

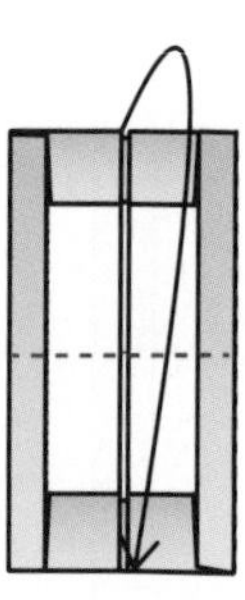

Valley fold the top edge down to meet the bottom so the paper is folded in half.

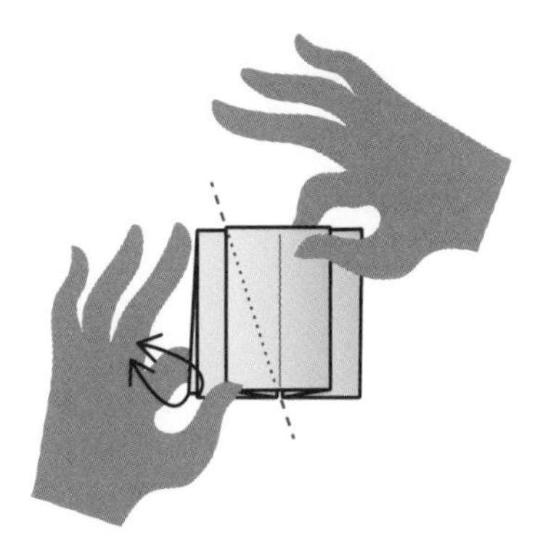

While pinching the top right corner section, pull out the bottom left corners in a swivel. Create the shape of the skirt by making the bottom wider.

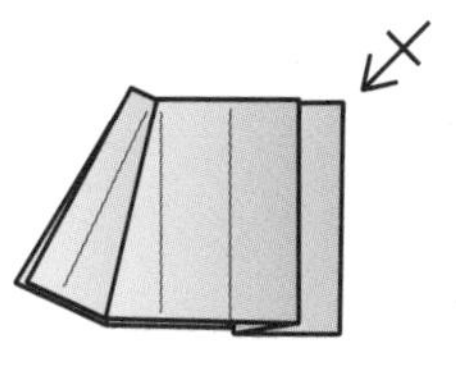

Repeat on the opposite side.

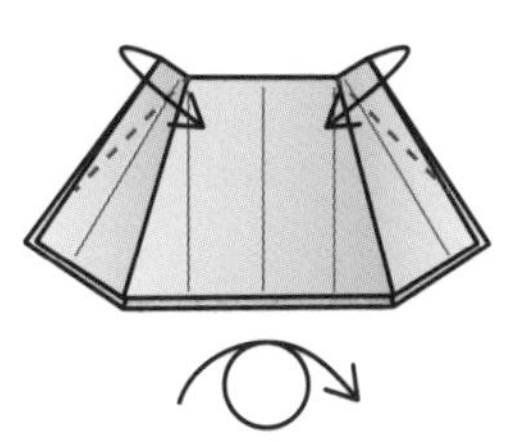

Shape the waist of the skirt by folding the flaps sticking out on the top in on a diagonal. (Note: You can also fold a narrow waistband to hold them in place.) Turn the paper over.

Enjoy your finished miniskirt!

Maxi Skirt

Maxi skirts can work in spring, summer, or fall, depending on how you choose to style them. Pair your skirt with a tank top and flip-flops in the summer, or a sweater or jean jacket to make it work year-round, especially in cooler fall temps. One of the easiest ways to make a maxi skirt pop is with a bold print, like this paper version, which features bright colors and a fun pattern. You can fold the skirt so the stripes are horizontal or vertical, depending on your personal style preference.

HOW TO FOLD

1

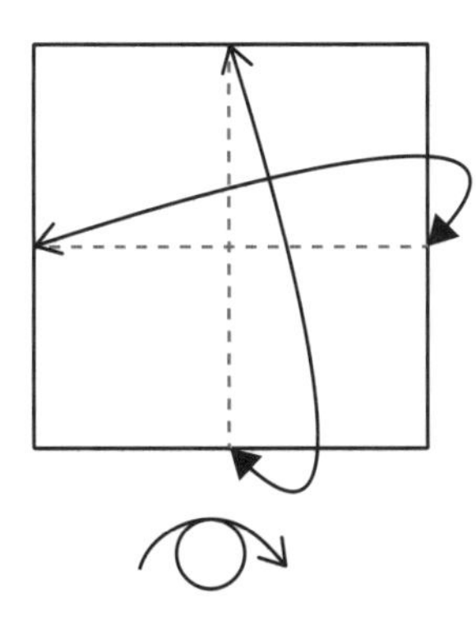

Fold the paper in half in both directions and then unfold. Turn the paper over. (Note: The side facing down will become the outside of the skirt; the other side will become the waistband.)

2

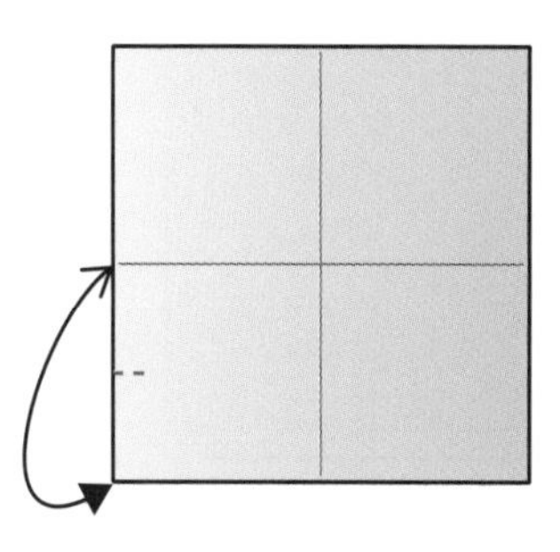

Bring up the bottom edge to the halfway crease, and pinch only the corner section to mark it as a landmark crease. Unfold.

3

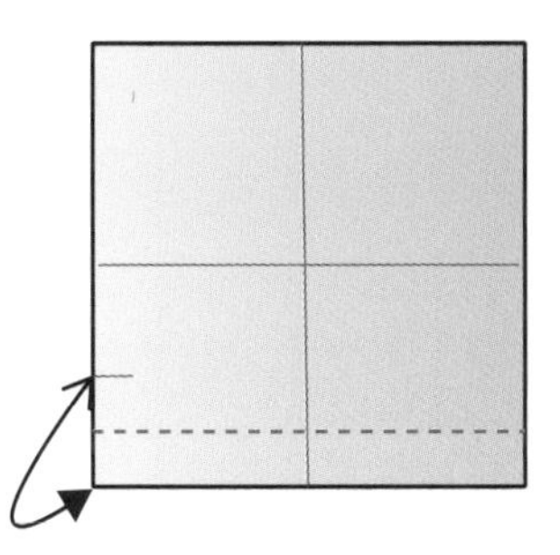

Fold the bottom edge to the landmark crease made in the previous step. Unfold.

4

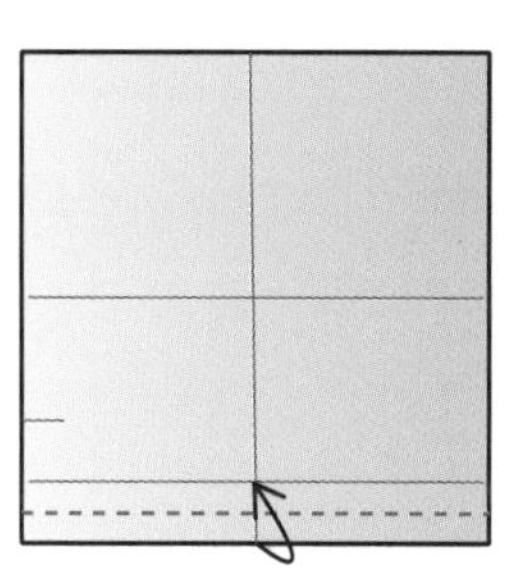

Fold the bottom edge up to the new crease made in the previous step.

5

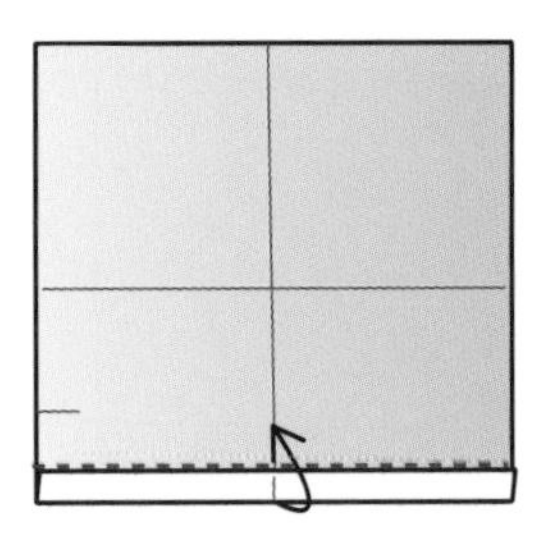

Fold the bottom edge up again on the existing crease to create the skirt's waistband.

6

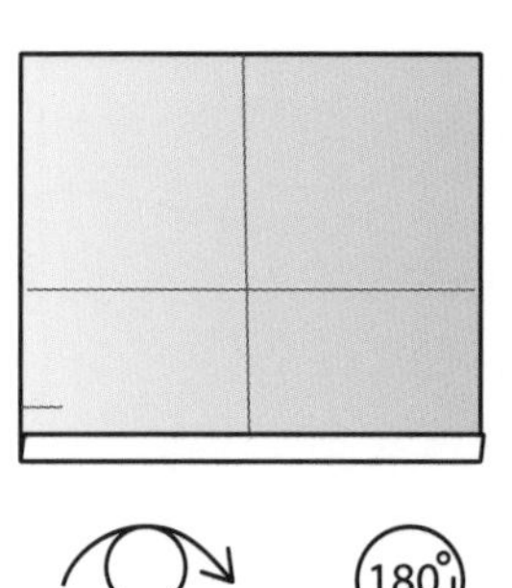

Turn the paper over and rotate it 180° so that the folds you just made are now at the top on the back.

7

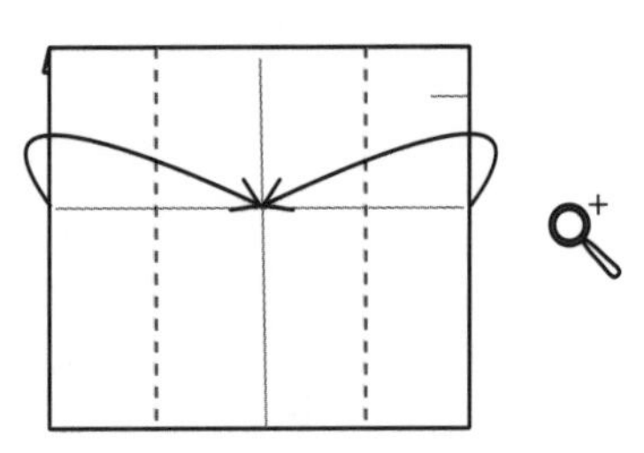

Fold the side edges into the center crease. (Note: The next step is a magnified view.)

8

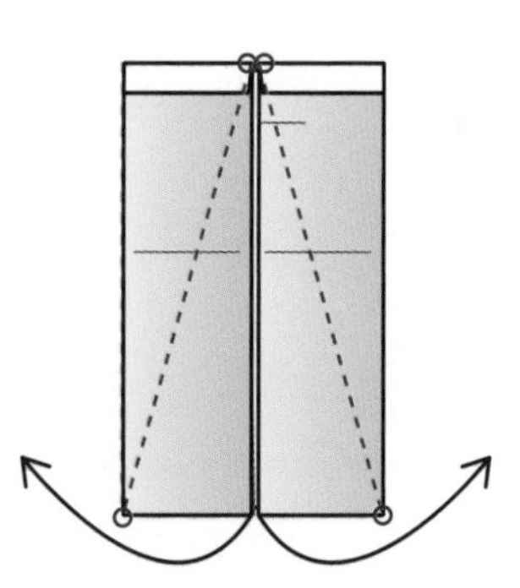

Fold the bottom corners out on a diagonal.

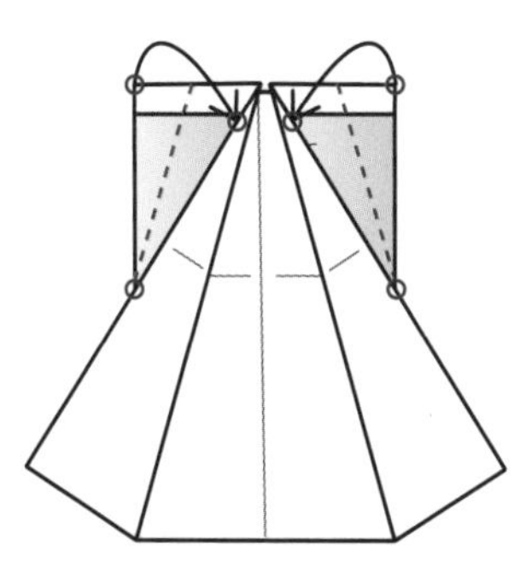

Taper the waistline of the skirt by folding the top corners in at an angle.

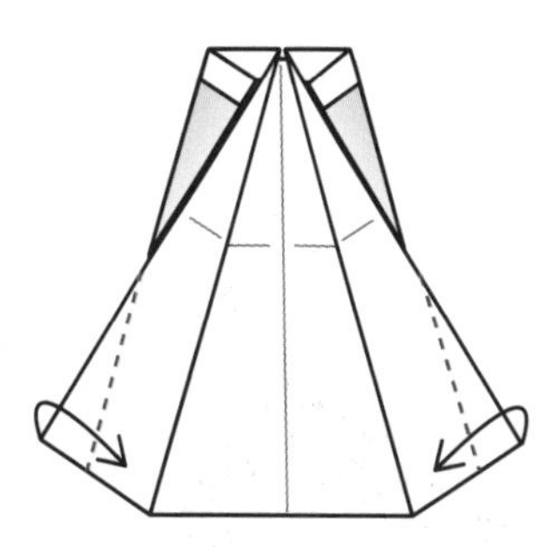

Shape the bottom of the skirt by folding the corners in as well.

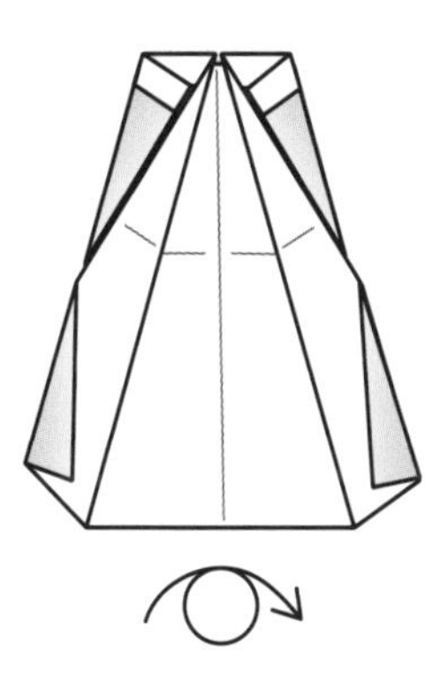

Turn the paper over.

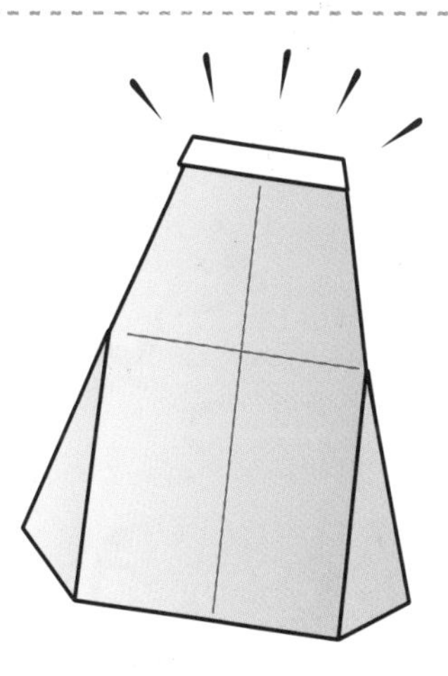

Enjoy your finished maxi skirt!

Pleated Skirt

Pleated skirts are a fun, feminine addition to any wardrobe. In order to balance the fullness of a pleated skirt, a fitted waistband is key. It's also important to choose a bright color or fun pattern to keep the skirt from looking too stuffy. This knee-length paper version utilizes an on-trend bird-print paper and complements it with a bright pop of color at the hem and waistband.

STYLE TIPS

- Pair your pleated skirt with a fitted T-shirt or blouse—make sure to tuck in whatever top you choose to show off the skirt's waistband!
- Wear with ballet flats for an easy, everyday outfit, or toss on a pair of heels to dress up your skirt!

HOW TO FOLD

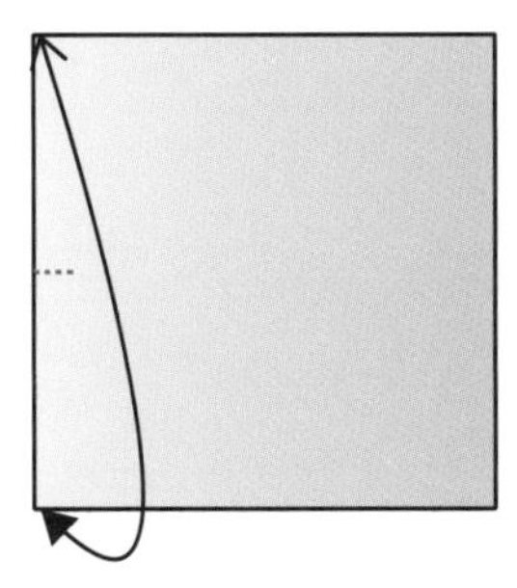

Bring the bottom left corner up to the top left corner and pinch fold the center point, then unfold. (Note: The side facing up will become the outside of the skirt; the side facing down will become the contrasting hem and waistband.)

2

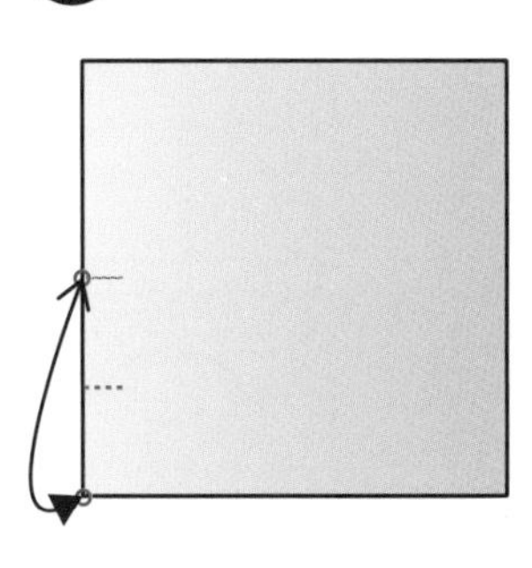

Fold the bottom corner up to the existing pinch crease to make a second pinch crease and then unfold.

3

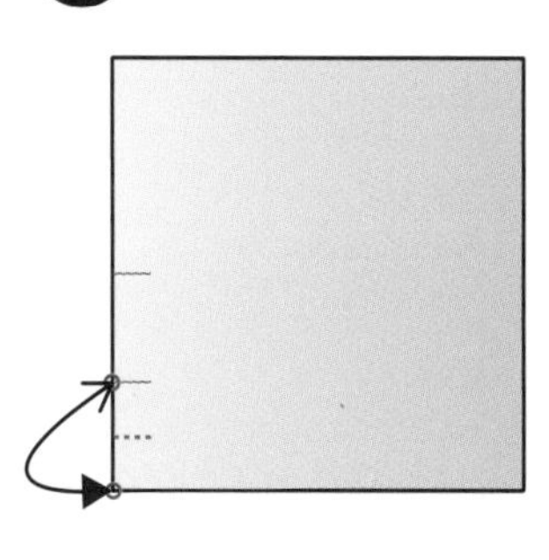

Make a third pinch crease by folding the bottom edge up to the crease made in step #2 and then unfold.

4

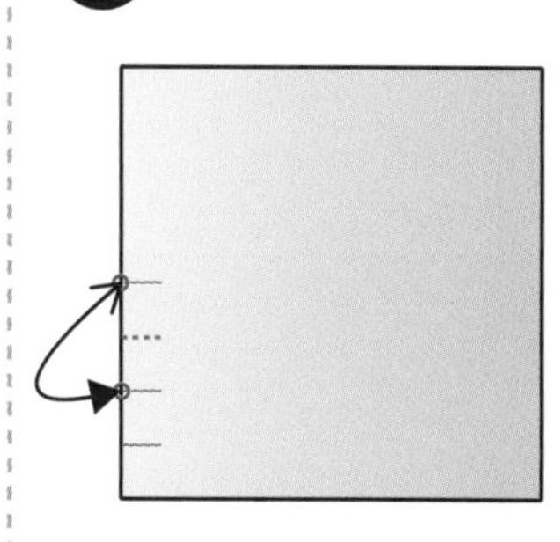

Pinch the midpoint between the center crease and the one below it and then unfold. (Note: You are dividing the bottom half of the paper into quarters.)

5

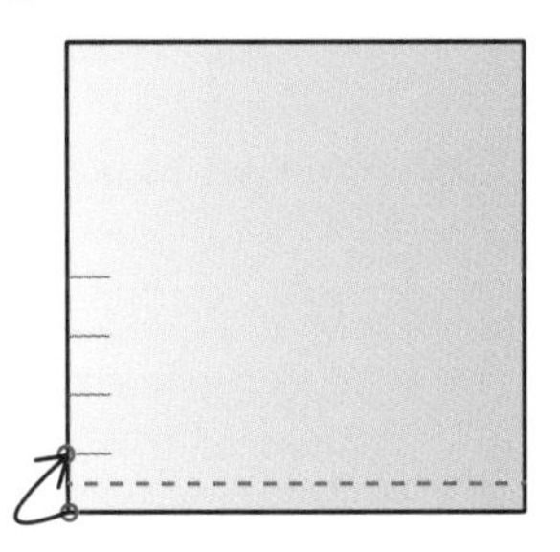

Fold the bottom edge up to the nearest pinch crease.

6

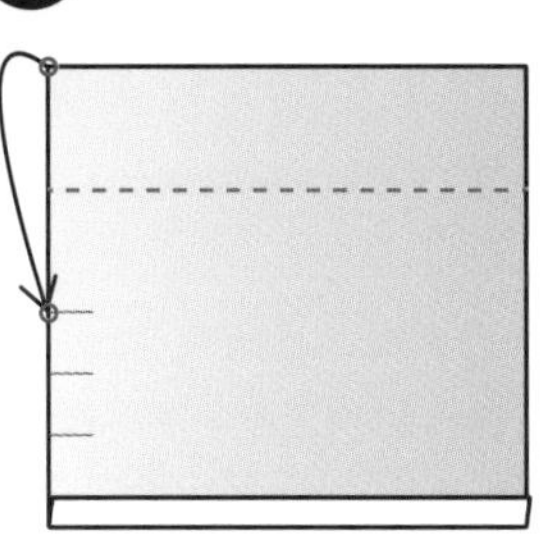

Fold the top edge down to the top pinch crease.

7

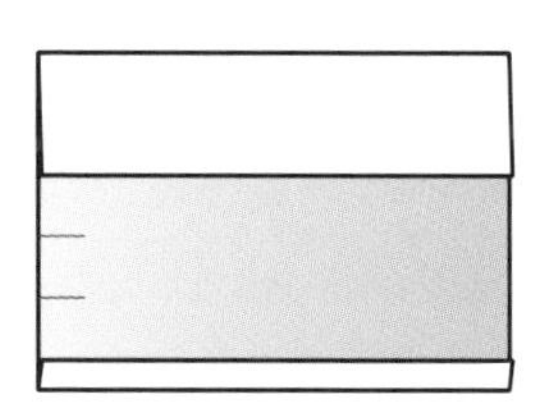

Turn the paper over.

8

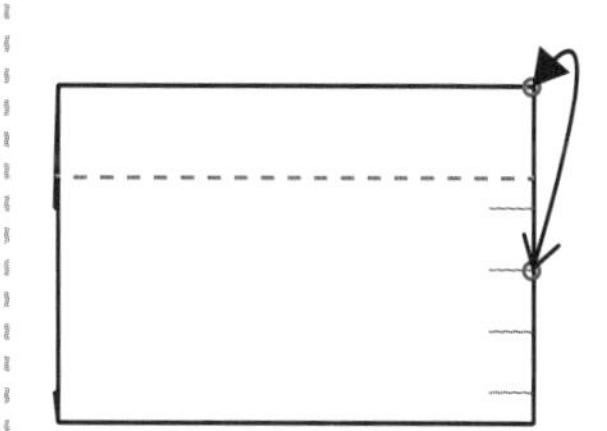

Fold the top edge down to the pinch crease just below the center crease and then unfold.

9

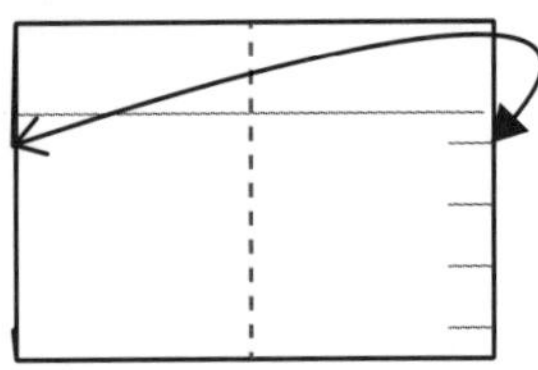

Fold the paper in half vertically and then unfold.

10

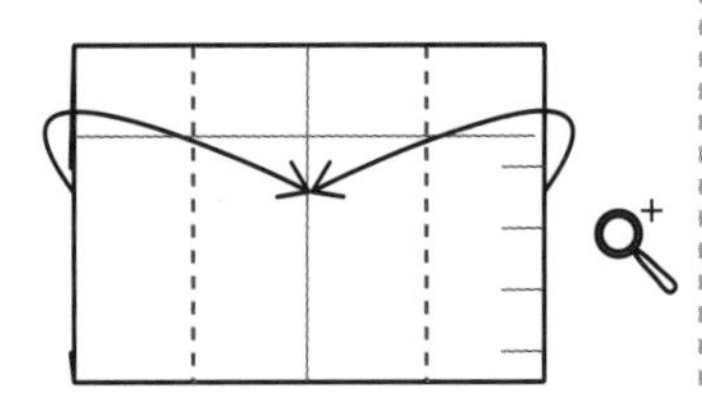

Fold the sides into the center crease. (Note: The next step is a magnified view.)

11

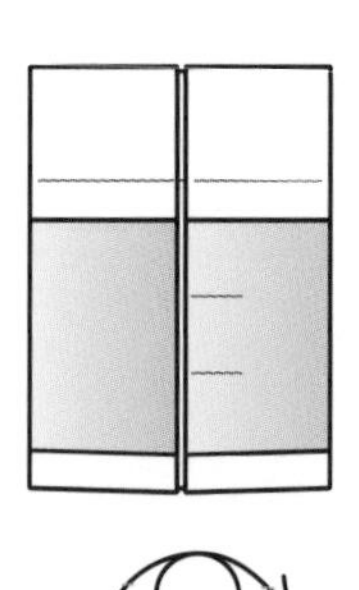

Turn the paper over.

12

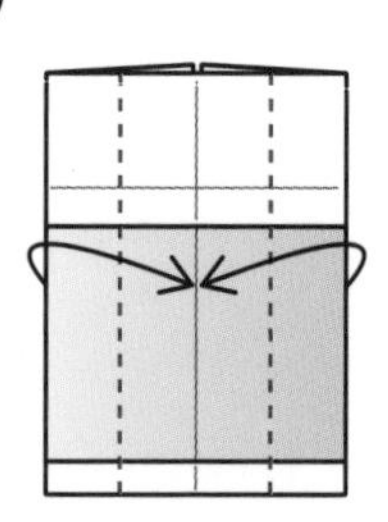

Fold the sides into the center crease.

13

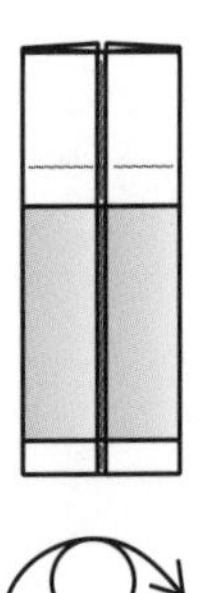

Turn the paper over.

14

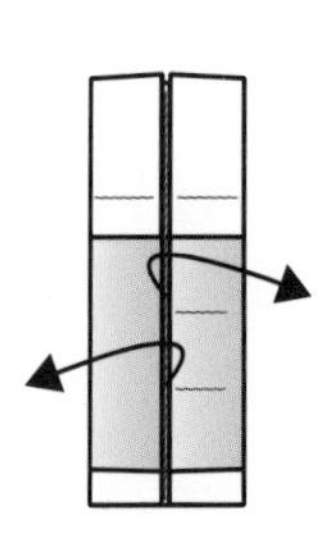

Open the center flaps out in the front. (See the next step for reference.)

15

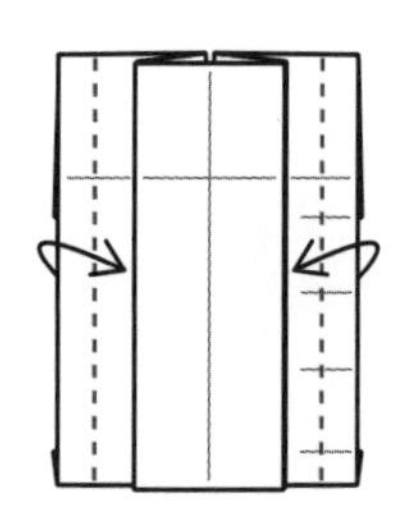

Fold the side edges into the folded edges.

16

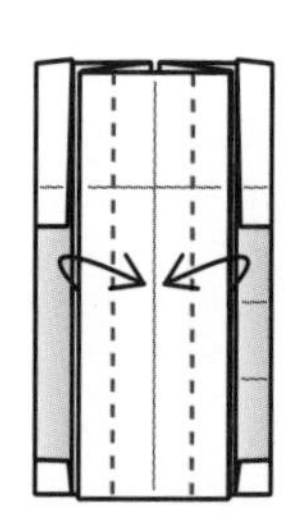

Bring the folded edges of the center section into the center crease.

Turn the paper over.

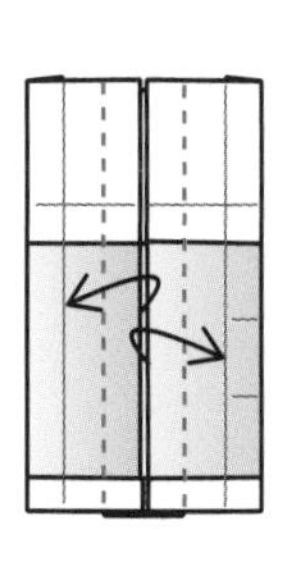

Bring the center folded edges out to the existing crease.

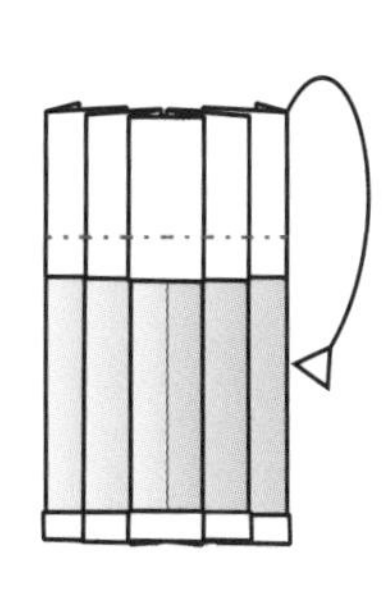

Mountain fold the top section to the back on the existing pre-crease. This should create an even color-changed band on both the top and bottom of the skirt.

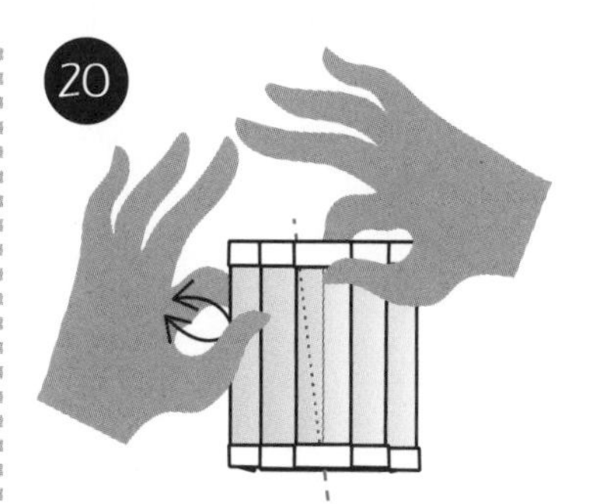

Pinch the top right sections together, and pull the bottom left corners together at the same time in a diagonal swivel. (Note: This will spread the bottom of the skirt into a wider base.)

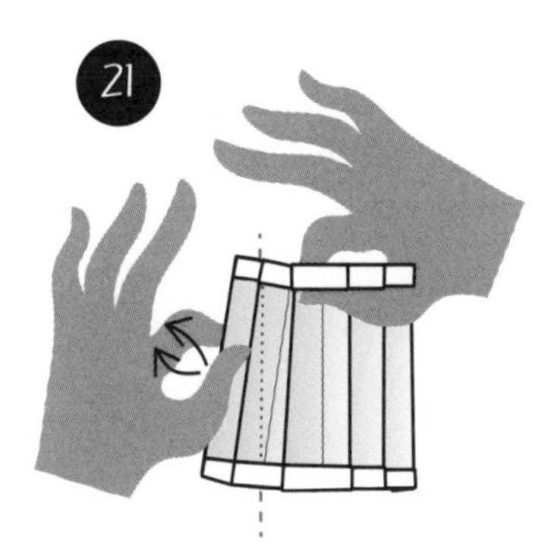

Move out to the next layer of pleats and repeat the diagonal swivel. (Note: The objective is to spread the bottom of the skirt out while swiveling the top section up.)

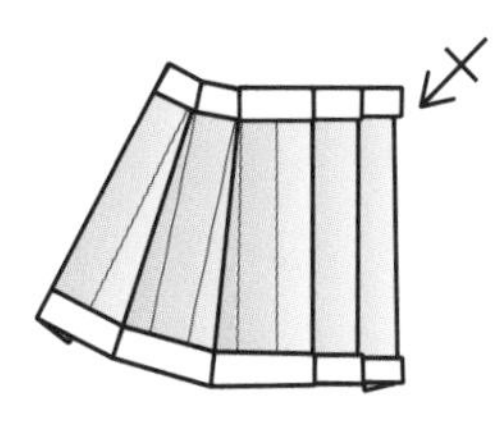

Repeat steps #20 and #21 on the opposite side.

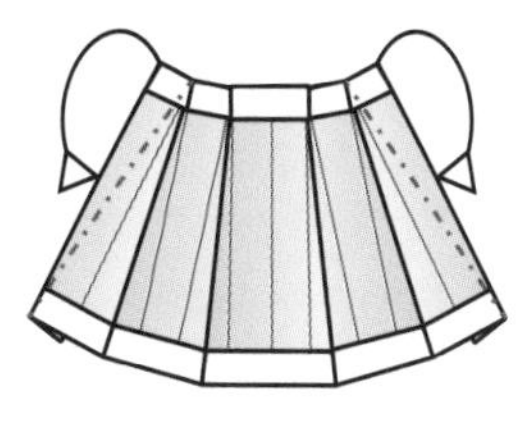

Mountain fold the sides to the back on a diagonal to shape the top of the skirt.

Enjoy your finished pleated skirt!

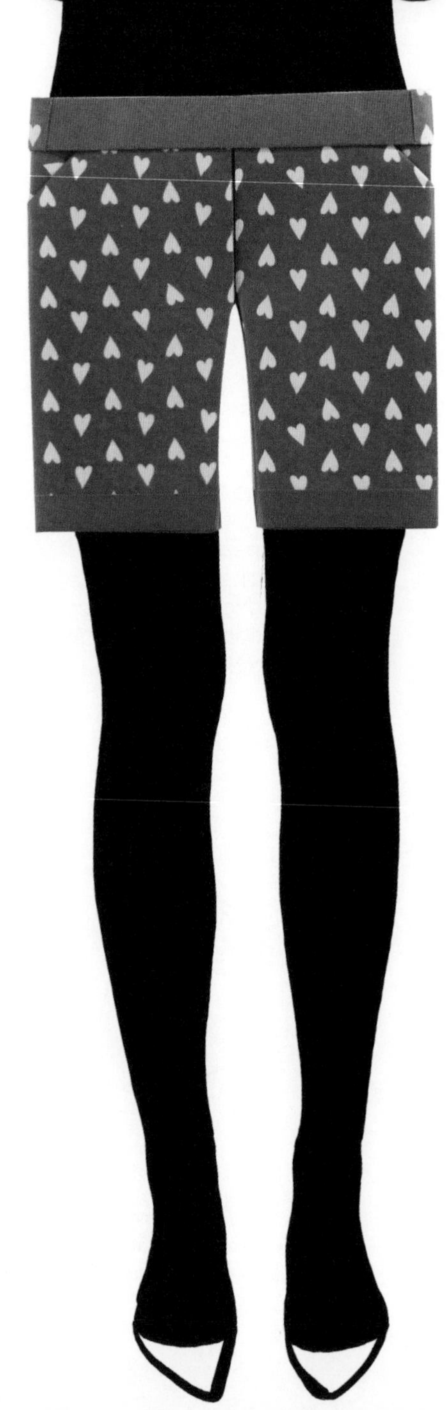

Shorts

Just as jeans are a go-to garment in the cooler months, **shorts** are a summer staple. Shorts can be a great, versatile addition to any wardrobe because they come in a wide range of fabrics, colors, and patterns. From basic denim cutoffs to dressy linen pairs, shorts can act as the base for any outfit. This paper pair features a fun, whimsical pattern and contrasting cuffs, but you can fold them in a variety of patterns or solid colors depending on what you plan to pair them with. Experiment to create as many different outfits as you'd like! You can also adjust the length and width based on your own style choices.

HOW TO FOLD

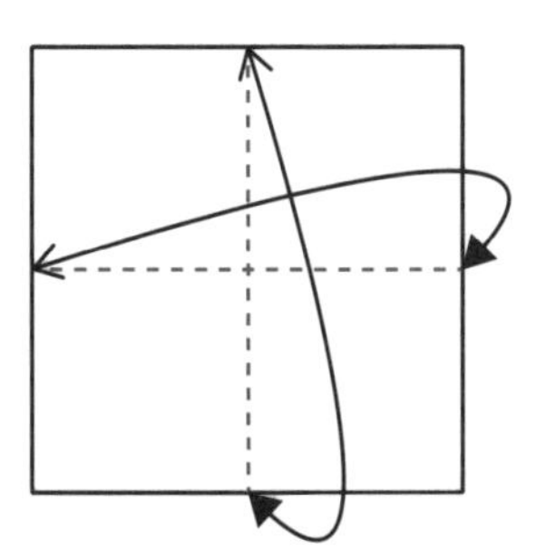

Fold the paper in half in both directions and then unfold. (Note: The side facing down will become the outside of the shorts.)

2

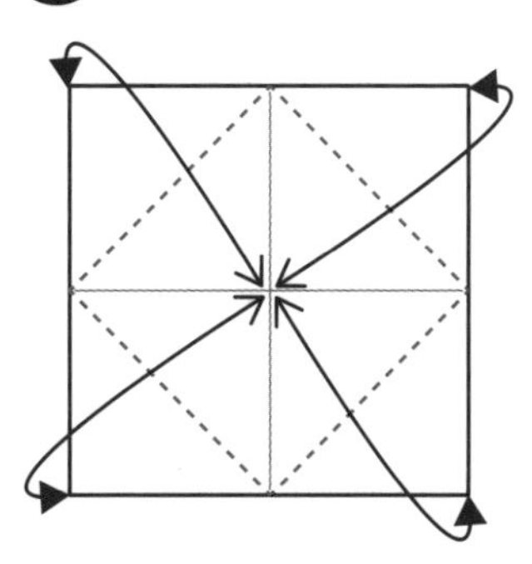

Fold all four corners into the center and then unfold.

3

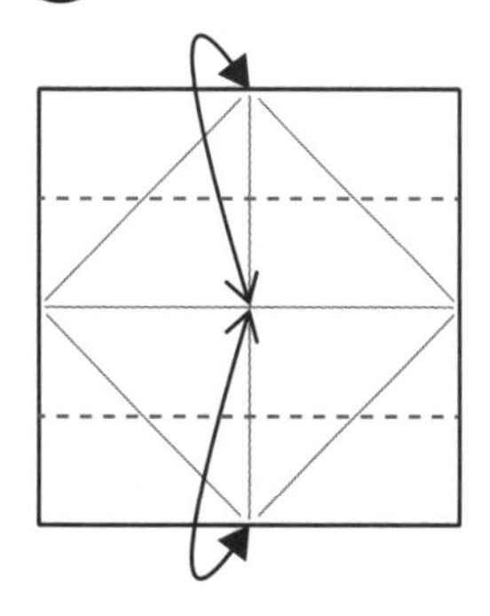

Fold the top and bottom edges into the center and then unfold.

4

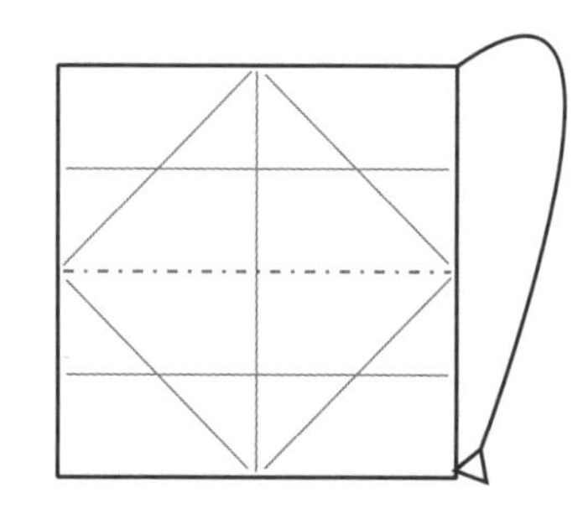

Mountain fold the paper in half to the back.

5

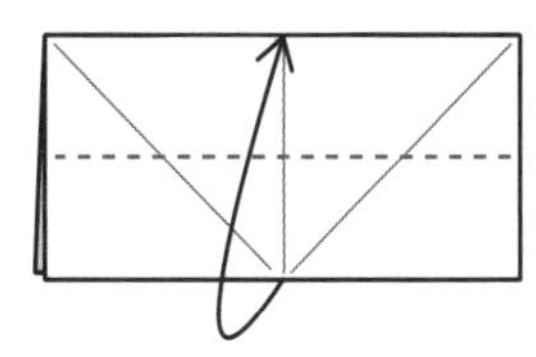

Fold the bottom edge up to meet the folded top crease.

6

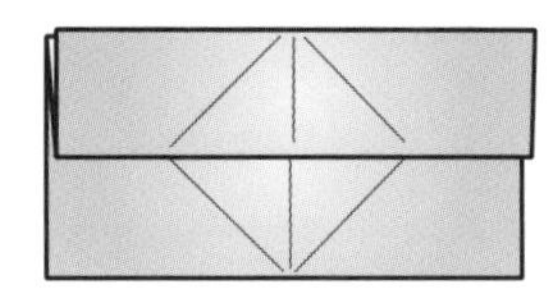

Turn the paper over.

7

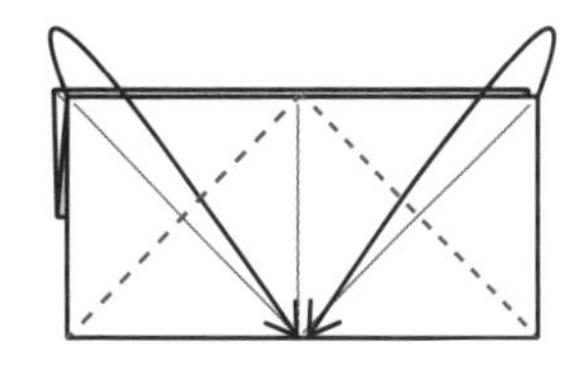

Fold the top corners down through all layers of paper.

8

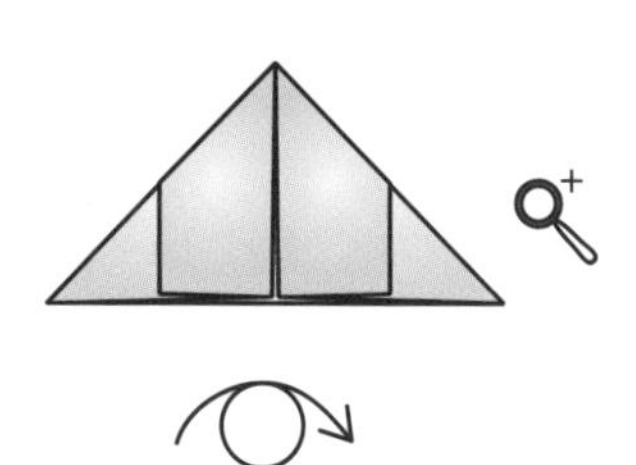

Turn the paper over. (Note: The next step is a magnified view.)

9

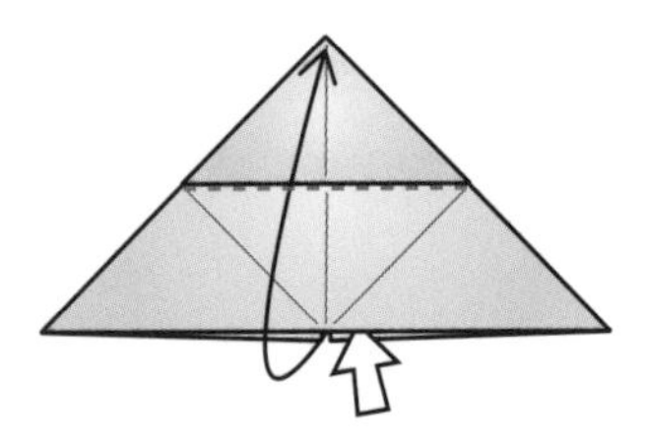

Lift the top layer and use the pre-creases to begin a squash fold.

10

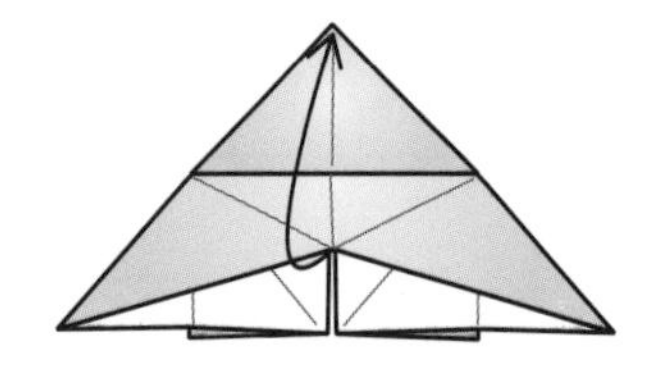

(Squash fold in progress.) Bring the center of the bottom edge up to the top point. (Note: The sides will also move up toward the top.)

11

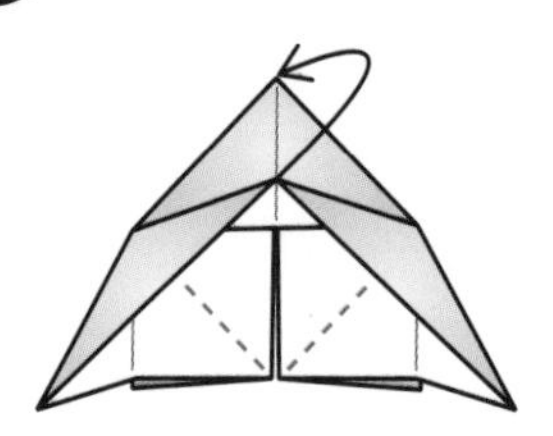

(Squash fold in progress.) Use the pre-creases in the bottom layer to help lift the corners to the top point.

12

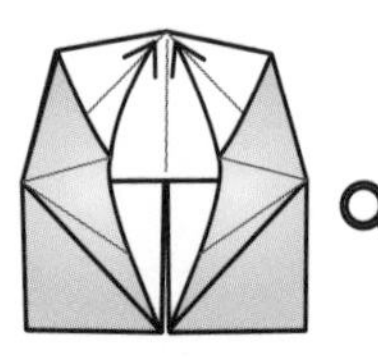

(Squash fold in progress.) Flatten the corners to form a square. (Note: The next step is a magnified view.)

13

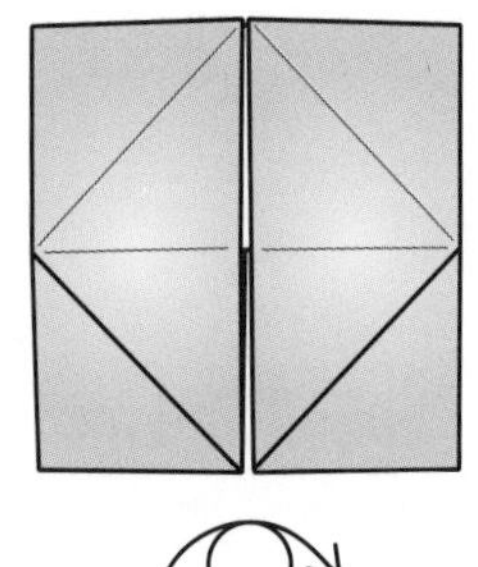

Turn the paper over.

14

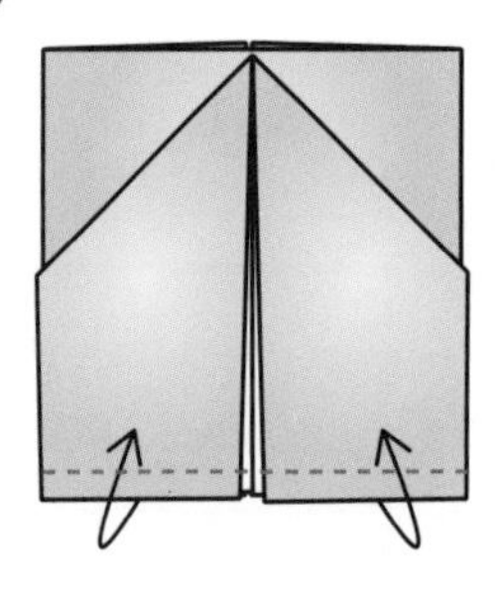

Fold the bottom edges up to make the cuffs. (Note: You can play around with the width of the cuffs by making this fold as wide or narrow as you'd like.)

15

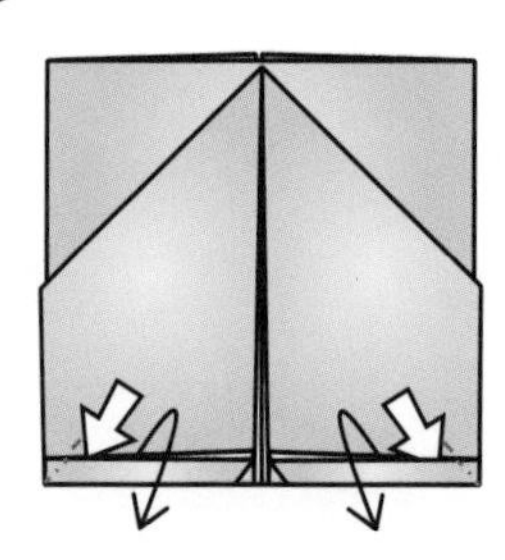

Open and squash each cuff so the contrasting color is visible. (See the next step for reference.)

16

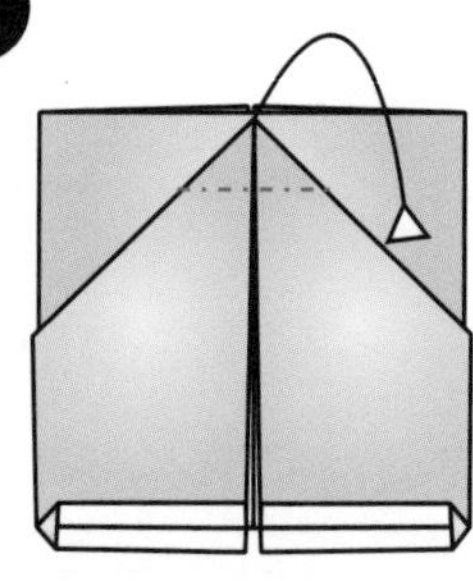

Mountain fold the top triangle to the inside. (Note: Folding this down farther will create shorter shorts and a wider waistband.)

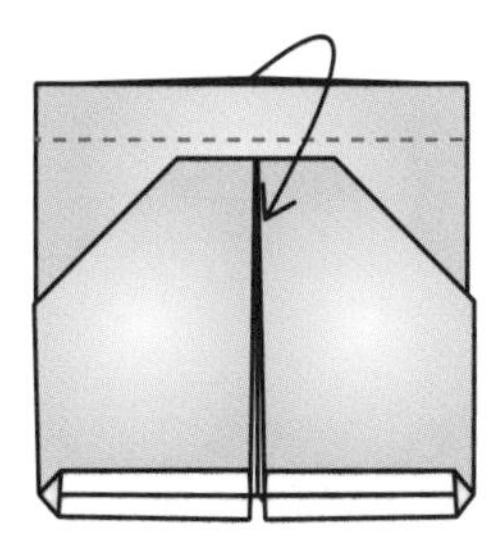

Fold the top section down to create the waistband.

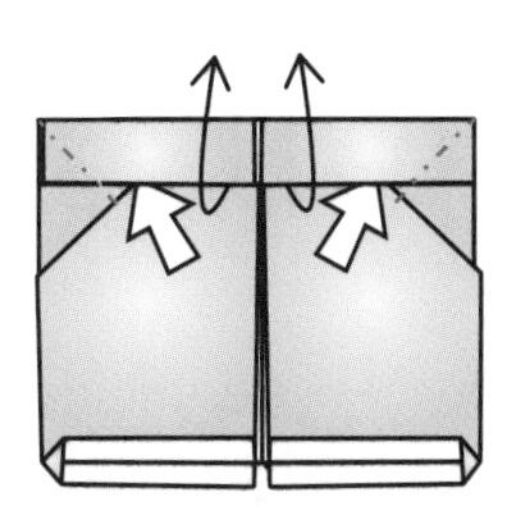

Open and squash the waistband so the contrasting color is exposed. (See the next step for reference.)

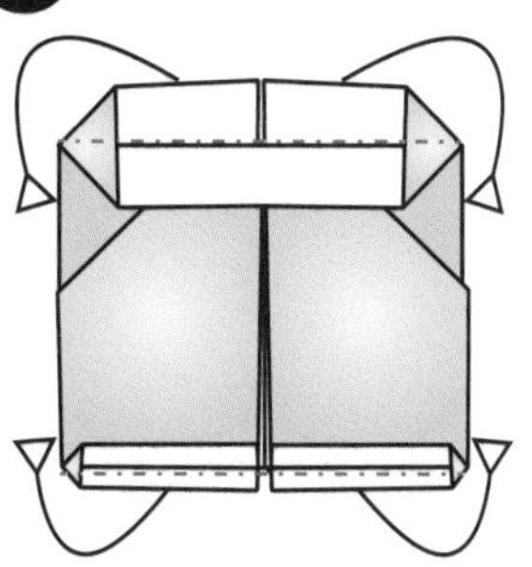

Mountain fold the top flaps on the waistband and bottom flaps on the cuffs to the back.

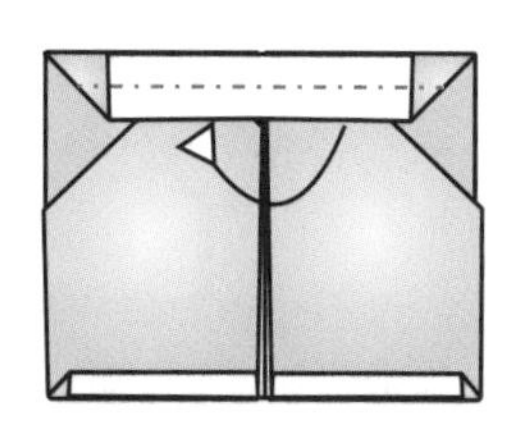

Mountain fold the top flap underneath to narrow the waistband.

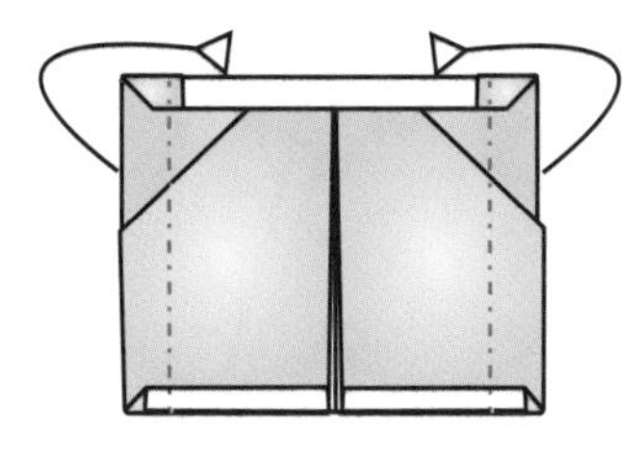

Mountain fold the sides to the back to narrow the width of the shorts.

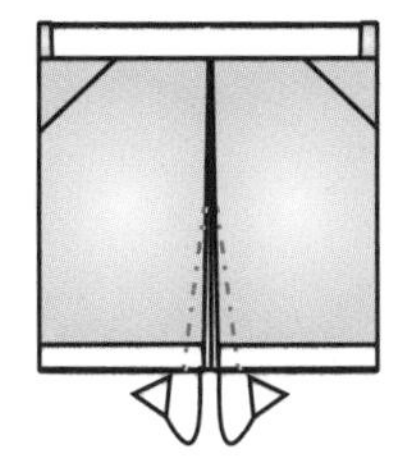

Shape and separate the legs by mountain folding the inside edges at a slight angle.

Enjoy your finished shorts!

Skinny Pants

Skinny pants are a great alternative to jeans when you want to spice up your look and try something different. This paper pair has a narrow leg and features a camo print, which can act as an unexpected neutral. Try folding the pants in a variety of colors and patterns to create an array of different looks. You can even use different textures to simulate leather leggings.

HOW TO FOLD

1

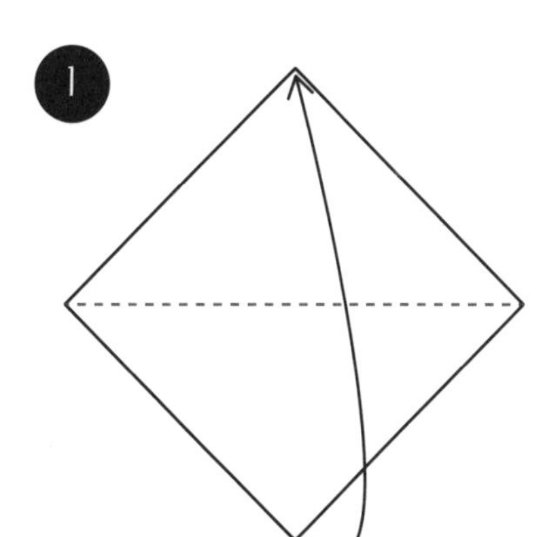

Fold the paper in half diagonally. (Note: The side facing down will become the outside pattern of the pants.)

2

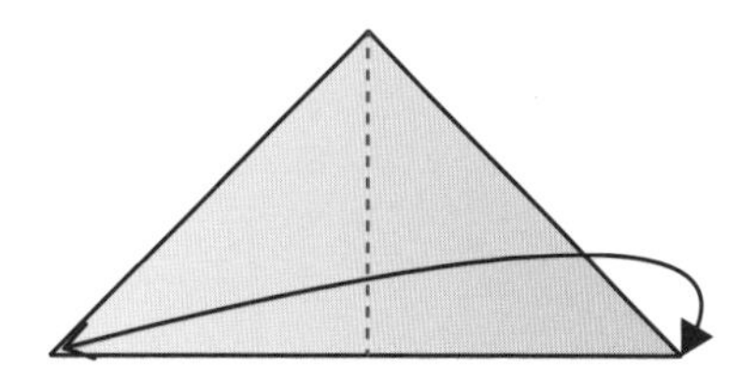

Fold in half again and unfold.

3

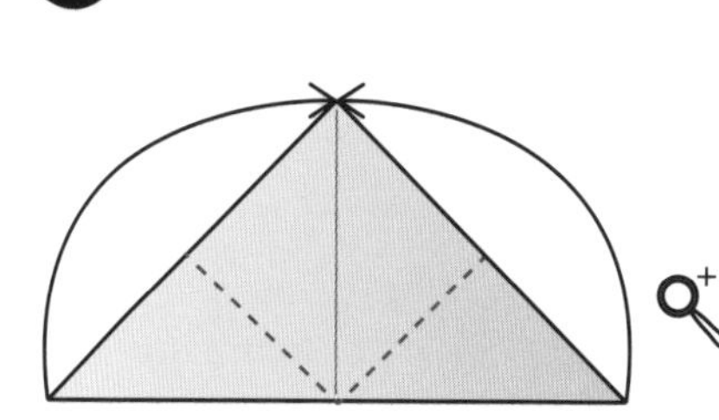

Fold both bottom corners up to the top of the triangle. (Note: The next step is a magnified view.)

4

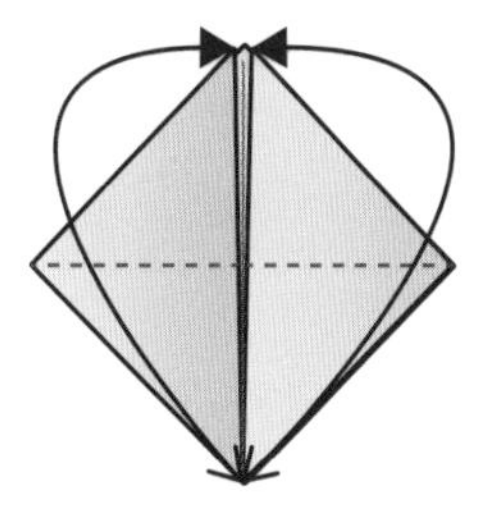

Fold the top corners down to the bottom and unfold.

5

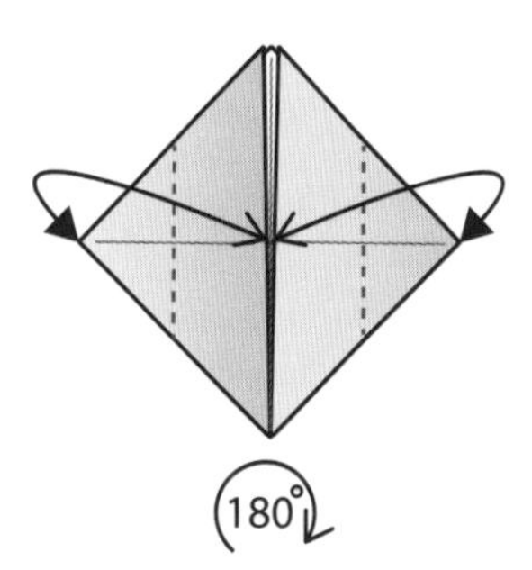

Fold both the left and right sides to the center and then unfold. Rotate the model 180°.

6

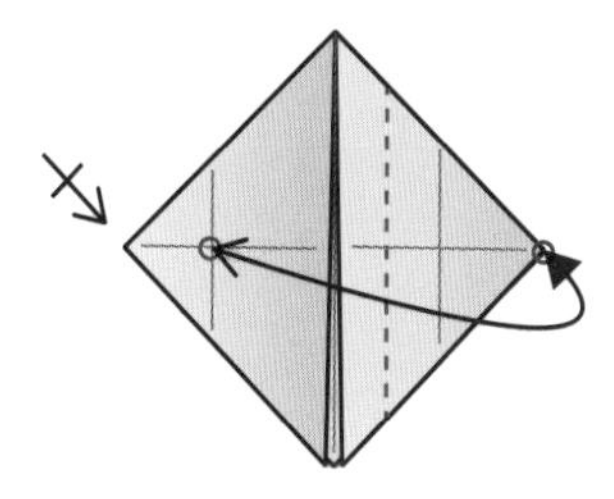

Fold the right corner to the crease on the left side and then unfold. Repeat this step on the opposite side.

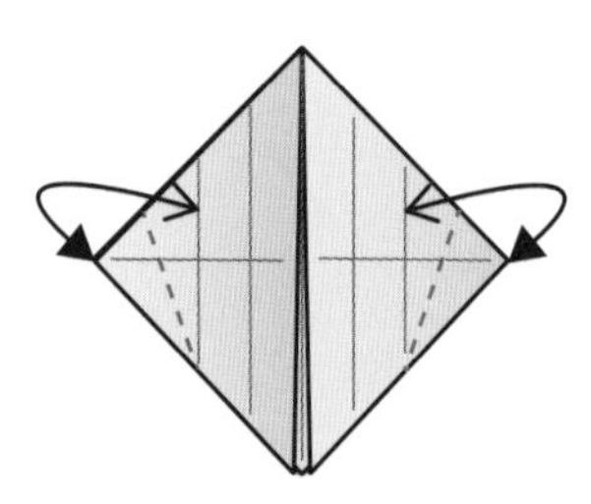

Fold a triangle on each side along the creases made in step #5 and unfold.

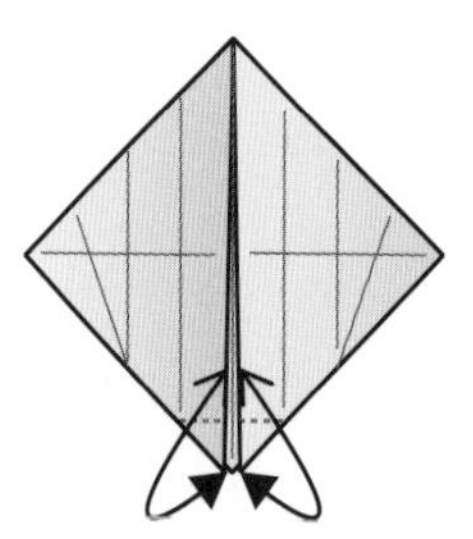

Fold the bottom corners up and then unfold. (Note: Use the creases made in step #6 as a reference for where to make this crease.)

9

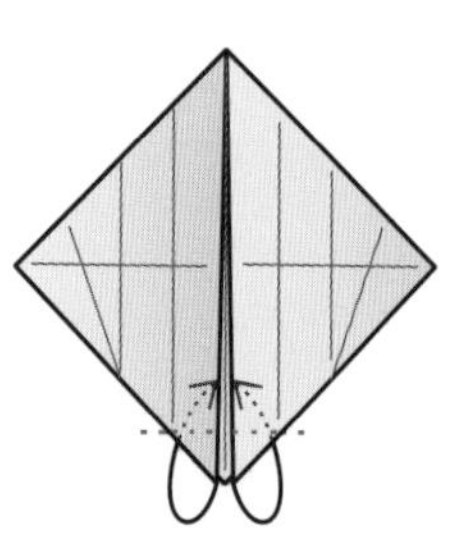

Inside reverse the bottom corners.

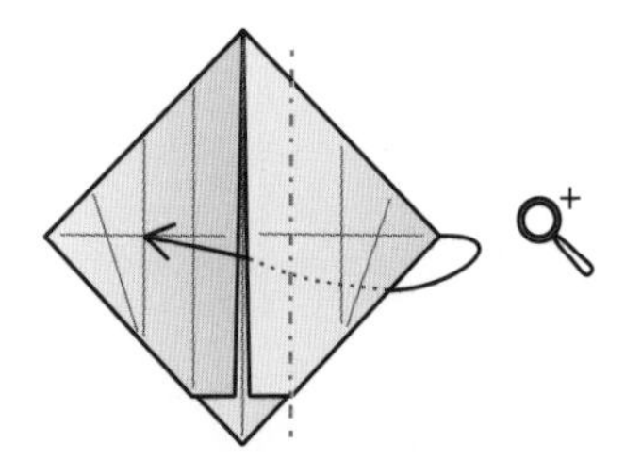

Inside reverse the right corner using the pre-creases from step #6. The corner will stick out on the inside. (Note: The next step is a magnified view.)

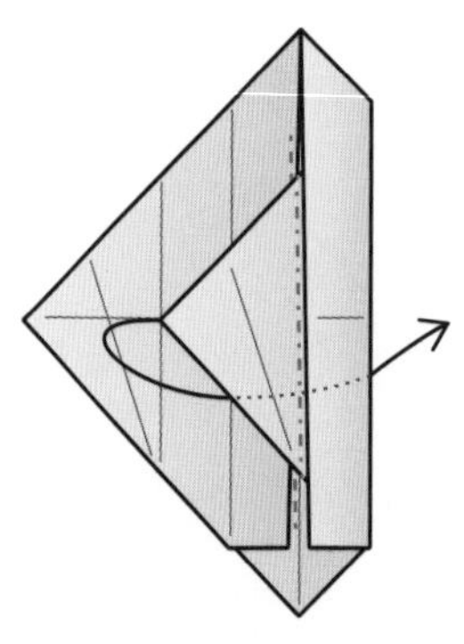

Inside reverse on the pre-creases made in step #5, so the triangle now sticks out to the outside.

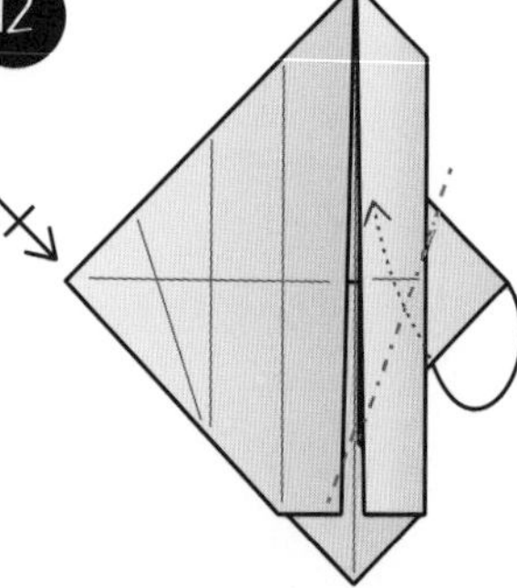

Using the pre-creases from step #7, inside reverse the triangle. Repeat steps #10–12 on the opposite side. (Note: There will still be a small point that will stick out on the sides.)

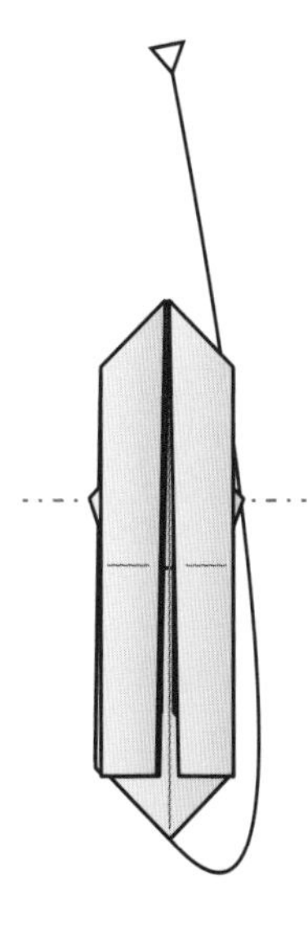

Mountain fold the back layer up as far as possible. (See the next step for reference.)

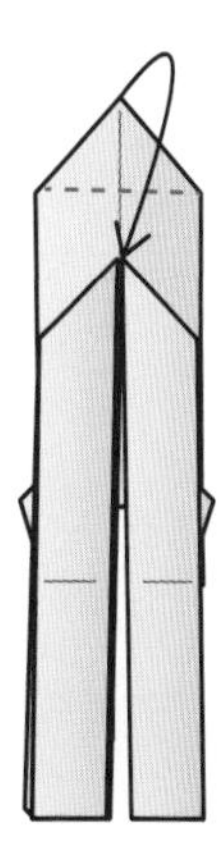

Fold the top corner down to create the waistband. (Note: The width of the waistband will be determined by how far you fold the paper past the center point.)

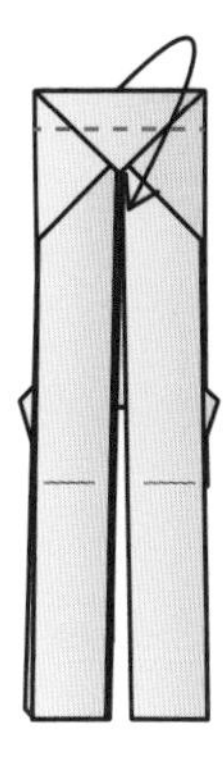

Fold the top edge down again to create the waistband.

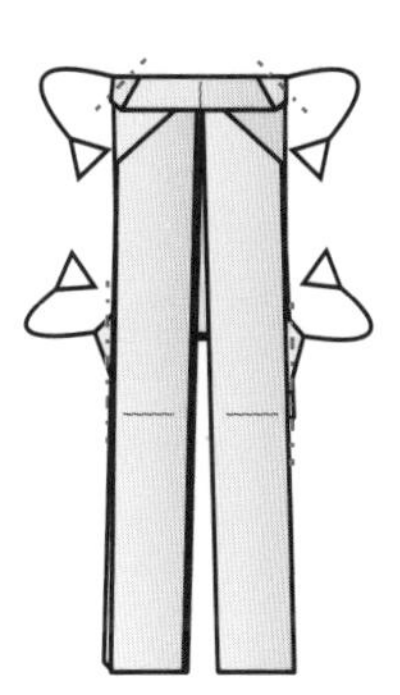

Mountain fold the top corners to shape the waistband, and then mountain fold the small triangular points that stick out on the sides.

Enjoy your finished skinny pants!

Jeans

Believe it or not, **jeans** have been around since the 1800s! This essential garment has gone through a serious style evolution in the past fifty years alone—flares, bell-bottoms, straight leg, skinny leg, and high-waist, just to name a few. Jeans today can be incredibly unique—from colored, patterned denim to perfectly distressed pairs. But no matter your style, the perfect pair of jeans is a must-have.

STYLE TIPS

- Jeans go with anything! Pair with heels for a night out or dress yours down with flats for a casual, everyday look.
- Blouses, sweaters, T-shirts, and jackets all work well with jeans—choose whatever you want to create your own personal style.

HOW TO FOLD

1

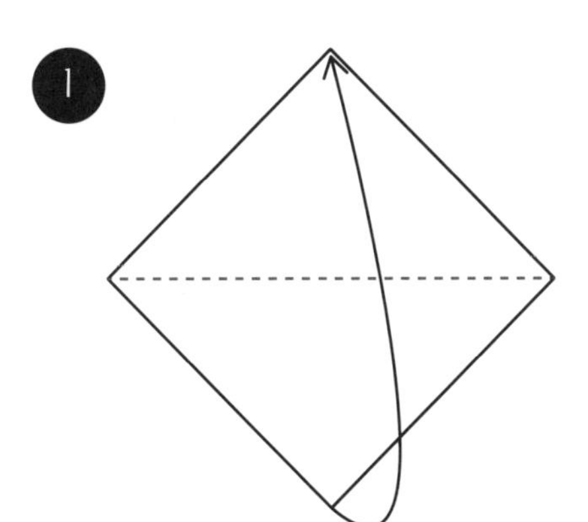

Fold the paper in half diagonally. (Note: Whichever side is facing down will become the outside of the jeans; the side facing up will be the waistband and cuffs.)

2

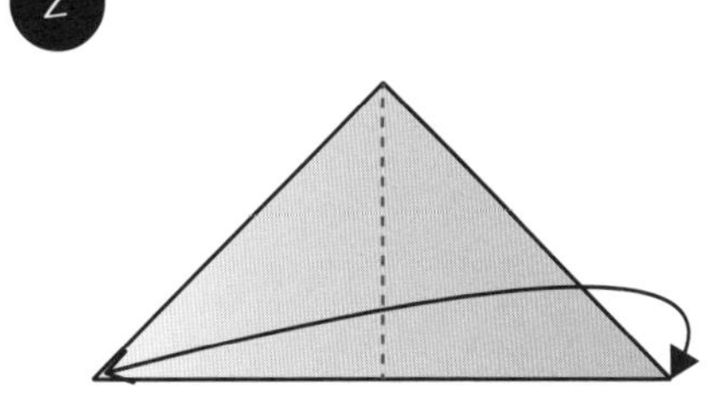

Fold the triangle in half and then unfold.

3

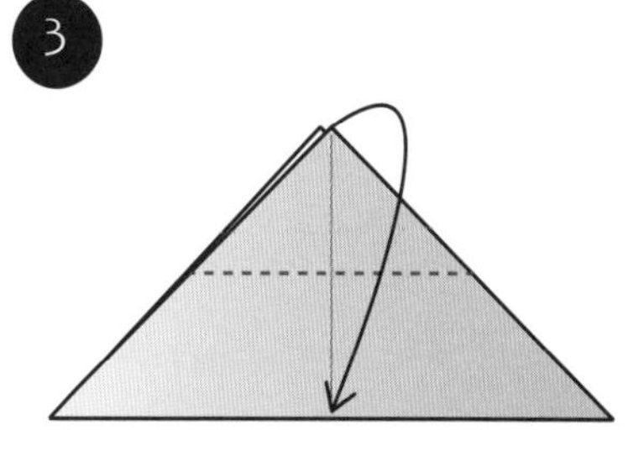

Fold the top corner down to the bottom. (Note: Only fold the top layer.)

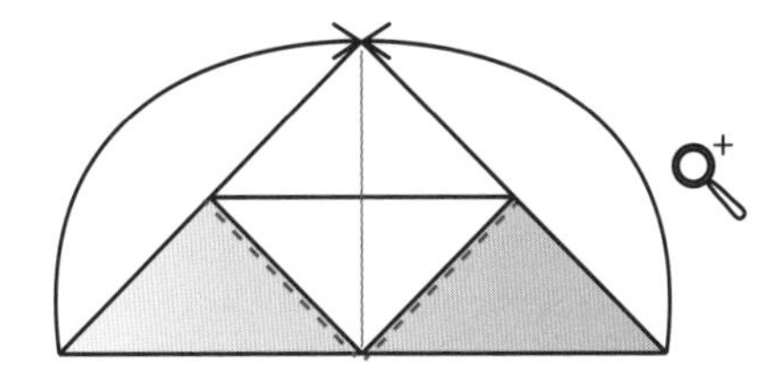

Fold both side corners up to the top point. (Note: The next step is a magnified view.)

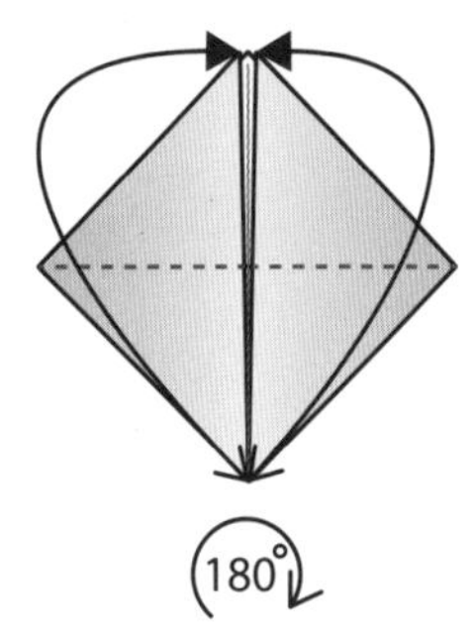

Fold the top corners (using only the top layer of paper) down to the bottom point and then unfold. Rotate the model 180°.

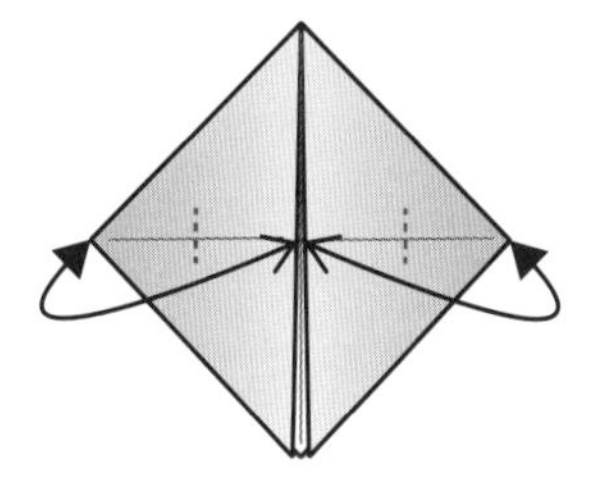

Pinch two landmark creases by bringing both side corners into the center and then unfold.

7

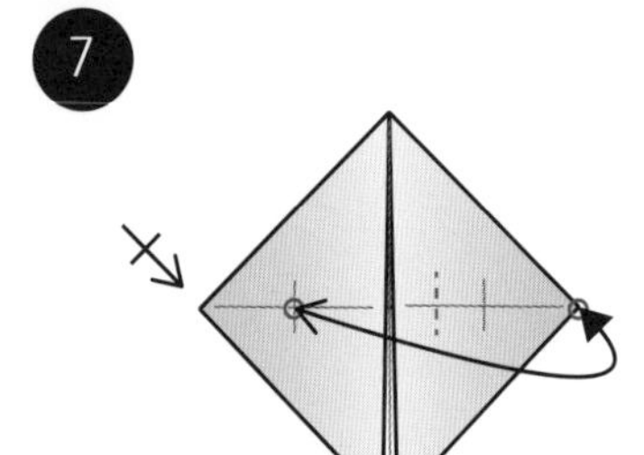

Fold the right corner to the landmark crease on the left side, make another pinch crease, and then unfold. Repeat this step on the left side.

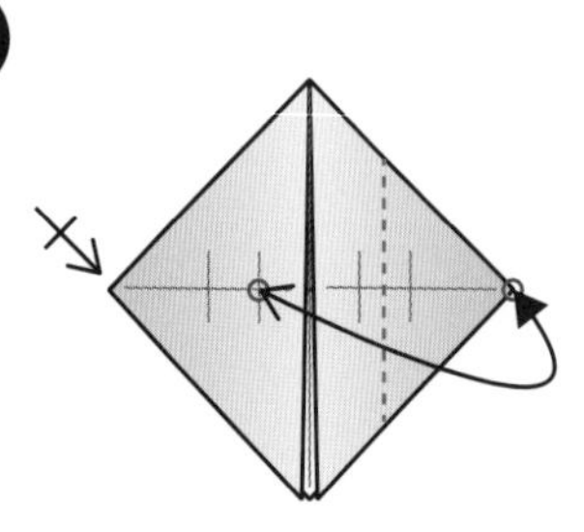

Fold the right corner to the nearest landmark crease on the left side and unfold. Repeat this step with the left corner.

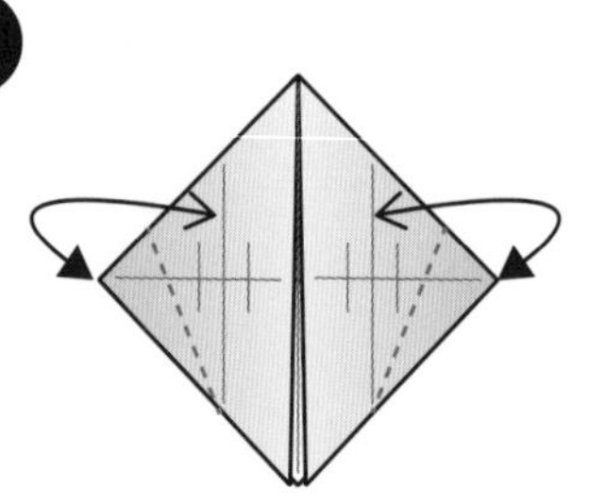

Fold and unfold diagonal creases on both sides by lining up the bottom side edges with the creases made in previous step.

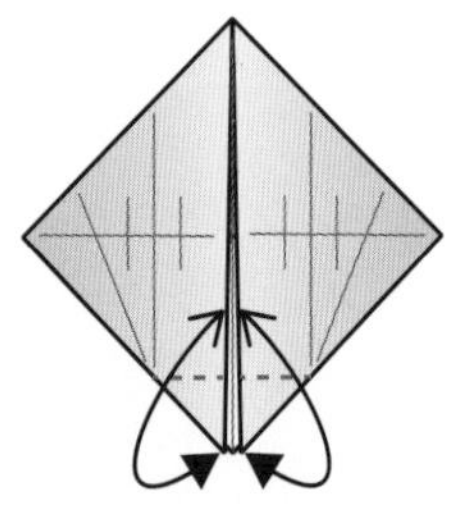

Fold the bottom triangles up and then unfold. Make these folds where the creases from steps #8 and #9 meet.

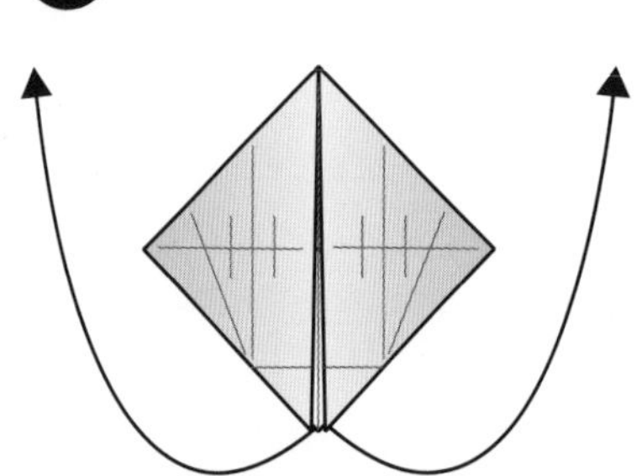

Unfold the top triangles back out to the sides. (See the next step for reference.)

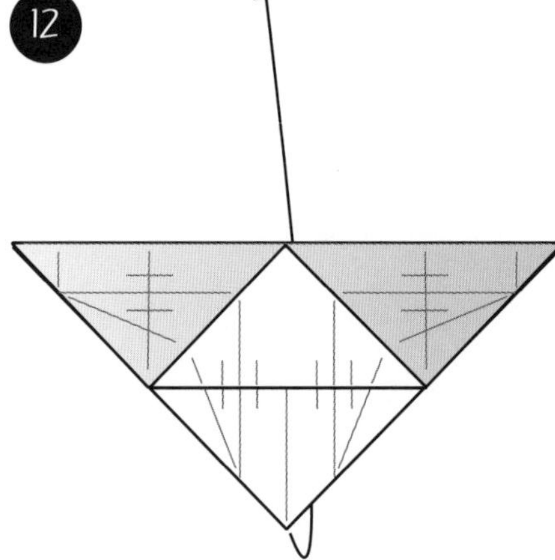

Unfold the bottom layer of paper to the back. (See the next step for reference.)

13

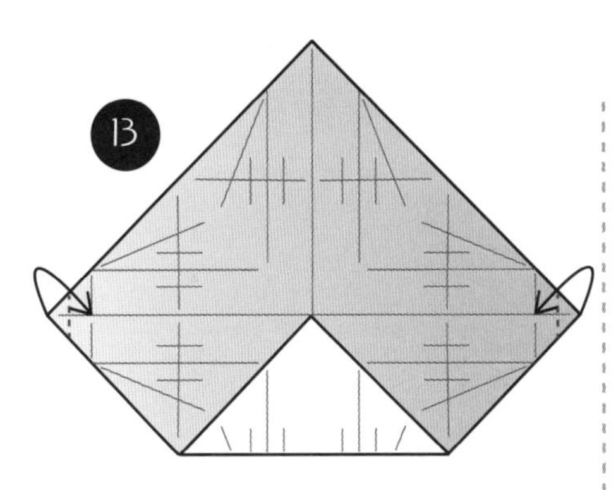

Fold the side corners in to meet the creases made in step #10.

14

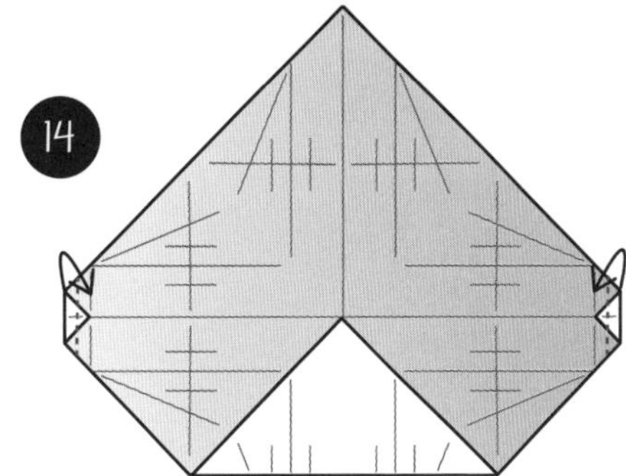

Fold in again, to the crease, through both layers.

15

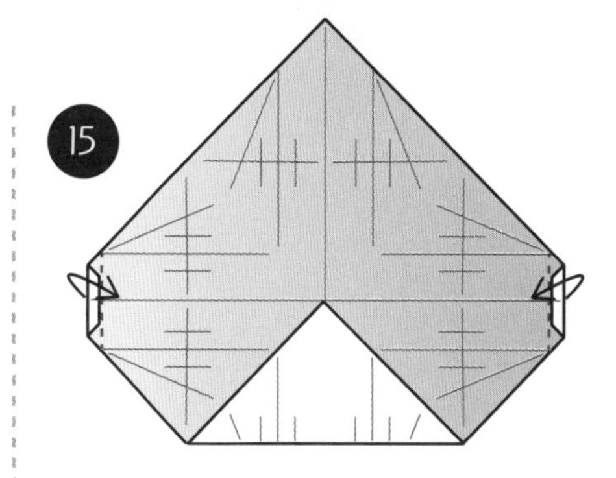

Fold in again, on the pre-crease. This will create a color-change cuff on the bottom of the jeans. (Note: If you don't want the color-change cuff, you can tuck the corners in on the other side.)

16

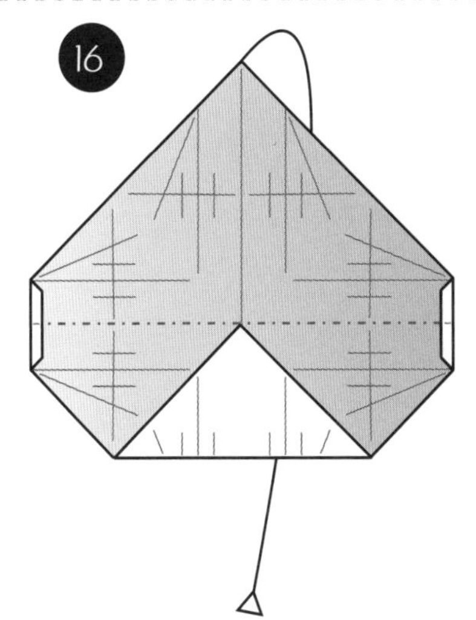

Mountain fold in half on the existing pre-crease.

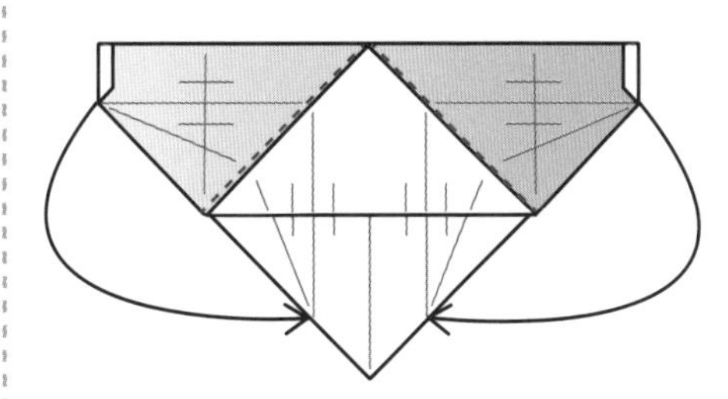

Fold the sides in along the pre-creases so the model once again looks like it did in step #10 with the cuffs folded in.

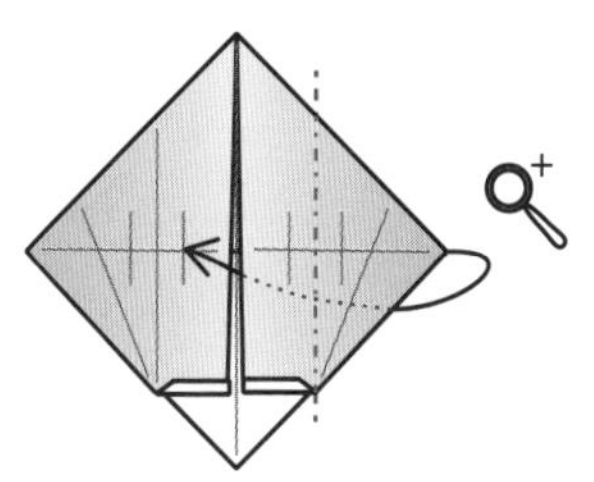

Inside reverse the right corner using the pre-crease from step #8. The tip of the triangle will stick out from the center. (Note: The next step is a magnified view.)

19

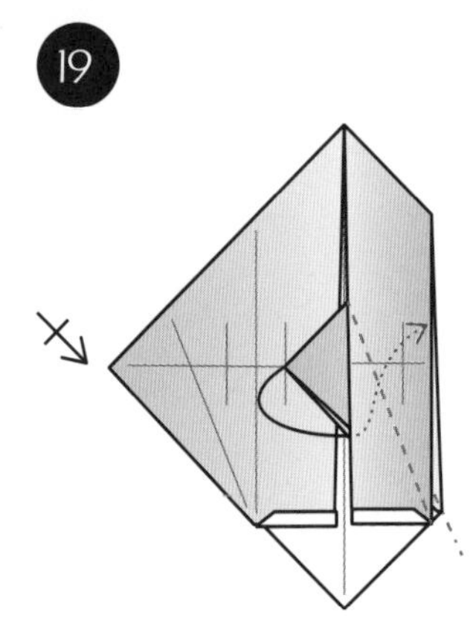

Using the diagonal pre-crease from step #9, inside reverse the triangle that is sticking out so it is hidden from view. Repeat steps #14 and #15 on the left corner.

20

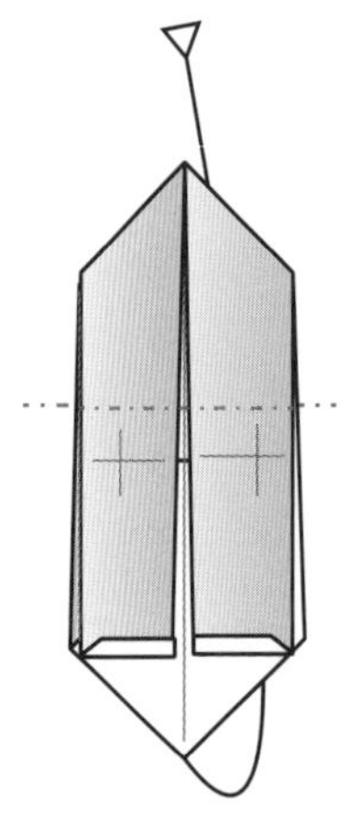

Fold the back section up as far as possible.

21

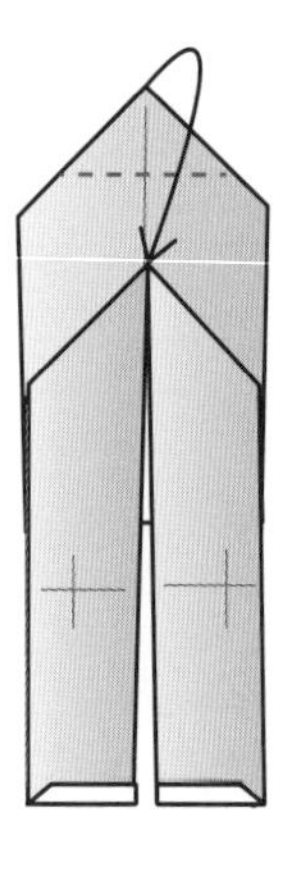

Fold the top corner down to the tip of the triangle point.

22

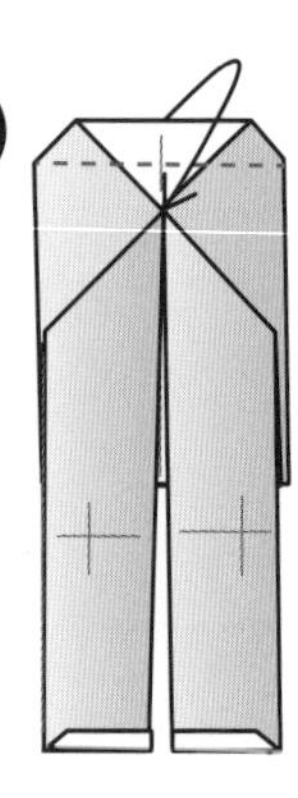

Fold the top edge down again.

23

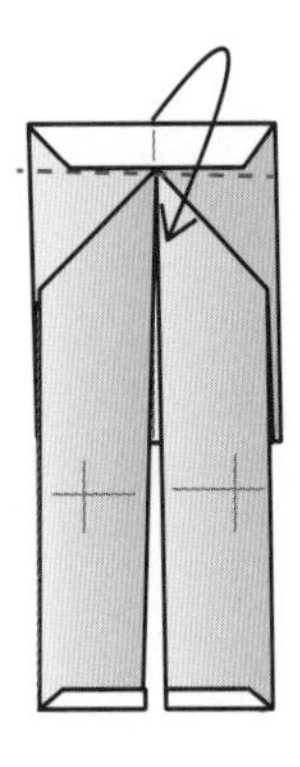

Fold down again, overlapping the triangle points.

24

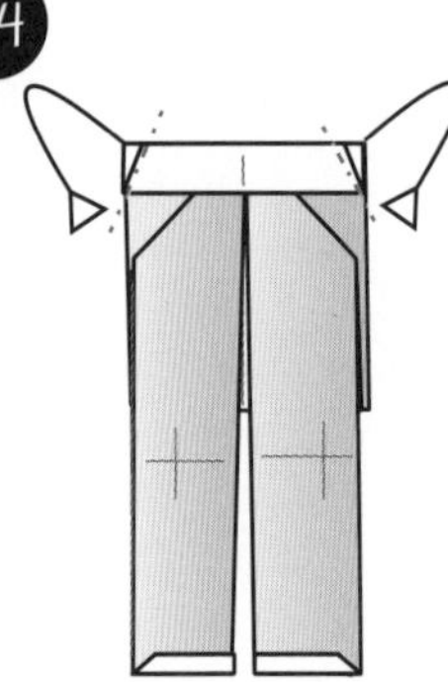

Mountain fold the corners to taper the waistband.

Enjoy your finished jeans!

Try folding your jeans in unexpected colors and patterns!

Dresses

Shift Dress

Shift dresses are easy to wear and a simple, classic wardrobe must-have for any fashionista. Although this paper version has a slightly nipped-in waist to give it shape, most shift dresses have no defined waist. That's why it's important to find one that fits correctly. Look for a dress that's neither boxy nor tight. A fun pattern or bright color can also make your dress stand out!

STYLE TIPS

- A simple shift dress can be dressed up or down—throw on a blazer or sweater for a more professional look, or add a casual jacket and flats for the perfect weekend outfit.
- Add some statement jewelry—like a bangle or necklace—to dress up your shift dress.

HOW TO FOLD

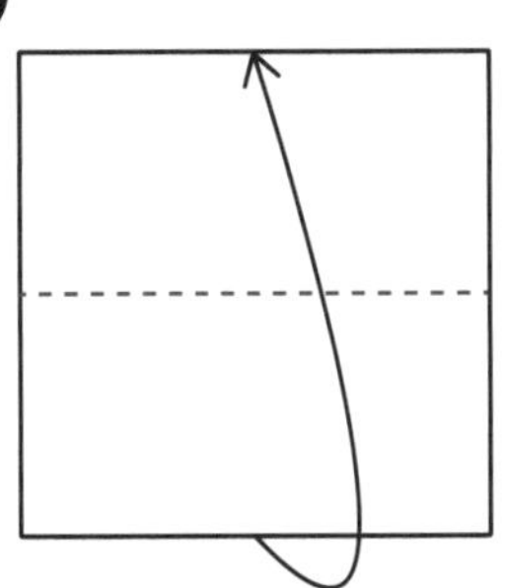

Fold the paper in half horizontally. (Note: The side facing down will become the outside of your shift dress.)

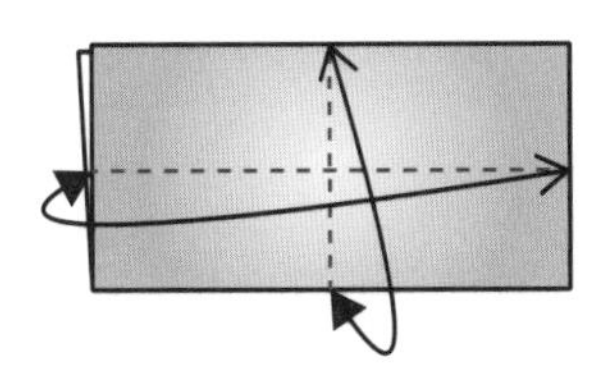

Fold in half again in both directions and then unfold.

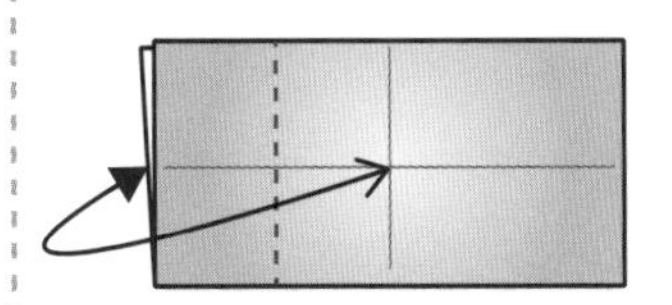

Fold the left side into the center crease and then unfold.

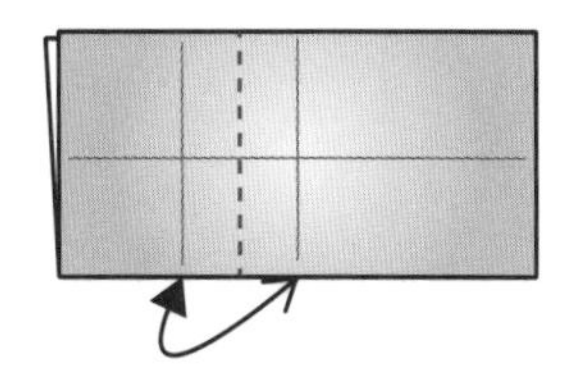

Fold from crease to crease (between the quarter and half creases) and then unfold.

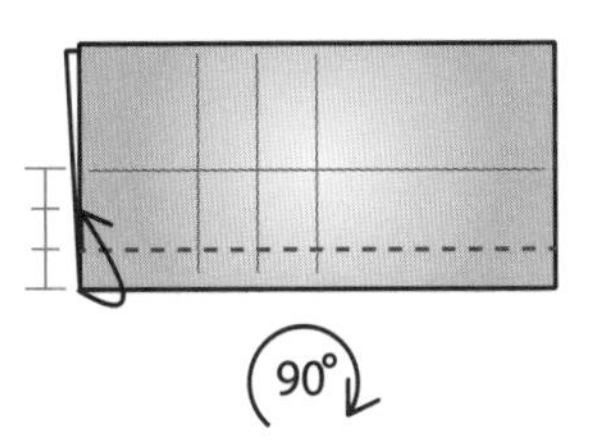

Fold the bottom edge up one-third of the way between the bottom of the paper and the center crease. (Note: You can experiment with what happens to the center of your shift dress depending on the width of this fold.) Rotate the paper 90°.

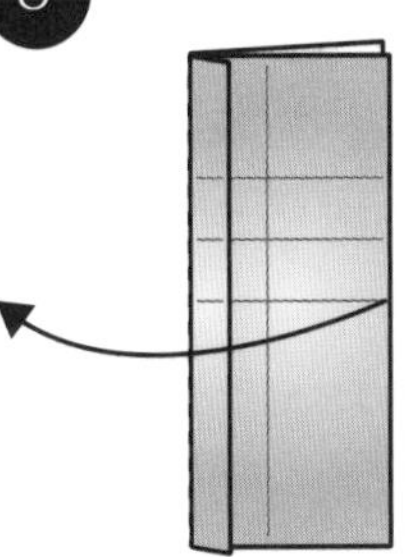

Unfold the paper back to the original square.

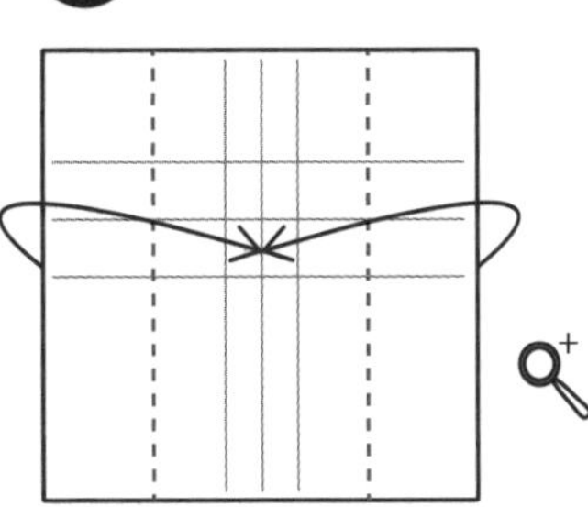

Fold the side edges into the center on the existing pre-creases. (Note: the next step is a magnified view.)

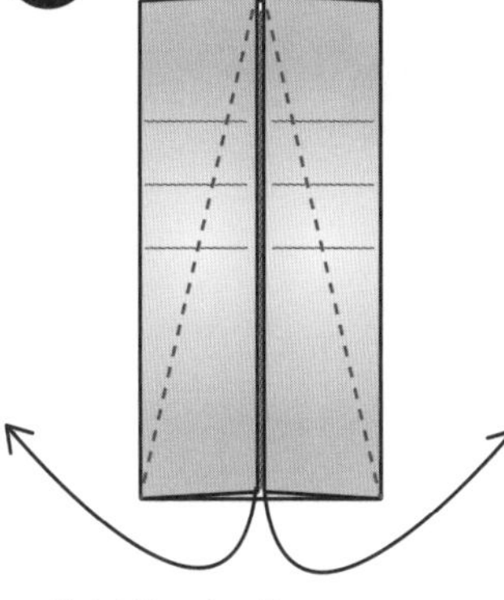

Fold the bottom corners out at an angle starting from the top center point. (See the next step for reference.)

9

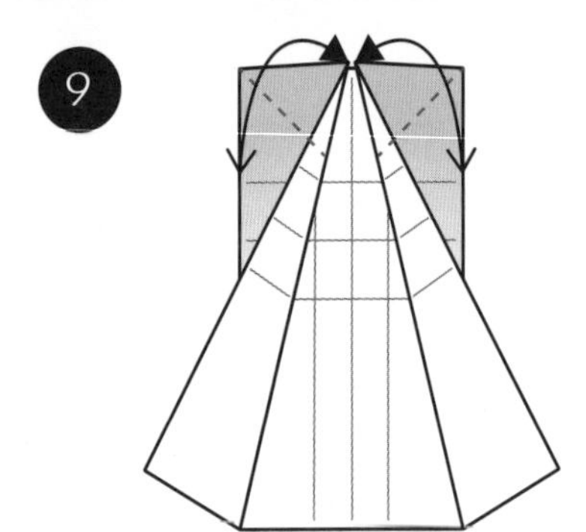

Using just the top layer of paper, fold the corners down at a 45° angle and then unfold. (Note: The corners will line up with the side folded edges.)

10

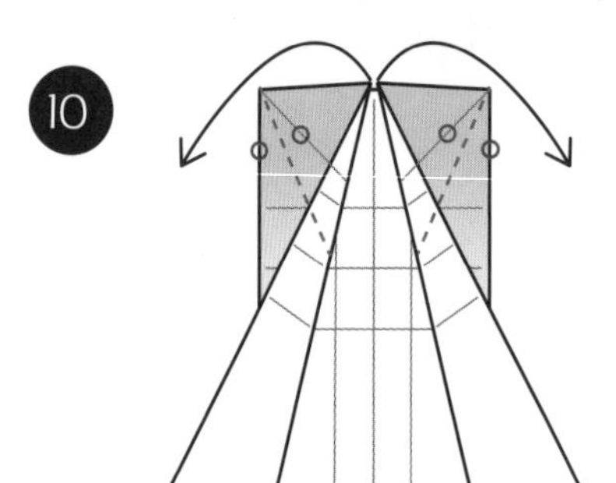

Fold the corner out to make the sleeves of your dress by lining up the crease from the previous step with the side folded edges. (See the next step for reference.)

11

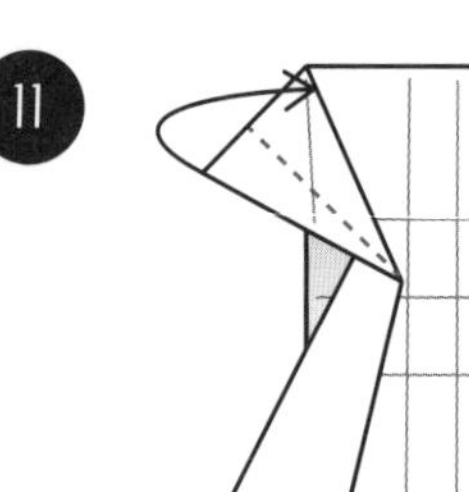

Angle bisect the triangle from the bottom point to make the sleeves smaller. Turn the paper over.

12

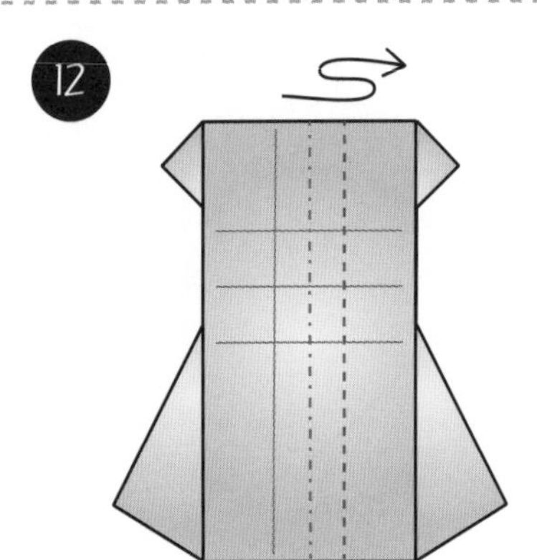

Pleat fold the center using the existing crease. (See the next step for reference.)

13

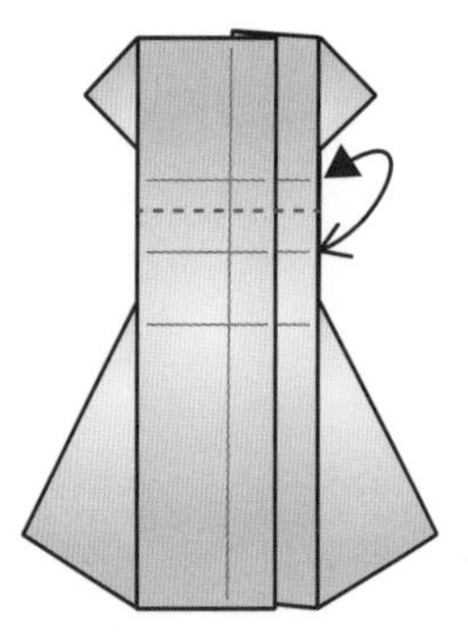

Make a new valley crease between the top two pre-creases and then unfold.

14

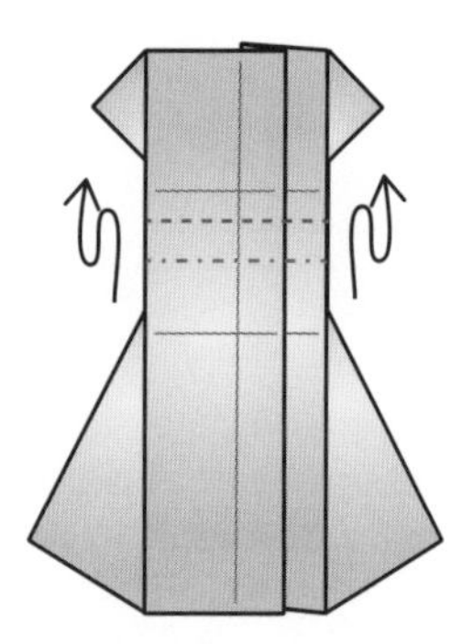

Pleat fold the center using the crease made in the previous step and the lower pre-crease. (Note: The mountain crease is on the bottom, and the valley crease is on top. See the next step for reference.)

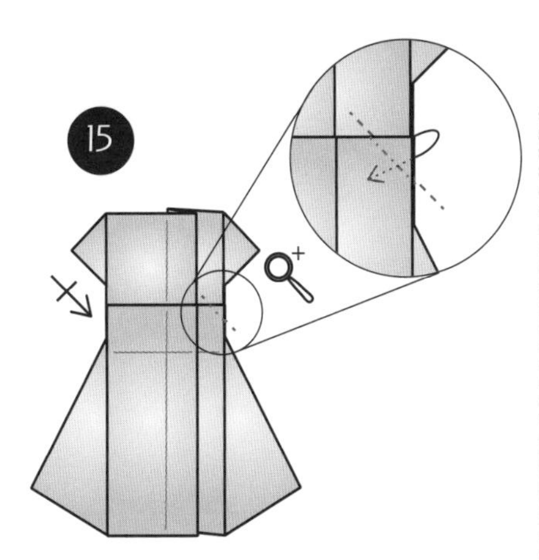

Fold and unfold, and then inside reverse the small corner to taper the dress and bodice. Repeat on the opposite side.

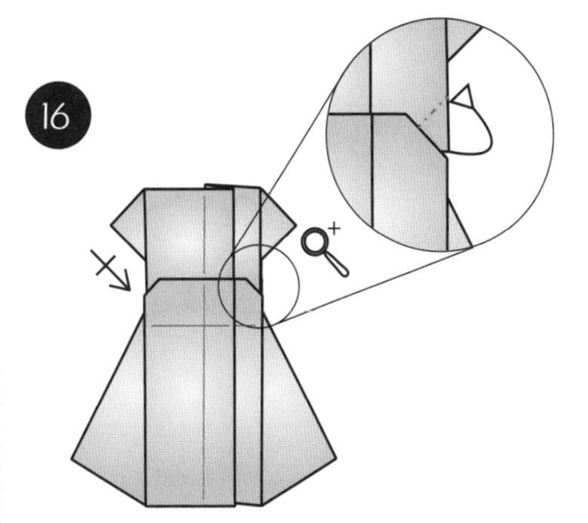

Mountain fold the small corner on the back layer. Repeat on the opposite side.

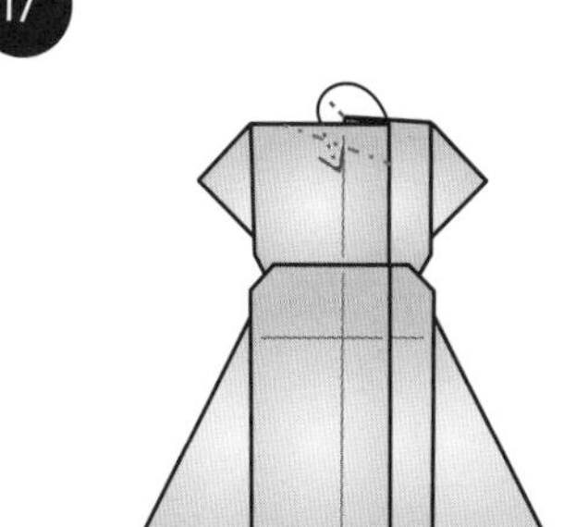

Fold and unfold, and then inside reverse the top of the bodice in an asymmetrical diagonal. (Note: This is to shape the top of the garment. See the next step for reference.)

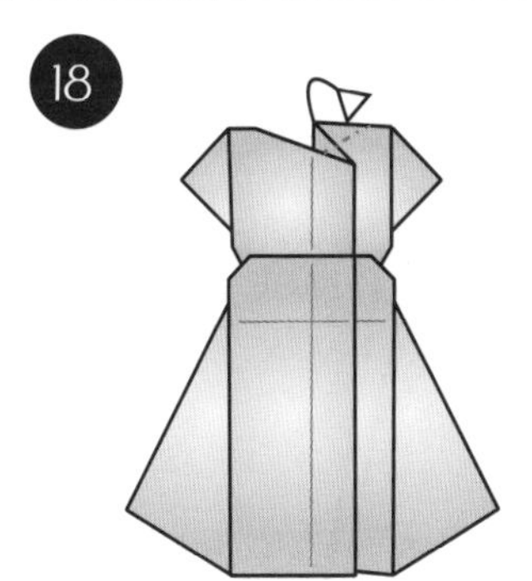

Mountain fold the upper corner of the back layer to finish shaping the V-neck.

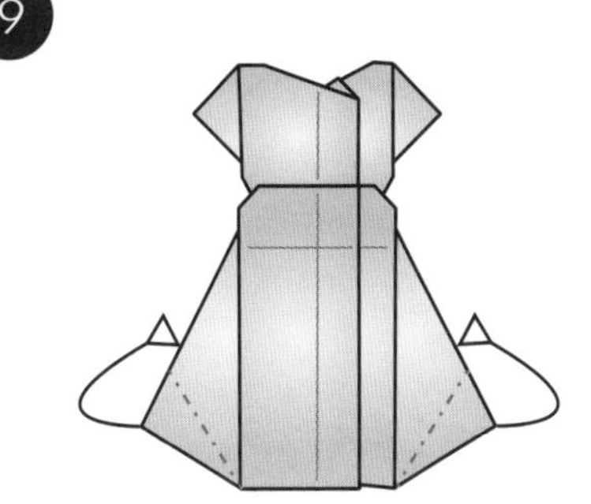

Mountain fold the bottom corners to shape the skirt.

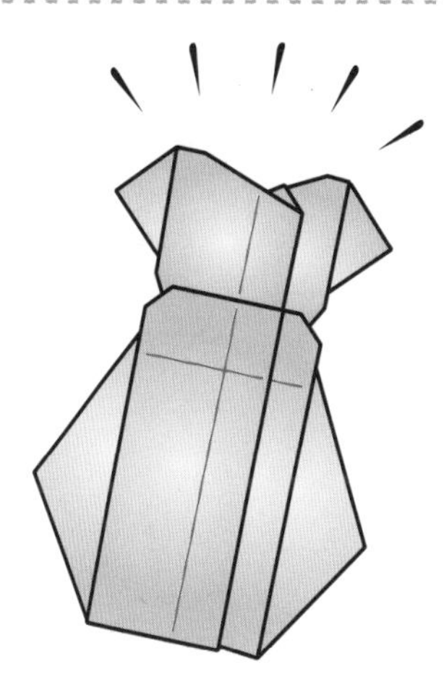

Enjoy your finished shift dress!

Sundress

Sundresses are the perfect summer attire—easy to wear, lightweight, and comfortable. Plus they come in a variety of fun, playful patterns. This paper version features a feminine floral print, but you can play around with an array of other patterns as well. For the most flattering fit, look for a sundress that hits at or just above the knee. A fitted waist, like the one on this model, also helps create an elegant silhouette.

STYLE TIPS

- Pair your sundress with a pair of heels to make it party-ready, or opt for a pair of flip-flops or flat sandals for a more casual look.
- Don't forget your sunglasses! Nothing completes a summer look like a cute pair of shades.

Pg. 130

HOW TO FOLD

1

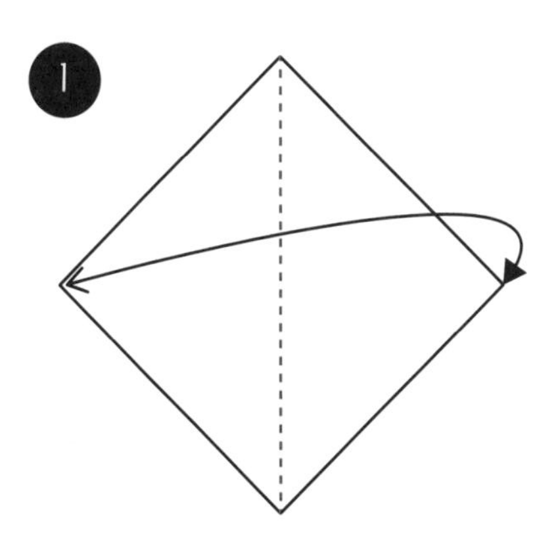

Fold the paper in half diagonally and unfold. (Note: The side that is facing down will become the pattern of your sundress.)

2

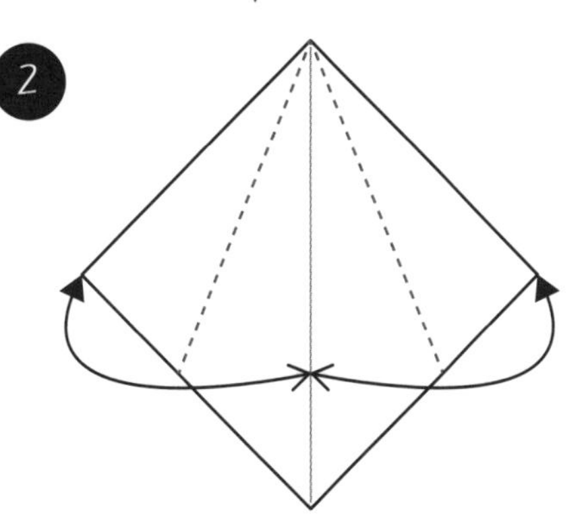

Fold the sides into the center crease and unfold.

3

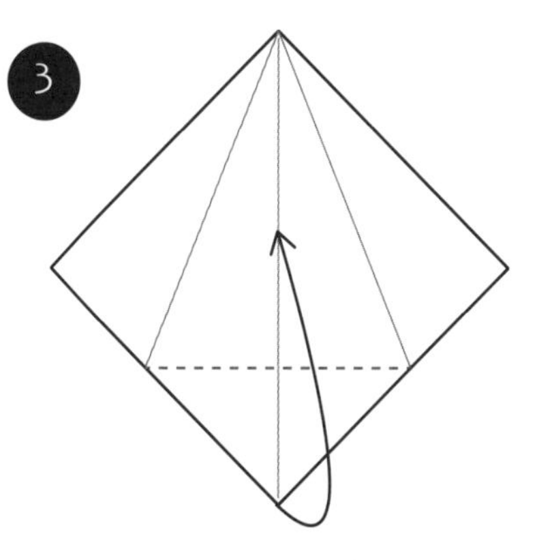

Fold the bottom triangle up using the bottom edge of the pre-creases made in the previous step as a landmark.

4

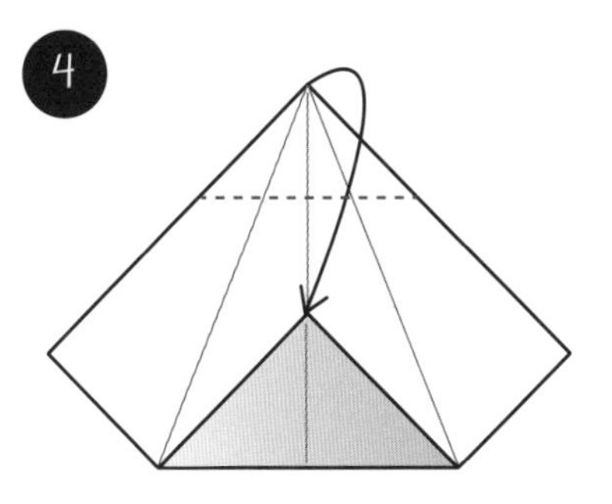

Fold the top corner down to meet the tip of the bottom corner.

5

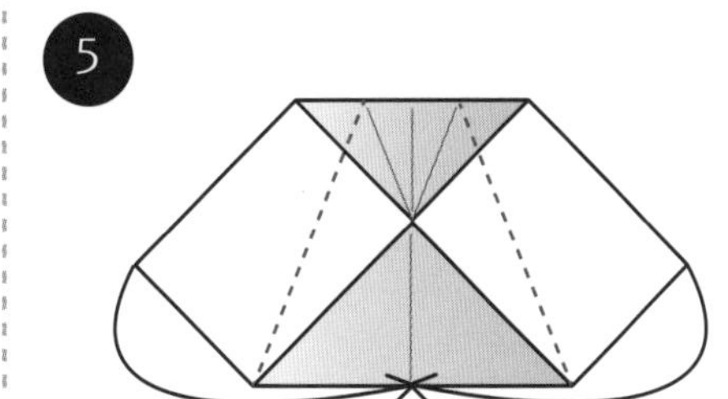

Fold the sides back in on the pre-creases made in step #2.

6

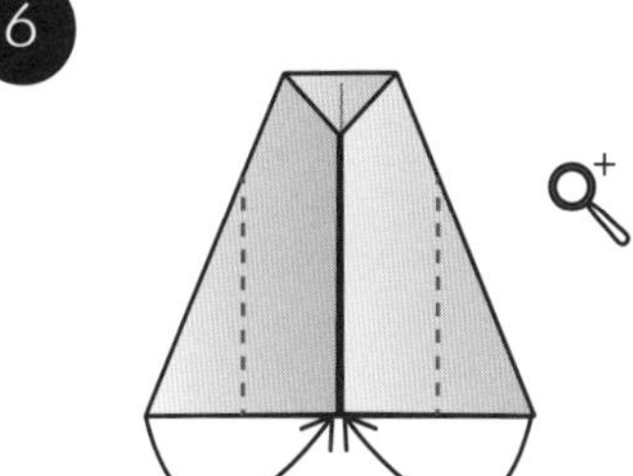

Fold the side corners into the center on the bottom. Be careful that the layers of paper don't shift. (Note: The next step is a magnified view.)

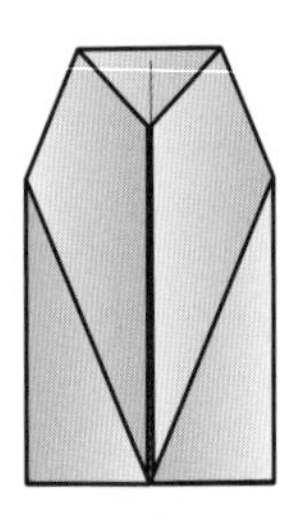

Turn the paper over.

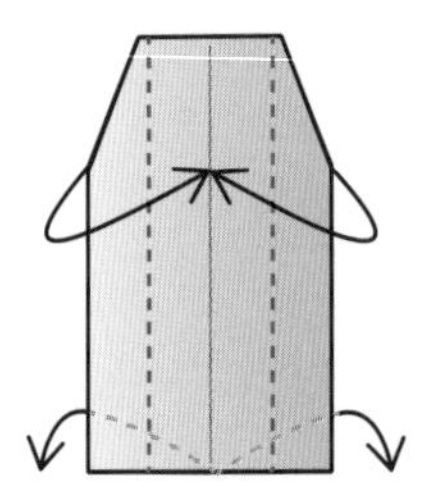

Fold the side edges into the center, allowing the corner flaps to flip out to the front as you make this crease. (See the next step for reference.)

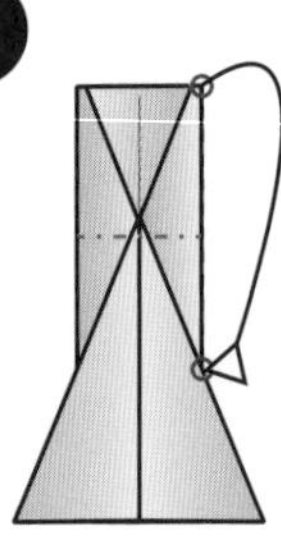

Mountain fold the top section to the back, using the circled points for reference. The crease will be slightly below where the top corners of the triangle meet.

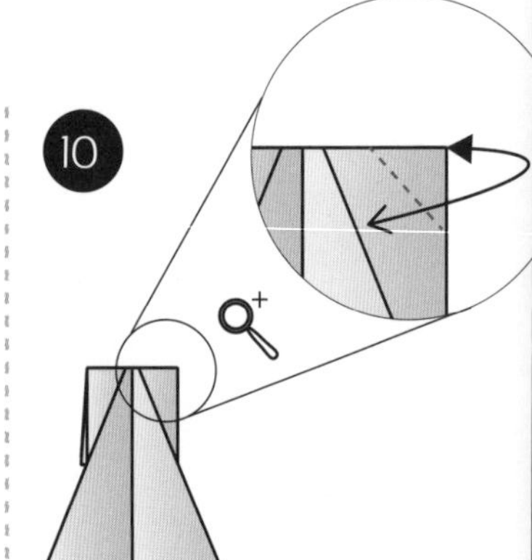

Fold and then unfold a small triangle on the top right corner. (See magnified view for reference.)

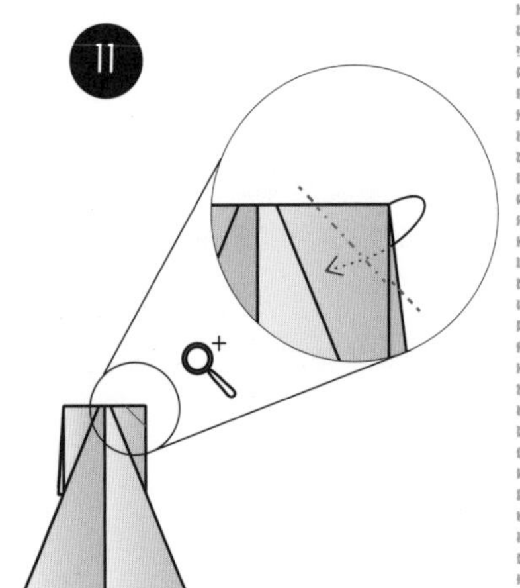

Inside reverse the corner.

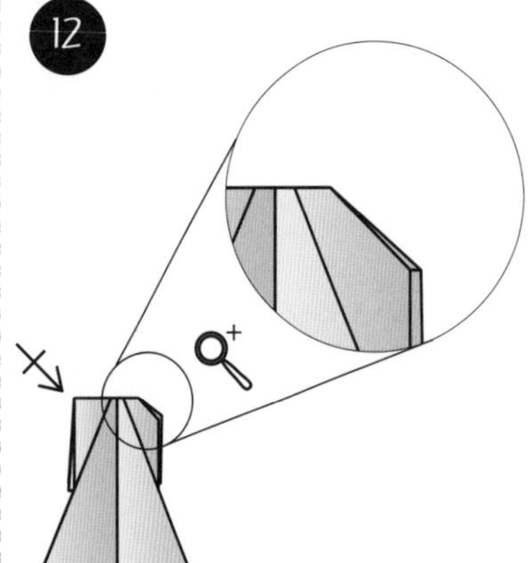

Repeat on the opposite side.

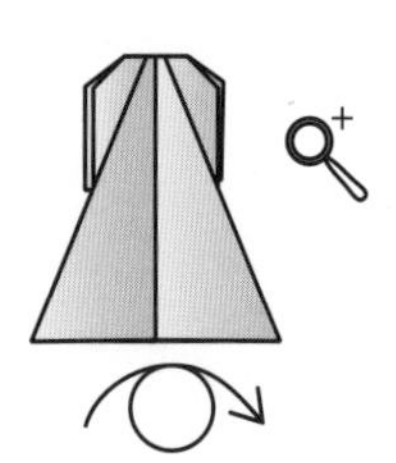

Turn the paper over. (Note: The next step is a magnified view.)

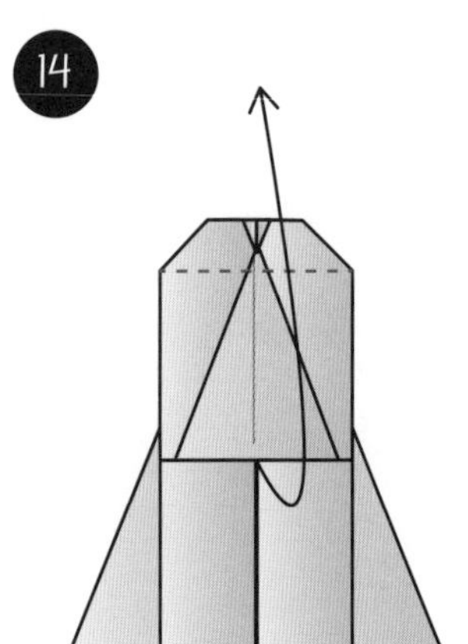

Fold up the flap at the base of the inside-reversed triangles.

15

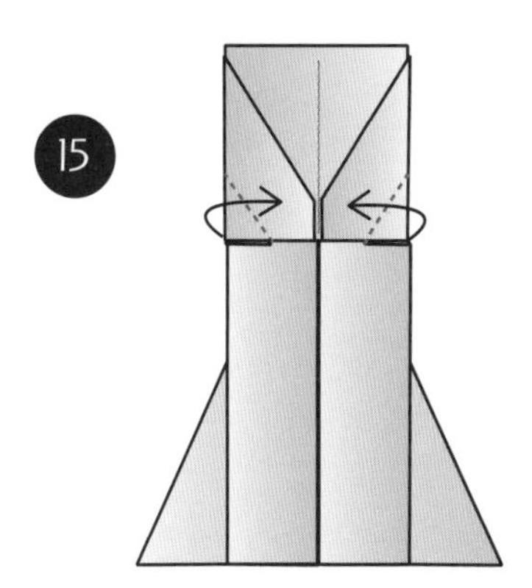

Fold in small triangles at each bottom corner. This will create a separation between the bodice and the skirt. (Note: You can taper it at more of an angle if you would like.)

16

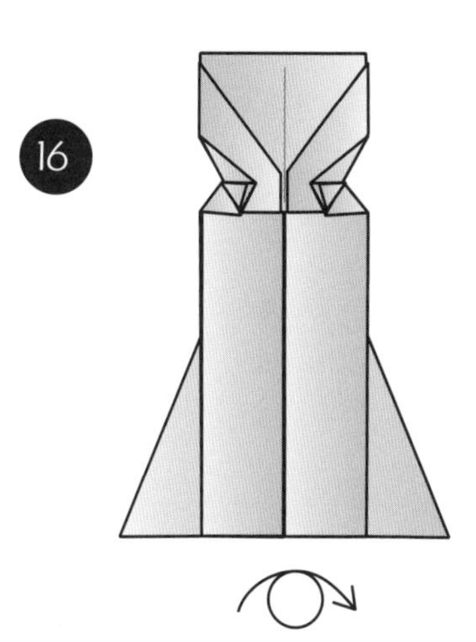

Turn the paper back over to the front.

17

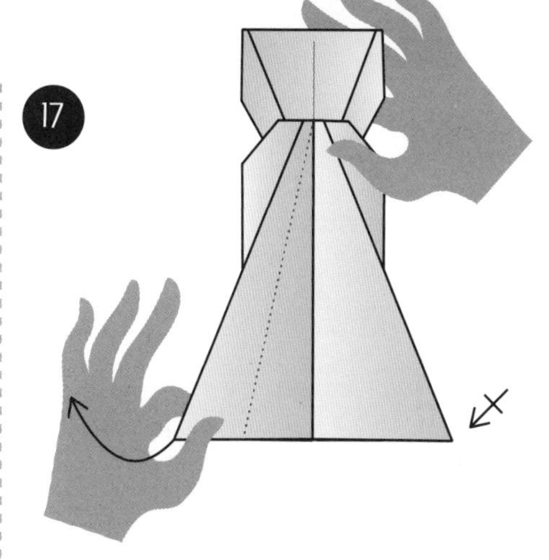

Hold the dress in the middle section near the right side as you pull the bottom left corner to spread the dress open wider. Repeat on the opposite side.

18

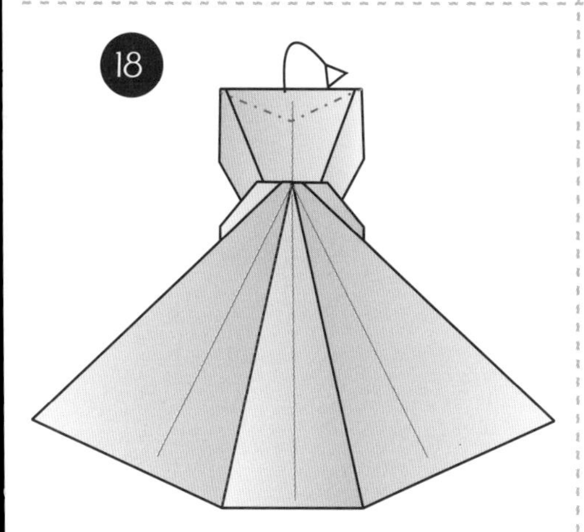

Optional: Mountain fold the top section in a V-line, similar to an inside reverse, to give the bodice more shape.

Enjoy your finished sundress!

Little Black Dress

The **LBD—**also known as the **little black dress**—is an absolute must for any fashionista's closet. The perfect LBD is both timeless and versatile, but finding a dress that stands out from the crowd is equally important. The asymmetrical details on both the skirt and bodice of this paper LBD help set it apart from your basic black dress, and the tapered waist makes for an extra flattering fit.

STYLE TIPS

- Don't forget the accessories—bold jewelry and a chic clutch to carry all your evening essentials are a must!
- Pair your LBD with a stylish pair of high heels for a full-on fancy ensemble.

HOW TO FOLD

1

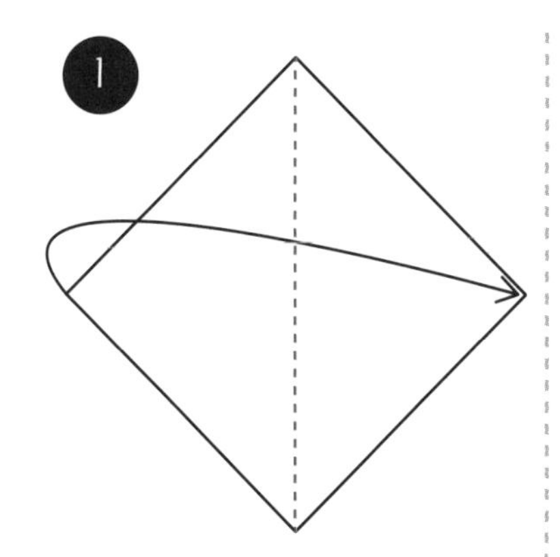

Fold the paper in half diagonally. (Note: The side facing down will become the outside of the dress.)

2

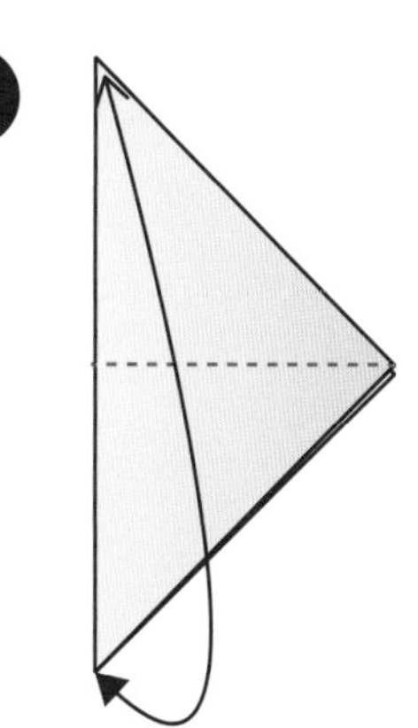

Fold the paper in half horizontally and then unfold.

3

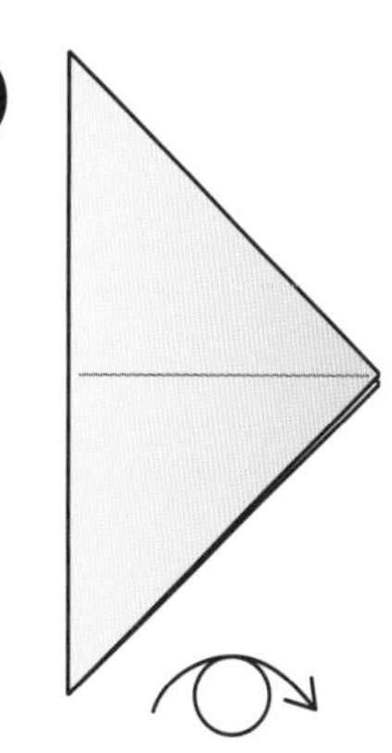

Turn the paper over.

4

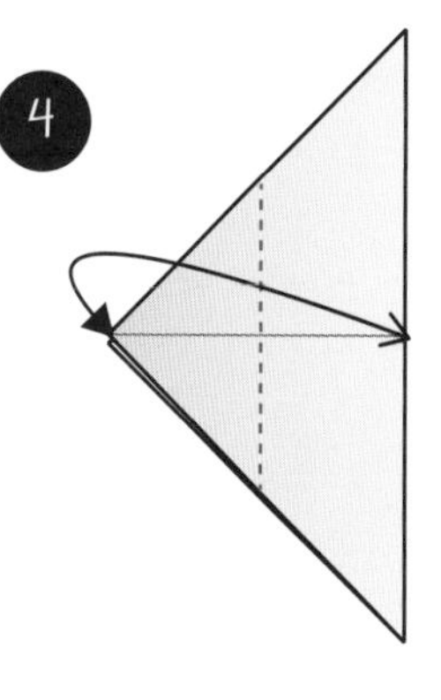

Fold the left corner to the opposite edge and then unfold.

5

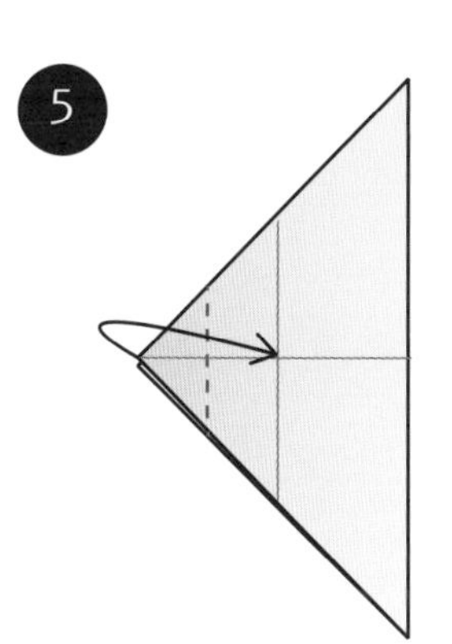

Fold the left corner (through both layers of paper) into the crease created in the previous step.

6

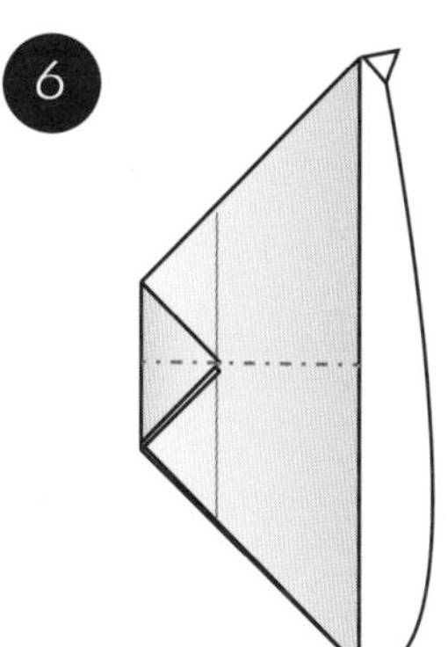

Mountain fold the paper in half on the existing pre-crease by folding the bottom corner to the back.

7

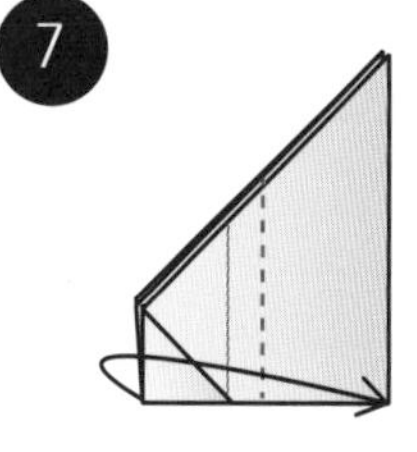

Fold the paper in half, bringing the left edge across to the opposite side. (Note: The next step is a magnified view.)

8

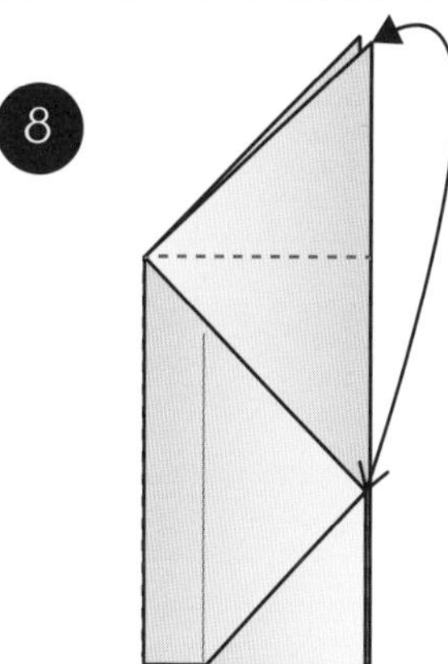

Fold the top corner down, through all layers, and then unfold. (Note: Use the upper point of the left triangle as a reference.)

Turn the paper over.

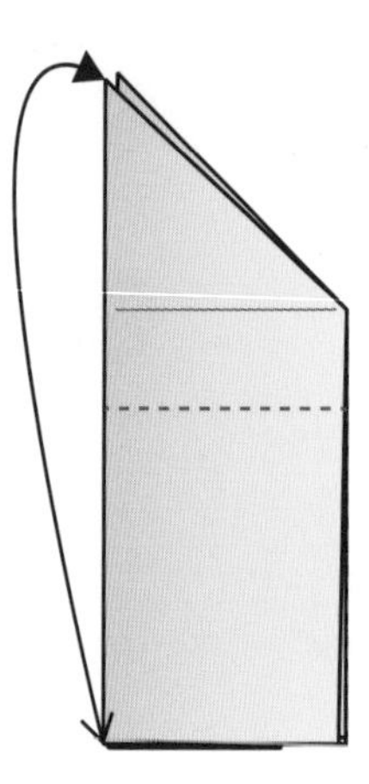

Valley fold the top corner down to the bottom and then unfold.

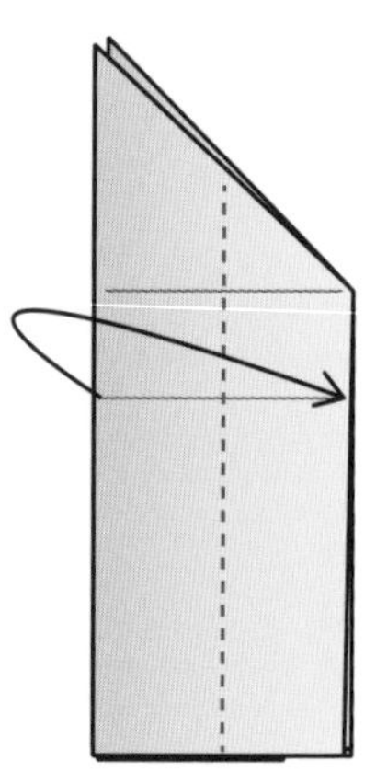

Valley fold the tall left side (the top double layers of paper) in half. (Note: This will leave the shorter bottom section in the back.)

12

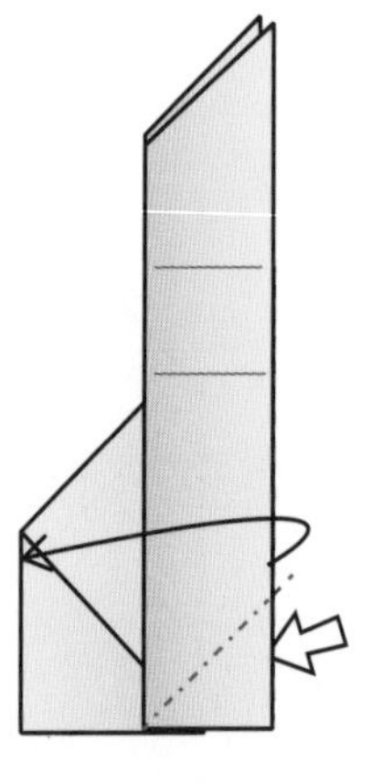

Open and squash fold by bringing only the top layer of the right side back to the left side. A pocket will open on the bottom to squash into an upside-down triangle. (See the next step for reference.)

13

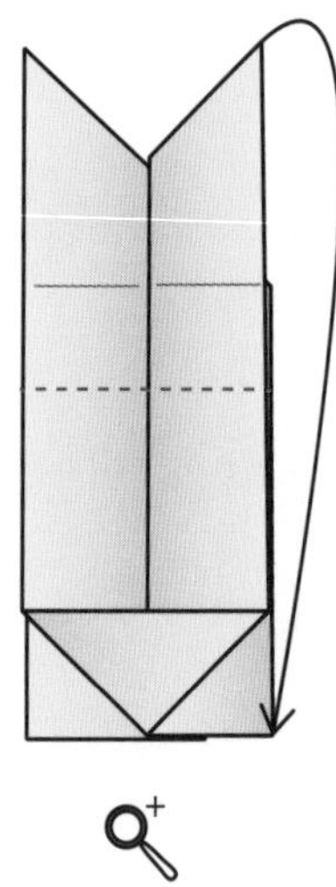

Valley fold the model in half horizontally using the preexisting crease. (Note: The next step is a magnified view.)

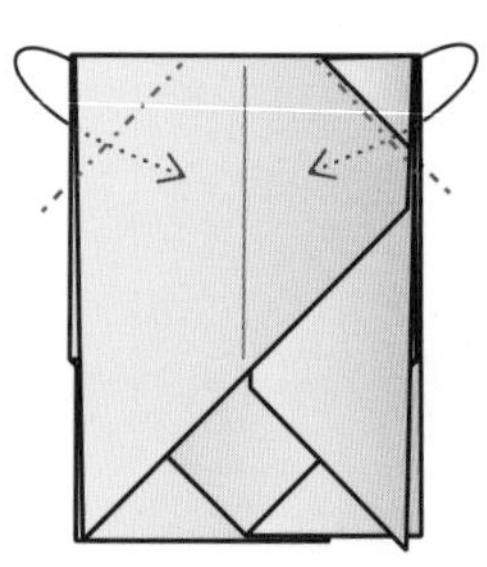

Pre-crease and inside reverse the upper left and right corners.

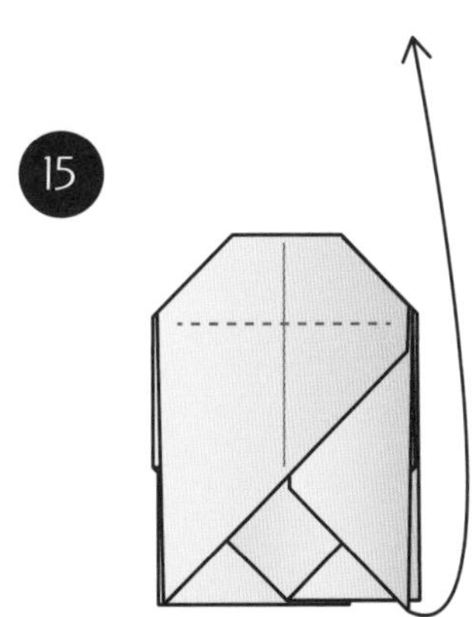

Fold the top layer back up on the existing crease to create the bodice of the dress. (See the next step for reference.)

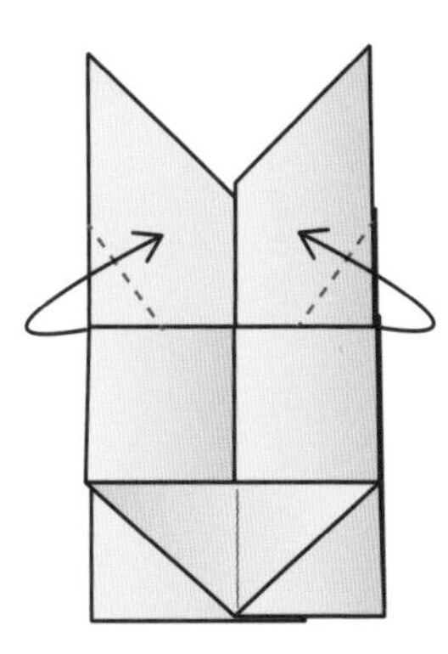

Valley fold the lower left and right corners of the bodice to shape the waistline of the dress.

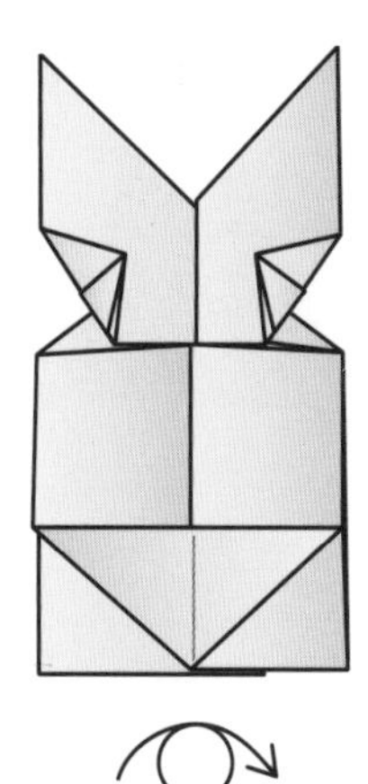

Turn the paper over.

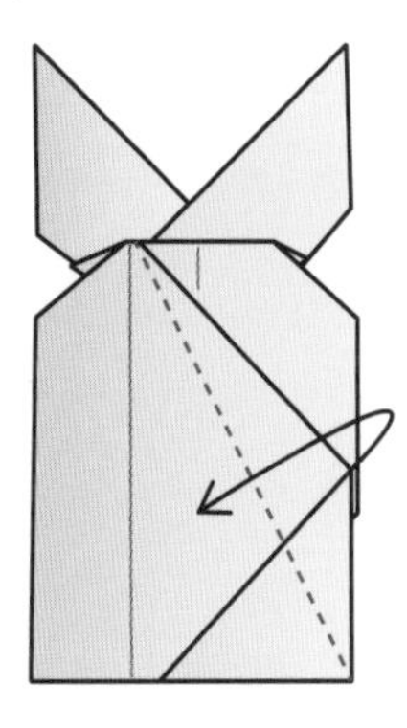

Valley fold the loose flap on the top, front layer of the skirt.

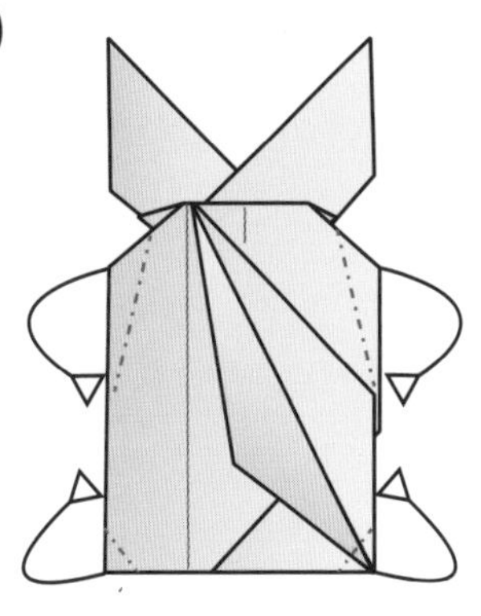

Mountain fold the upper and lower corners of the skirt to the back to shape the bottom of the dress.

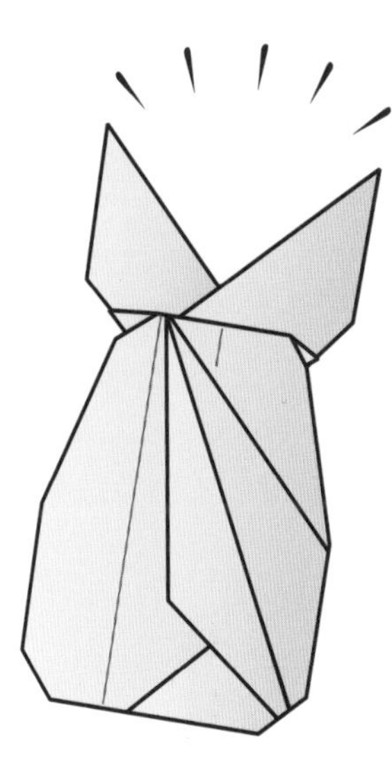

Enjoy your finished LBD!

Ball Gown

A **ball gown** can be a lot of things—classic, simple, elegant, beautiful, and timeless—but no matter what, it's always the perfect piece for a special formal occasion. With a bold skirt and art deco-inspired bodice, this paper version captures all those qualities and more. Feel free to jazz it up with glitter, jewels, and bling to make it even more special!

STYLE TIPS

- Dress your ball gown up with a pair of high heels.
- Don't forget to grab a clutch to hold all your evening essentials!

HOW TO FOLD

1

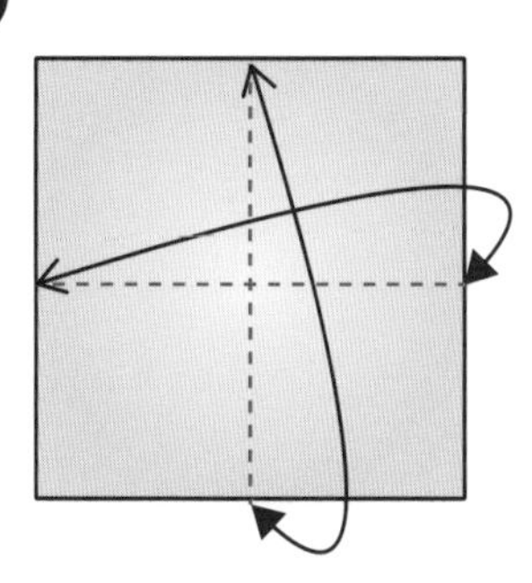

Fold the paper in half in both directions and then unfold. (Note: The side facing up will become the bottom of the ball gown; the opposite side will become the bodice.)

2

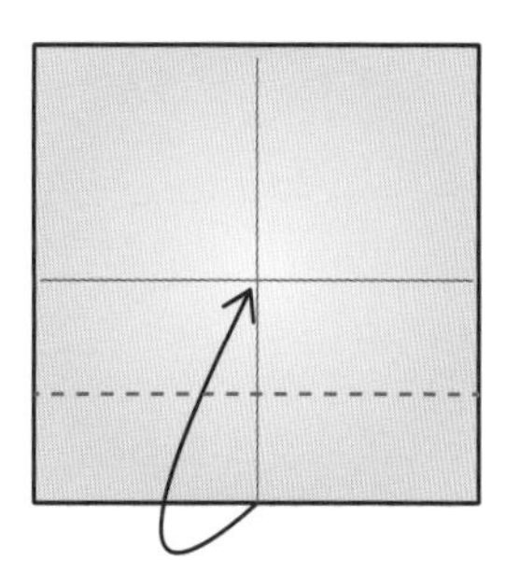

Fold the bottom edge up to the center crease made in the previous step.

3

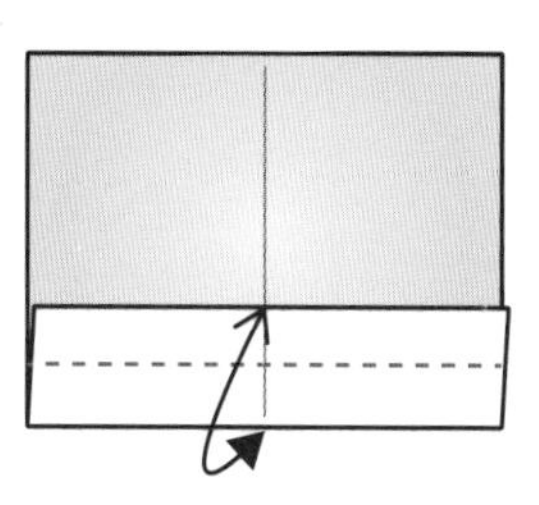

Fold the bottom edge, now two layers thick, up again to the meet the center crease. Then unfold the paper back to the original square.

4

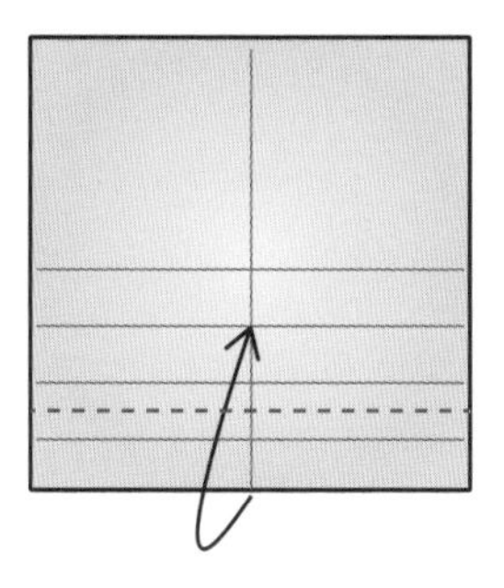

Fold the bottom edge up, using the third crease from the bottom as a landmark. (See the next step for reference.)

5

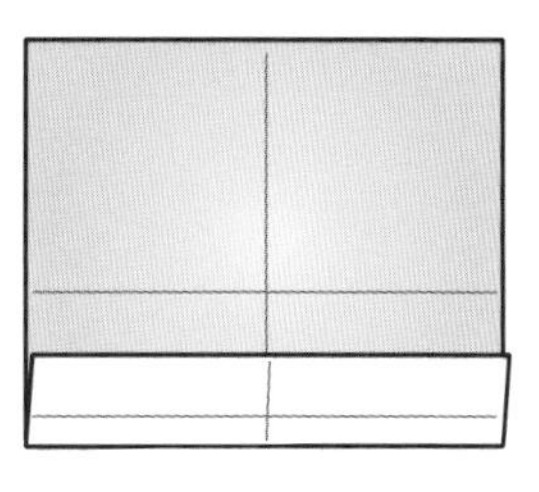

Turn the paper over.

6

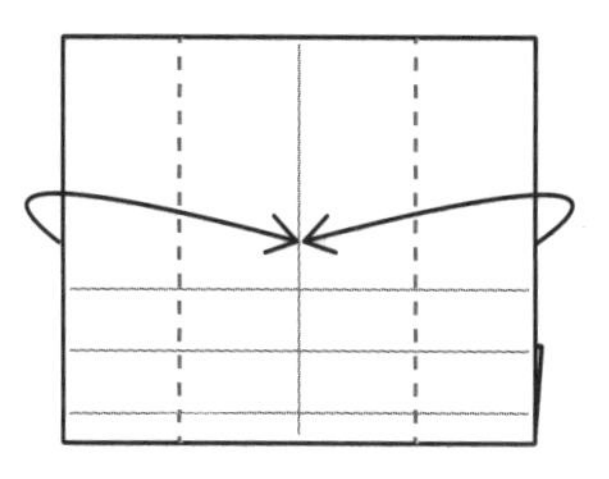

Fold both side edges into the center. (Note: The next step is a magnified view.)

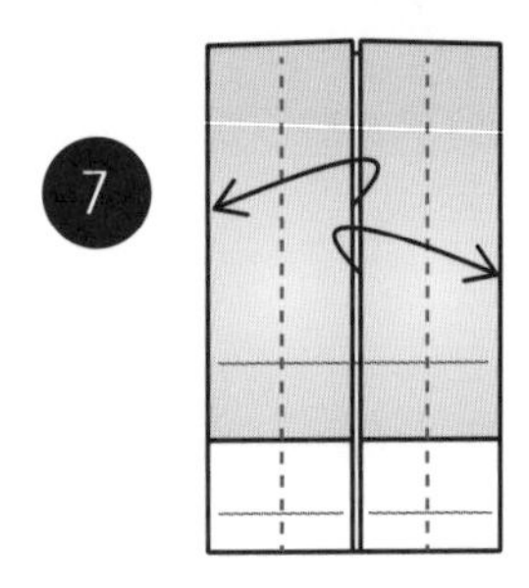

Valley fold the edges back out to the sides.

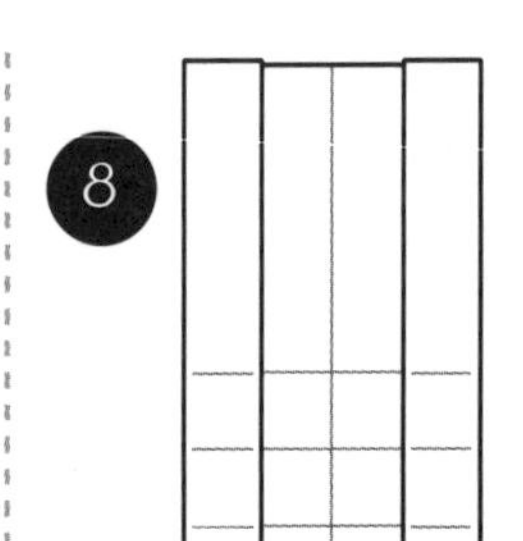

Turn the paper over.

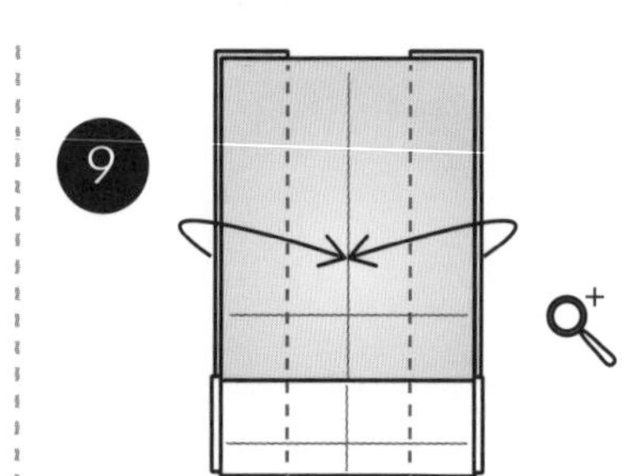

Fold both sides into the center. There will now be many pleated layers. (Note: The next step is a magnified view.)

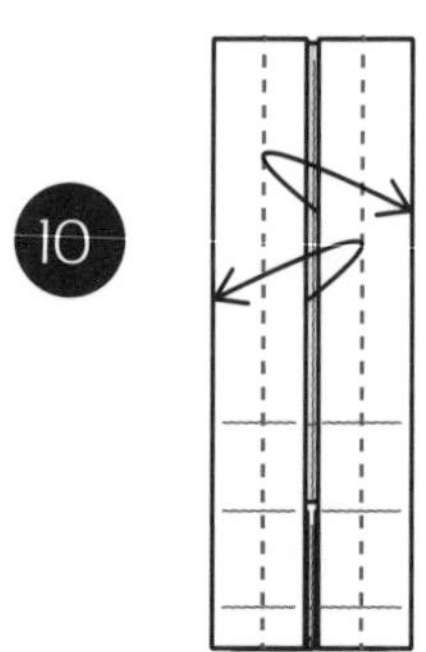

Fold only the top layers out to the sides. (See the next step for reference.)

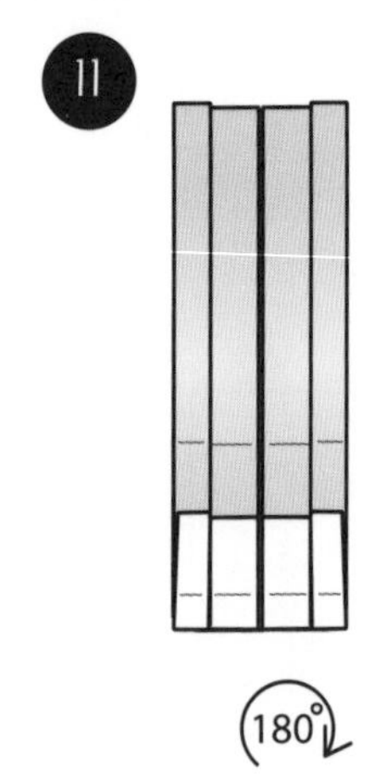

Rotate the paper 180° so the color-changed section is at the top. This top section is the bodice of the dress.

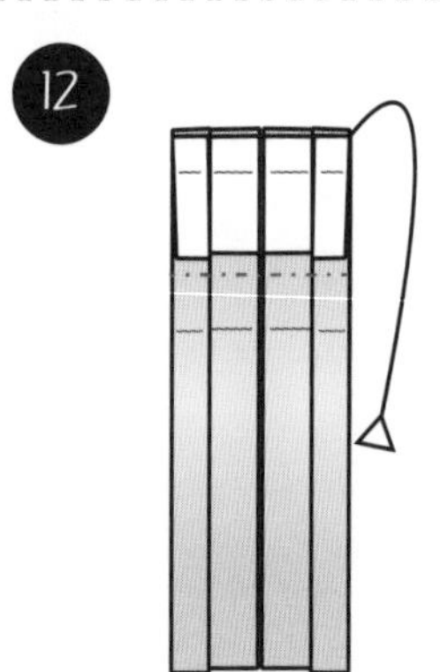

Mountain fold the top section behind on the existing pre-crease in preparation for folding the bottom of the dress.

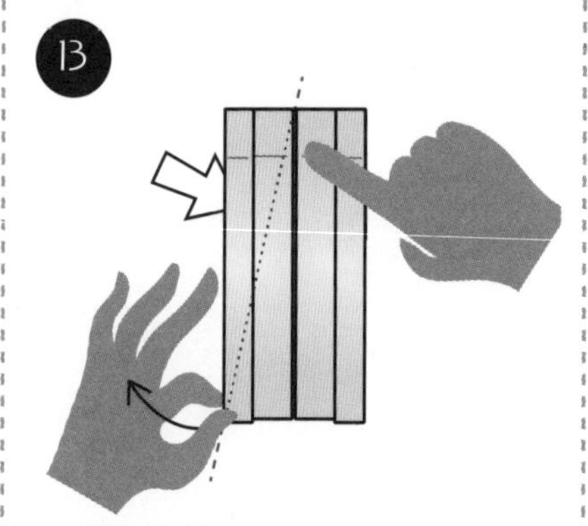

Pinch the bottom left corner and spread open to shape the dress. Make a new crease, pulling as far as you can without tearing the paper. It will help to hold down the top right side of the paper. (Note: Keep the model flat on the table and only lift the left side as you spread-squash.)

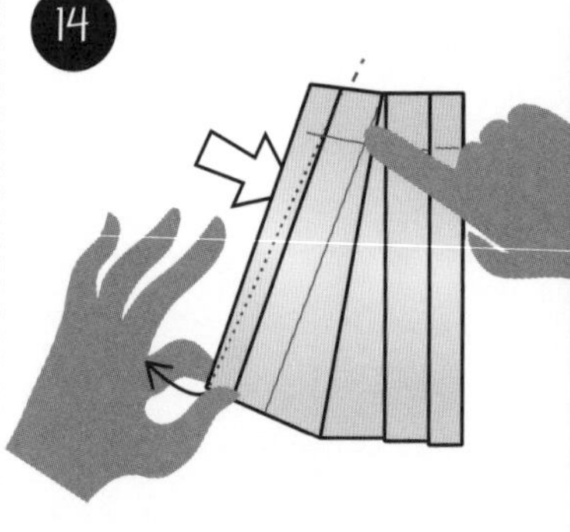

Spread-squash the small section on the edge, similar to the last step. (Note: It will help to hold down the right section.)

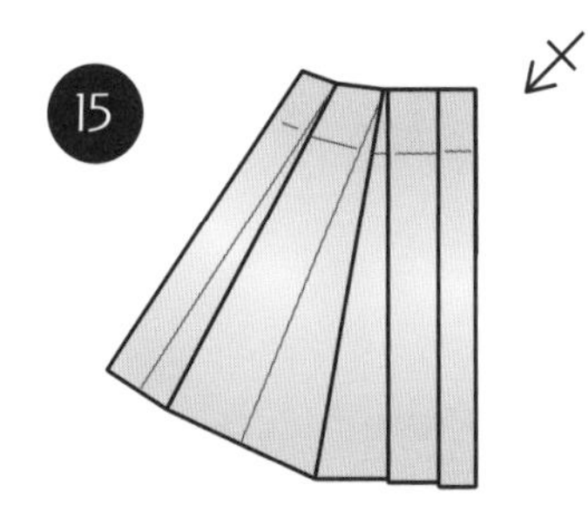

Repeat the spread-squashes from steps #13–14 on the opposite side.

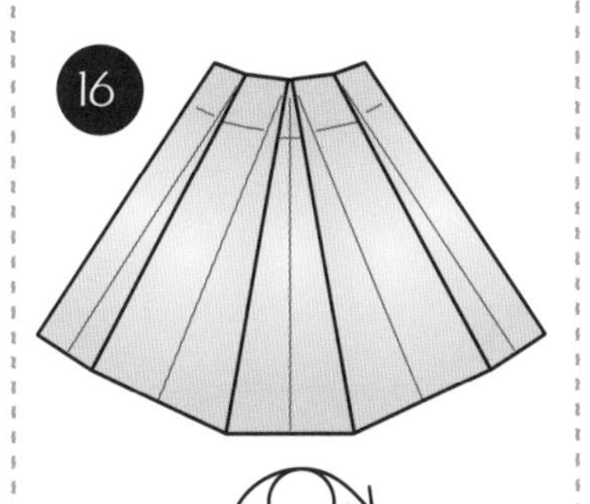

Turn the paper over.

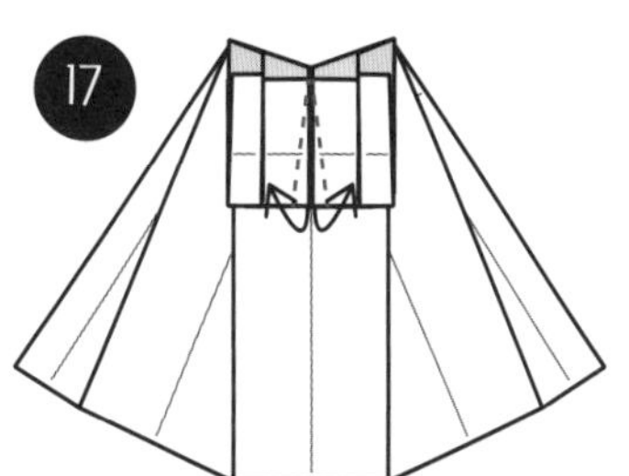

Fold the inner folded edges of the bodice in at a diagonal.

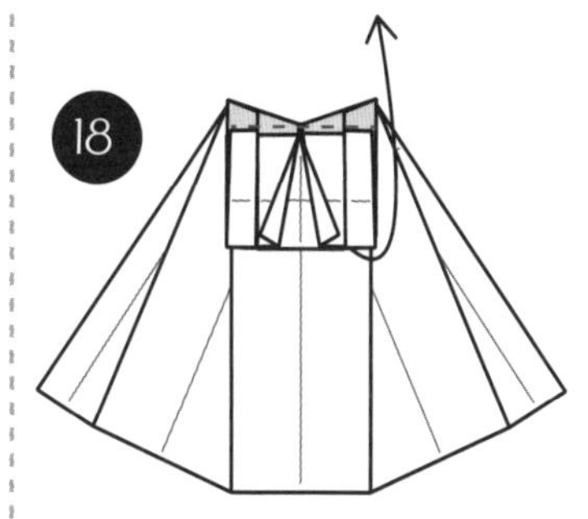

Fold the top section back up while keeping the spread-squashed parts of the dress flat.

Fold the top corners to shape the bodice of the dress. (Note: There are three folded corner layers. If it's too thick to fold them all at once, you can fold them in one at a time.)

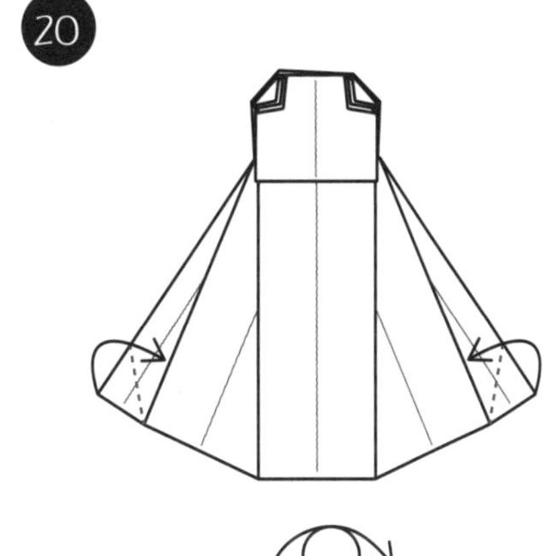

Fold the bottom corners to shape the skirt and turn the paper over.

Enjoy your finished ball gown! (Note: You can shape the ball gown as you'd like, making the skirt and bodice of the dress fuller or more tapered, depending on your personal taste.)

Prom Dress

The dress you wear to prom has to be just right—the right color, the right shape, the right fabric, and the right style! This paper **prom dress** has an elegant sweetheart neckline and just the right amount of flair in the skirt! Try folding it with contrasting colors on each side to make it pop and play up the color change.

STYLE TIPS

- Pair your prom dress with a fun pair of high heels in a contrasting hue for a bright pop of color.
- Make sure to grab a fun bag—like a stylish purse or clutch—to hold all your belongings.

HOW TO FOLD

1

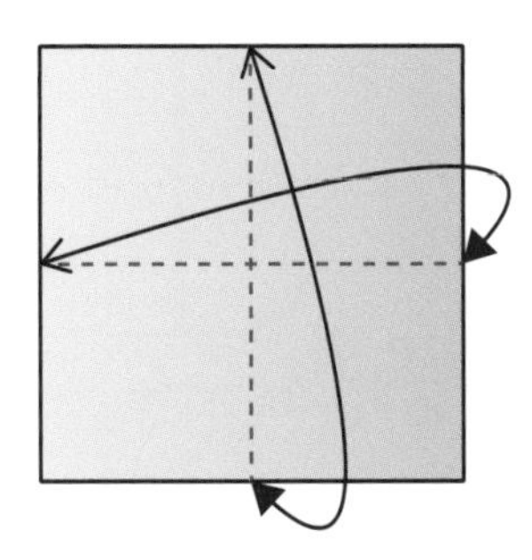

Fold the paper in half in both directions and unfold. (Note: The side facing up will become the outside of your prom dress; the side facing down will become the contrasting neckline.)

2

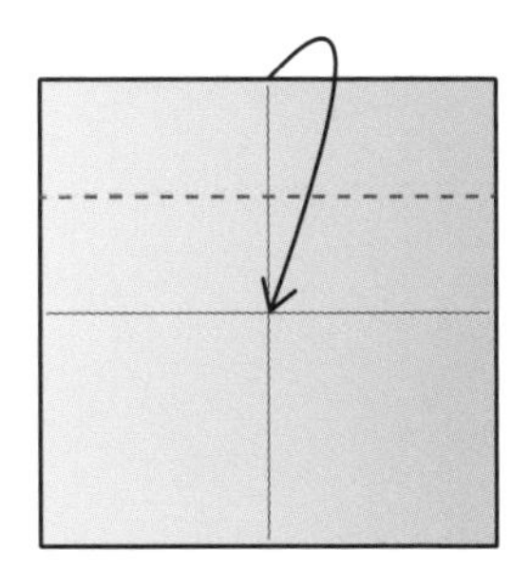

Fold the top edge down to the center crease.

3

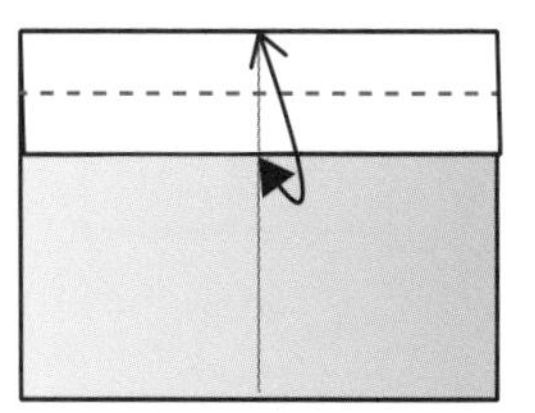

Fold the edge back up to the top and then unfold.

4

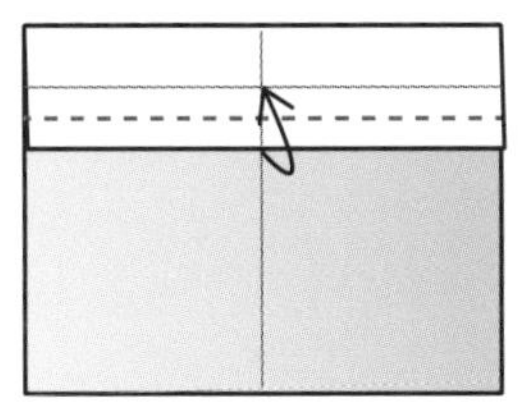

Fold the bottom edge up to the new crease made in the previous step.

5

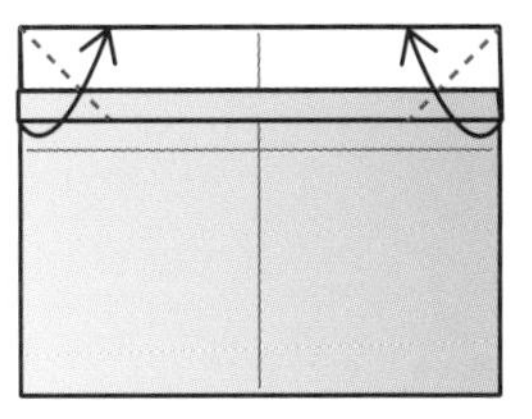

Fold the outside corners in, lining up the outside edge with the top of the paper.

6

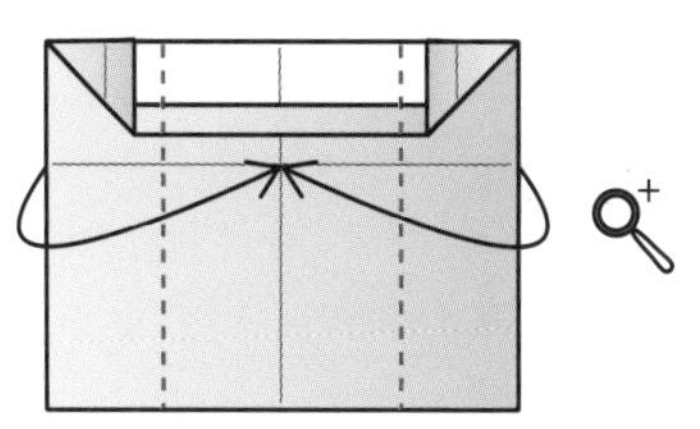

Fold the side edges into the center crease. (Note: The next step is a magnified view.)

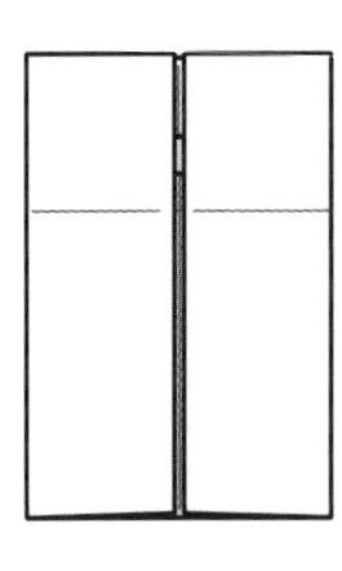

Turn the paper over.

8

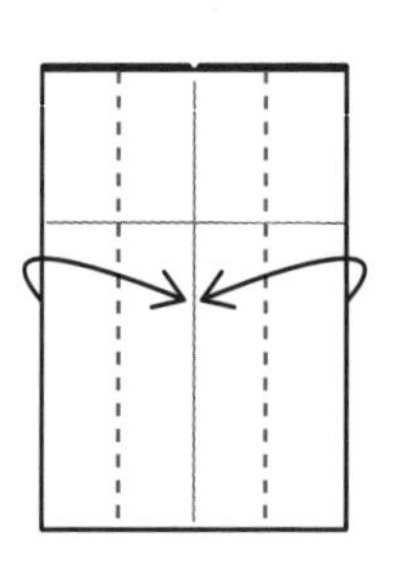

Fold the sides into the center crease.

9

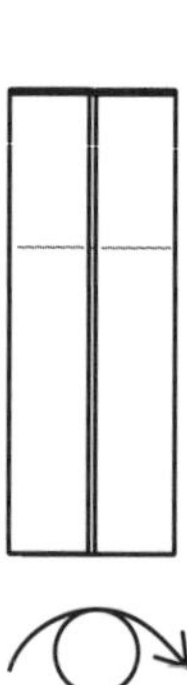

Turn the paper over.

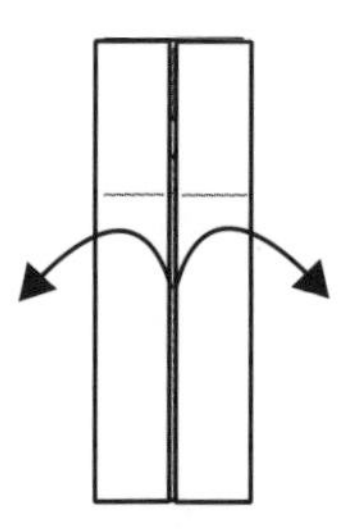

Open the front flaps back out to the sides.

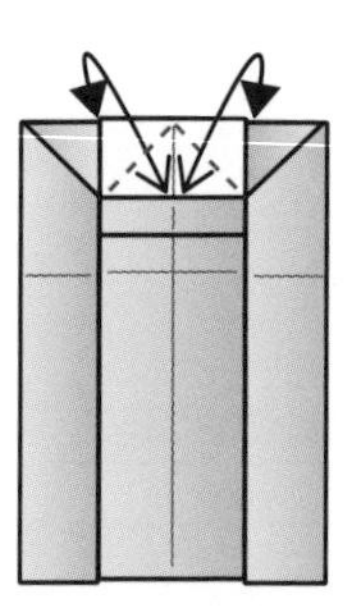

Using only the color-change section at the top, fold the top corners down and then unfold.

12

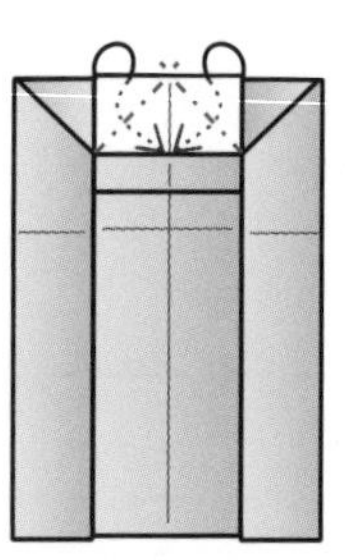

Inside reverse the corners using the pre-creases made in the previous step.

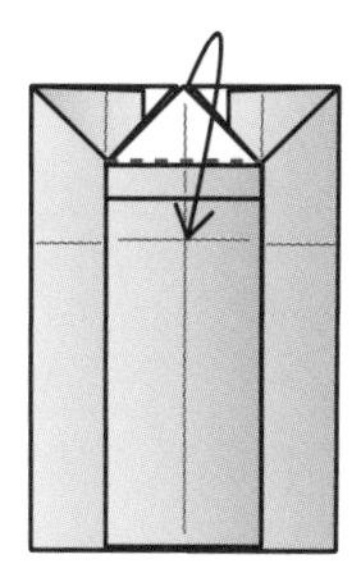

Fold the top triangle flap down.

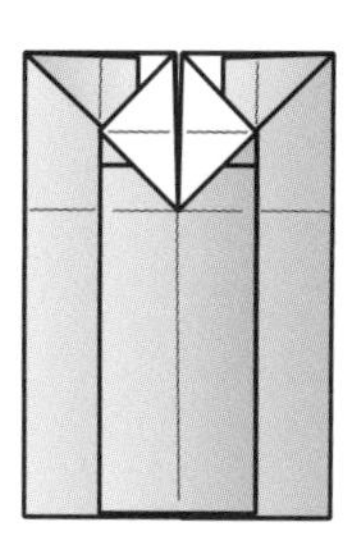

Turn the paper over.

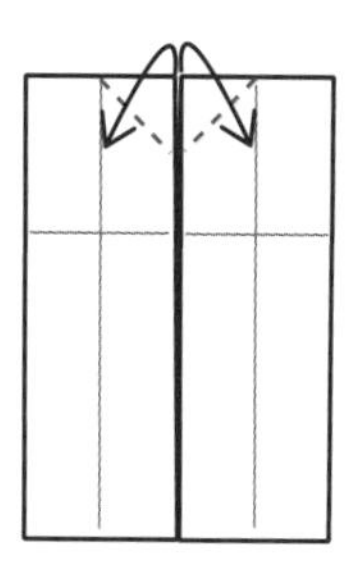

Fold the center corners down, using the pre-crease as a reference. (Note: There will be a small colored triangle in the back layer that also needs to be folded down. See the next step for reference.)

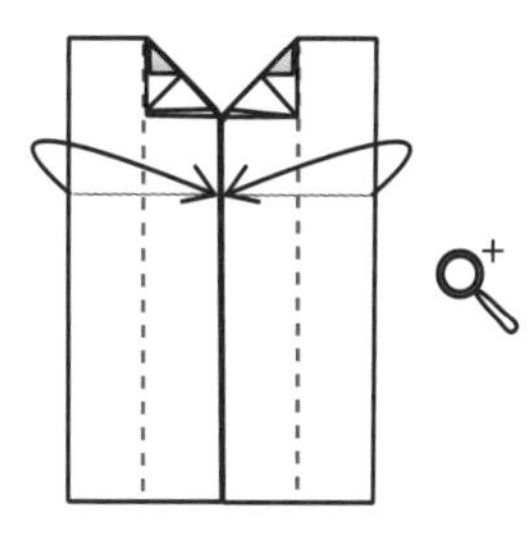

Reverse the existing pre-creases and fold the sides into the center. (Note: The next step is a magnified view.)

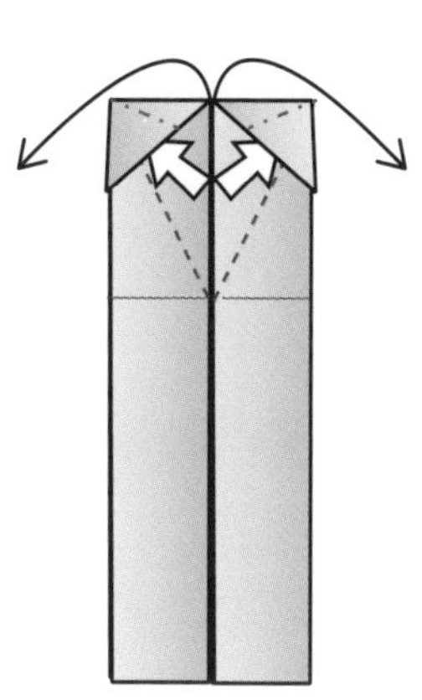

Open and squash the pockets at the top, using the pre-existing horizontal crease as a reference for the diagonal. This will be an asymmetrical squash fold. (See the next step for reference.)

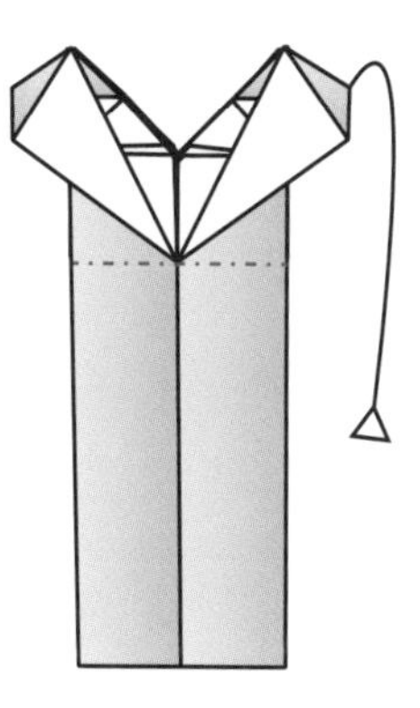

Mountain fold the top section to the back on the existing pre-crease.

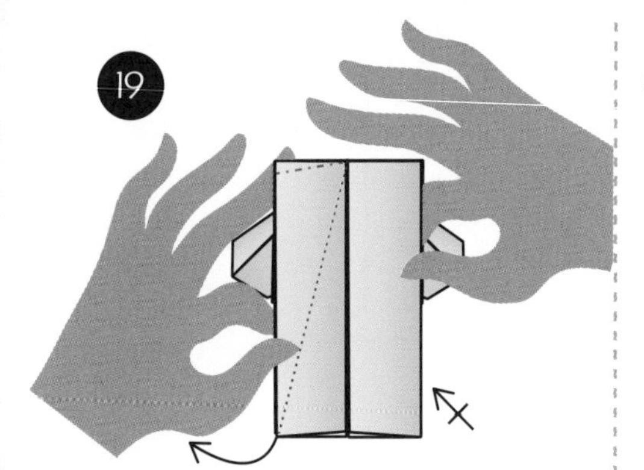

Pinch the upper right corner as you slide the front layer out from the bottom left corner, making a new diagonal crease. Repeat on the opposite side.

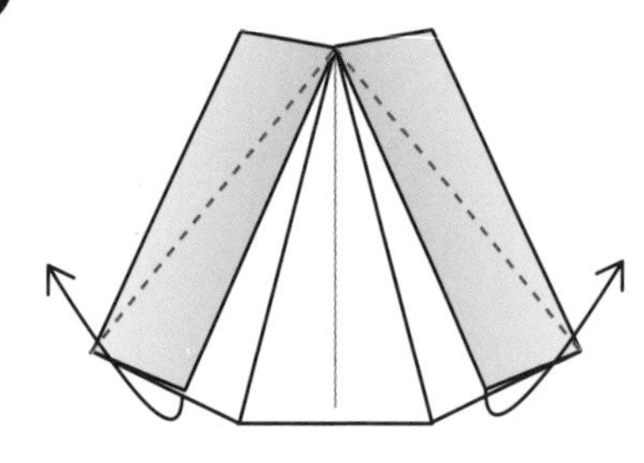

Fold the top layer flaps out at an angle, widening the skirt.

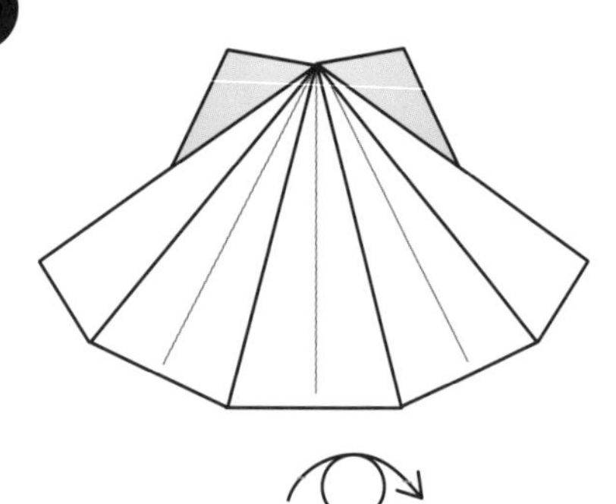

Turn the paper over.

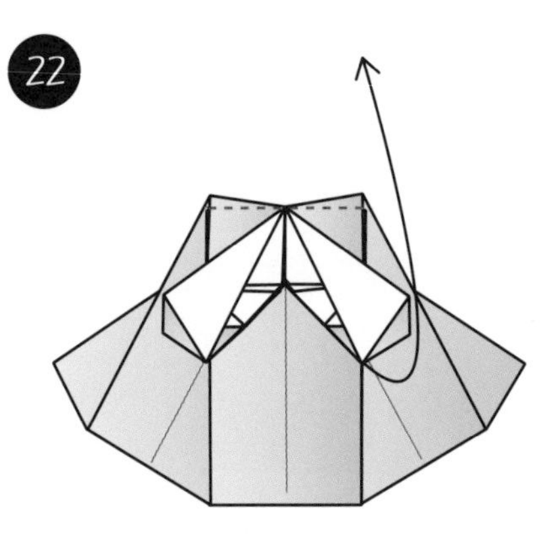

Fold the front section back up to the top on the existing pre-crease.

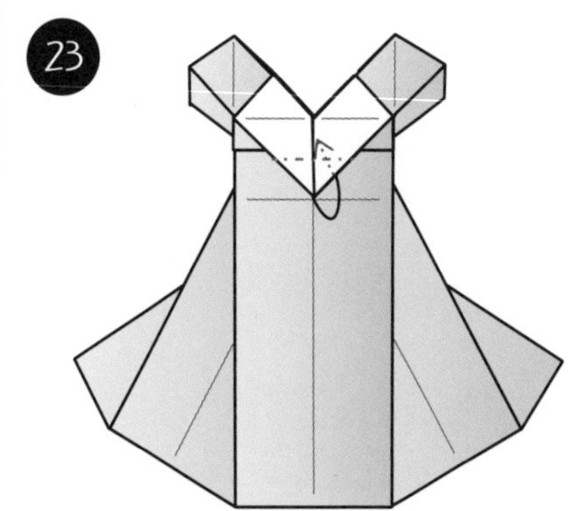

Optional: You can either leave the top section as a heart shape or tuck the bottom corner under the pocket below.

Enjoy your finished prom dress!

Summerwear
and
Outerwear

The **romper** started off as a child's onesie, but these days it's a versatile garment that can be dressy or casual, depending on how you wear it and what accessories you pair it with. This paper version uses both sides of the paper to create a distinct top and bottom. Try folding it with different types of patterns and combinations for a variety of looks!

STYLE TIPS

- Toss a sweater or jacket over your romper to take it from summer to fall.
- Pair your romper with flats for a daytime look or heels for an evening outfit.

HOW TO FOLD

1

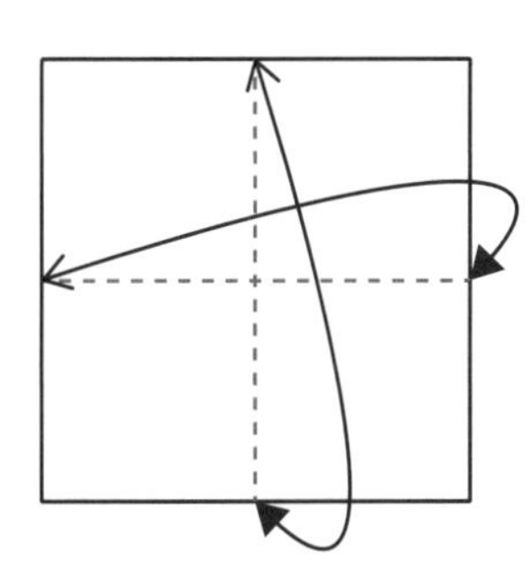

Fold the paper in half in both directions and then unfold. (Note: The side facing up will become the top half of your romper; the side facing down will become the bottom half.)

2

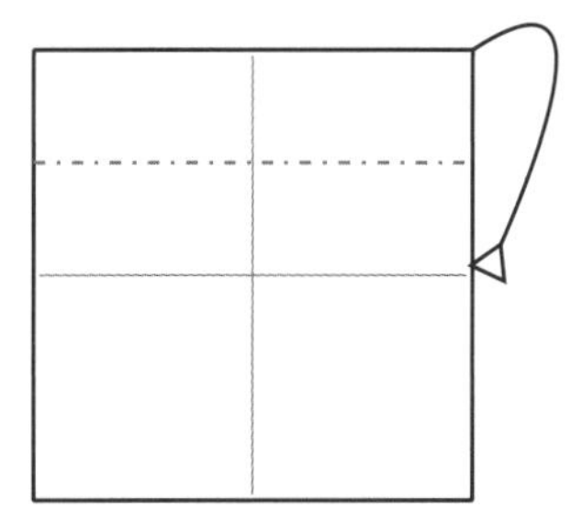

Mountain fold the top edge to the back to meet the center crease.

3

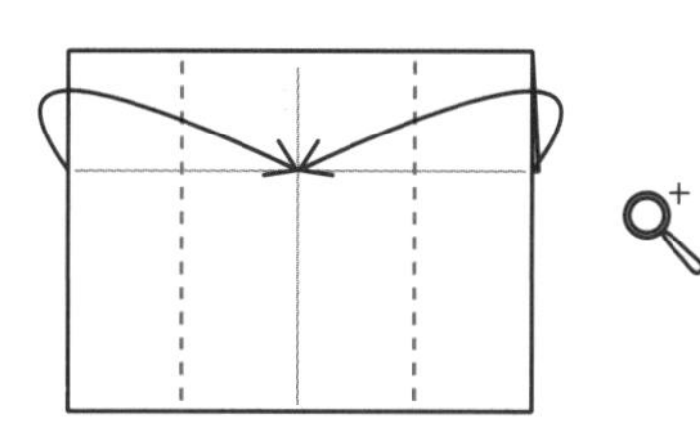

Fold the sides into the center crease. (Note: The next step is a magnified view.)

4

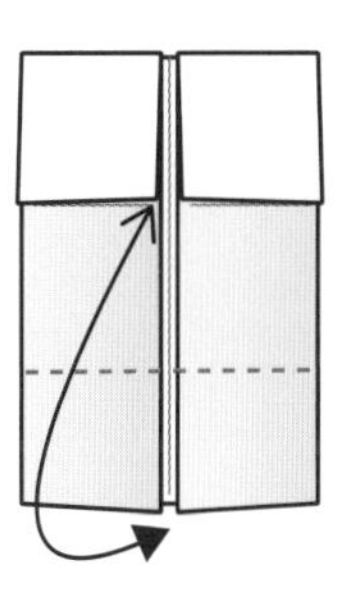

Fold the bottom edge up and then unfold.

5

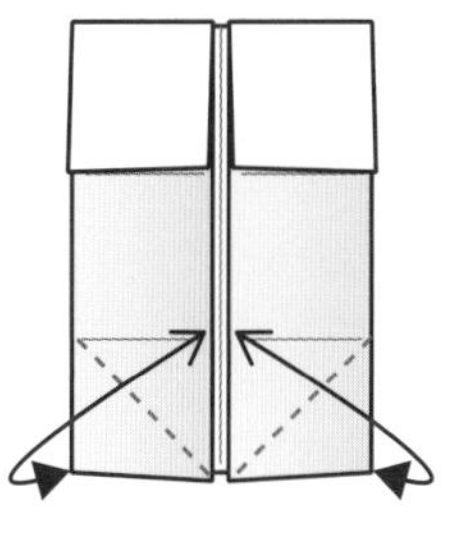

Fold the bottom corners in and then unfold.

6

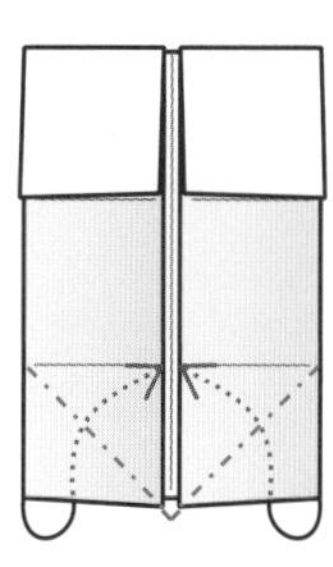

Inside reverse the corners.

7

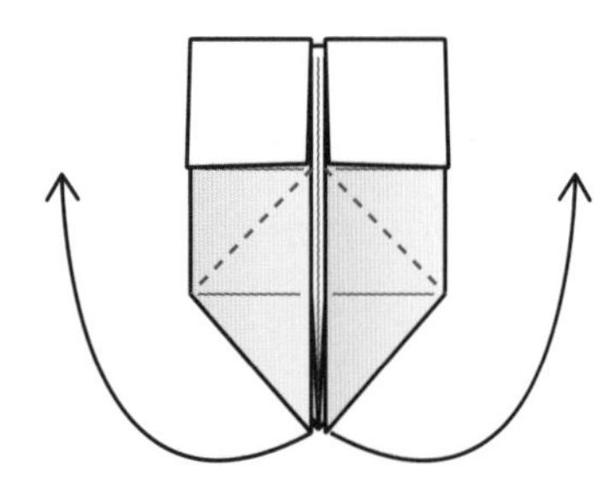

Pinch the bottom two corners in the front and pull out to the sides to make a boat shape. (See the next step for reference.)

8

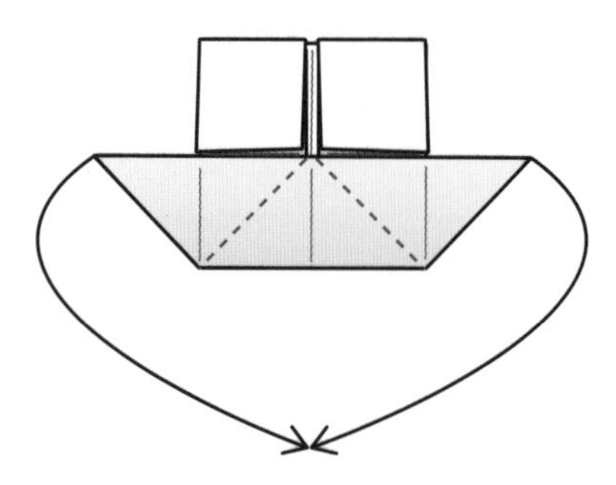

Fold the corners down to the bottom.

9

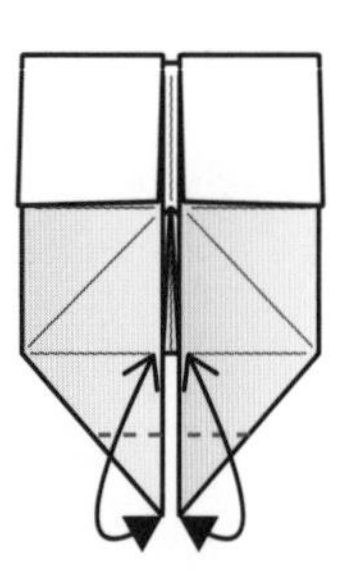

Fold the bottom corners up to meet the existing pre-crease and then unfold.

10

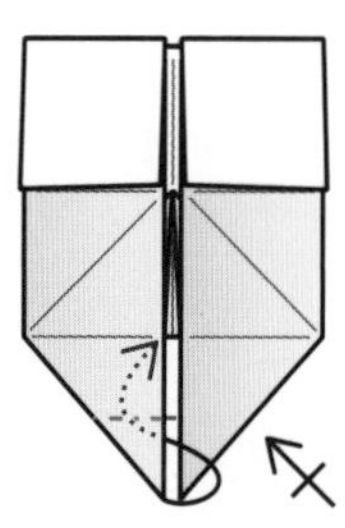

Inside reverse to tuck in the bottom left corner. Repeat on the opposite side.

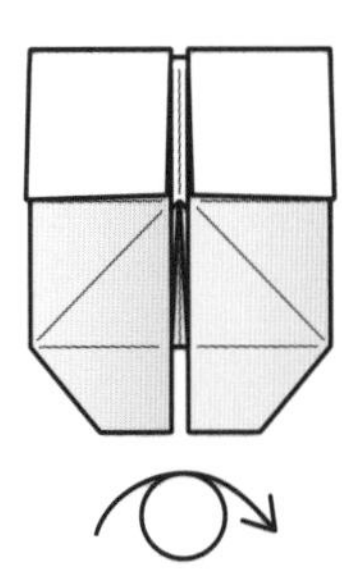

Turn the paper over.

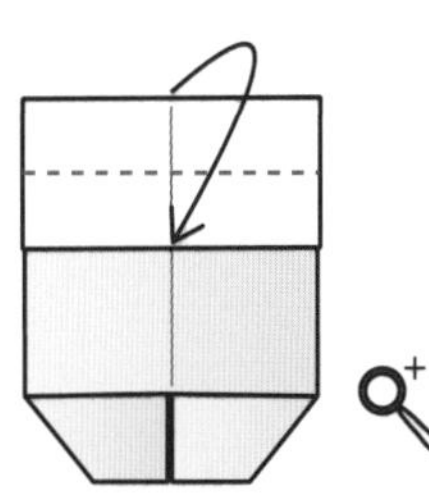

Fold the top edge down to the bottom of the top section. (Note: The next step is a magnified view.)

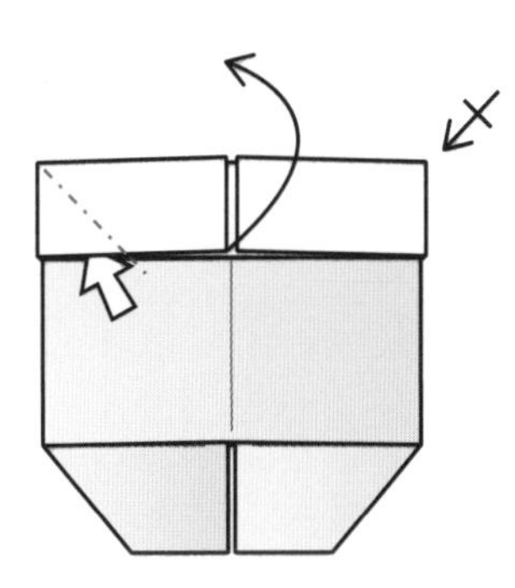

Pre-crease the corner, open the pocket, and squash fold. Repeat on the opposite side.

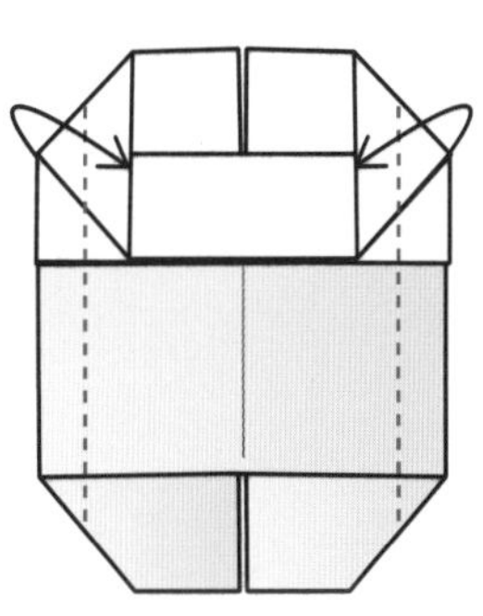

Fold in the side edges.

15

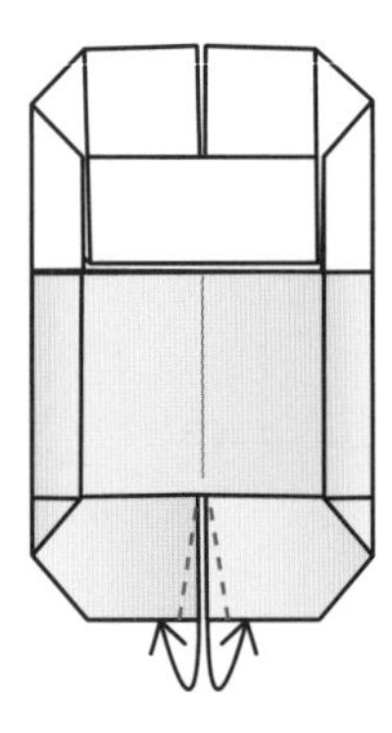

Fold thin triangles (through all layers) to separate the legs of the shorts.

16

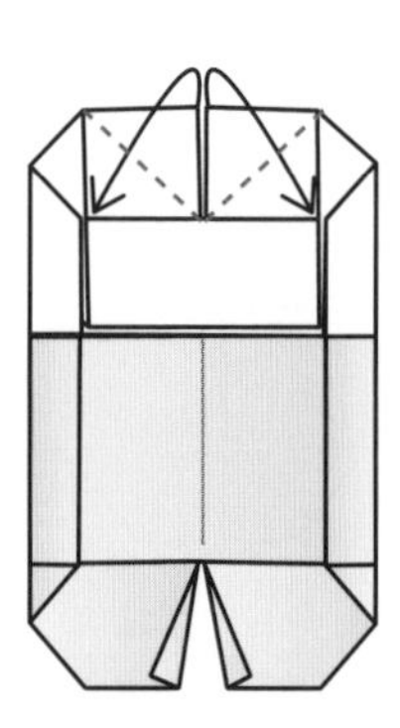

Fold down the center corners to create the neckline of the romper.

17

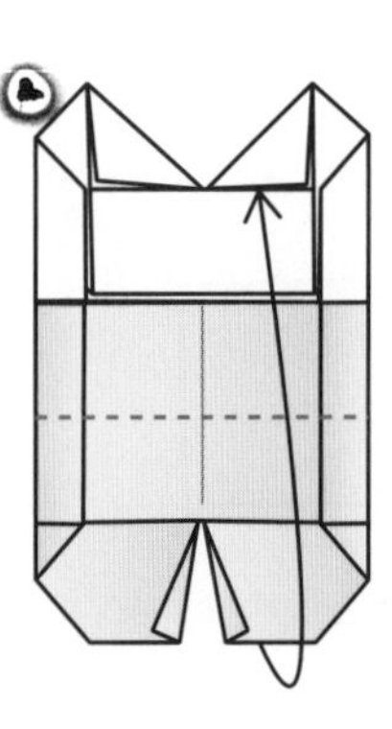

Fold the bottom edge up.

18

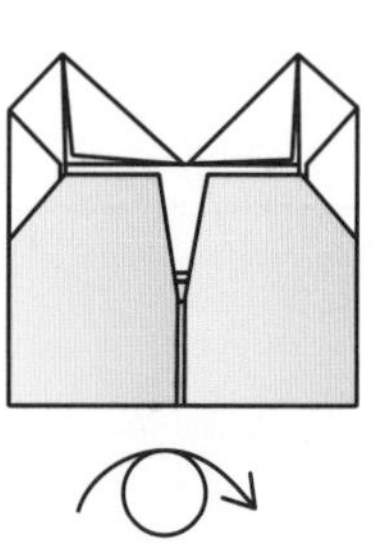

Turn the paper over.

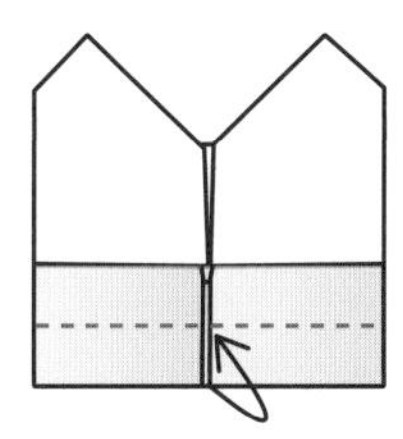

Fold up to create a pleat, bringing the back shorts section to the front while doing so.

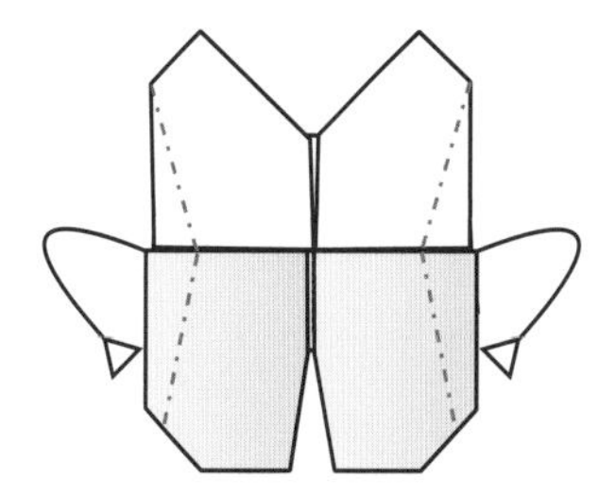

Mountain fold the sides in at an angle to taper and shape the waistline of the romper.

Optional: Fold the center sections out to create a decorative detail along the neckline.

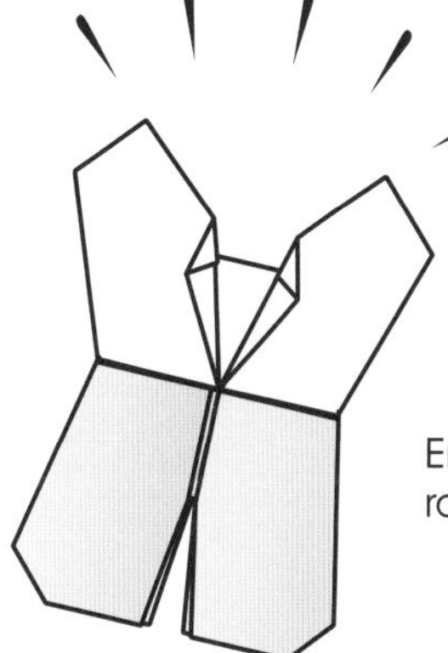

Enjoy your finished romper!

Swimsuit

Swimsuits have had a long evolution, from early bathing suits with long sleeves and skirts designed to shield skin from the sun to the itty-bitty bikinis seen today. But a classic one-piece swimsuit, like this paper version, is always in style. A tapered waist makes for a flattering fit, and the fun palm print is trendy and modern. It could even be worn with shorts or a skirt!

STYLE TIPS

- Your swimsuit will pair perfectly with a comfy pair of flip-flops and a cool pair of sunglasses.
- Don't forget a tote bag to throw your essentials in when heading to the beach or pool!

Pg. 96

HOW TO FOLD

1

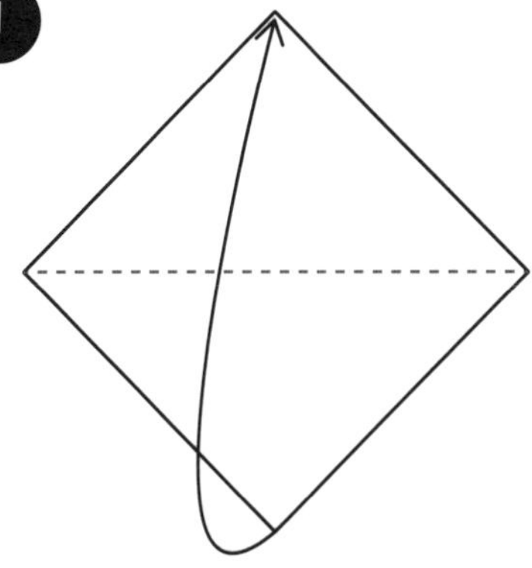

Fold the paper in half diagonally. (Note: The side facing down will become the pattern of the swimsuit.)

2

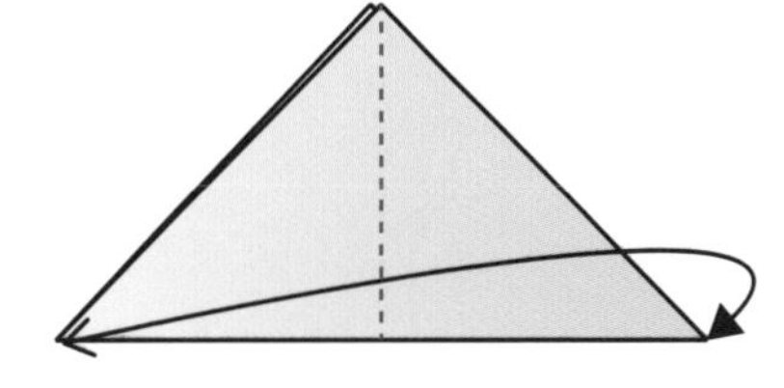

Fold in half again and then unfold.

3

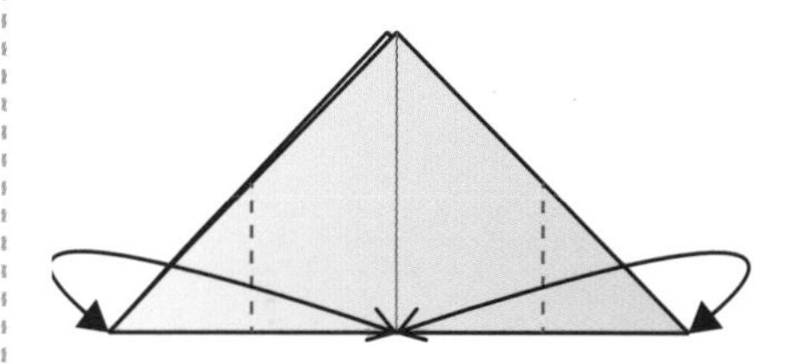

Fold the side corners into the center crease and then unfold.

4

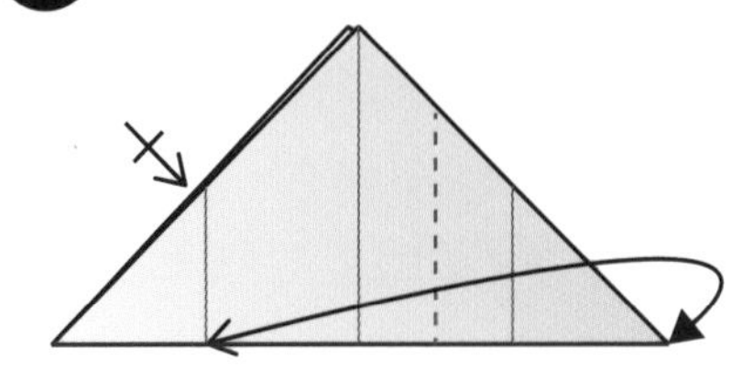

Fold one corner into the crease made in the previous step and then unfold. Repeat on the opposite side.

5

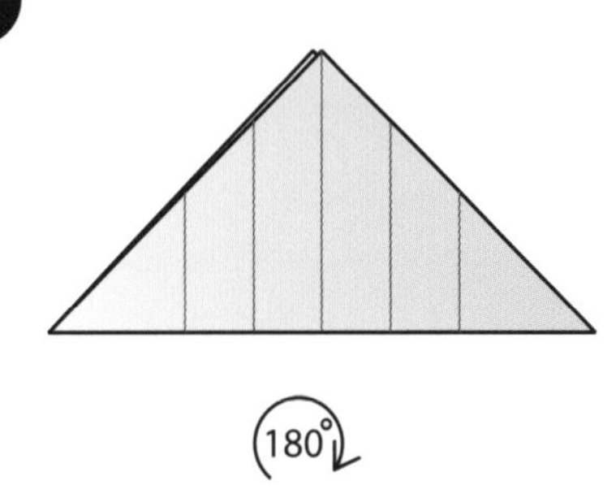

Rotate the paper 180°.

6

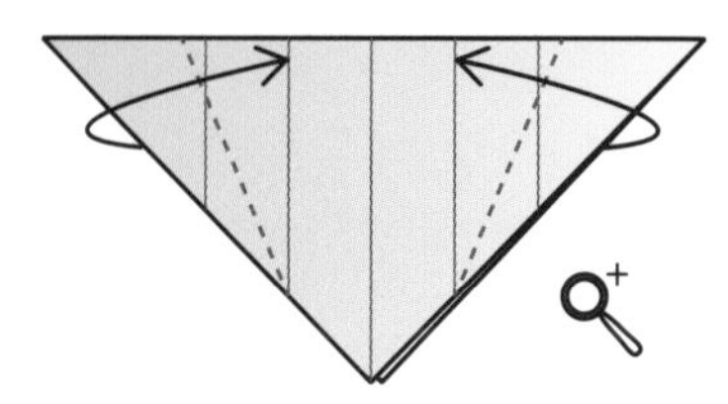

Fold the corners up to line up with the crease made in step #4. (Note: The next step is a magnified view.)

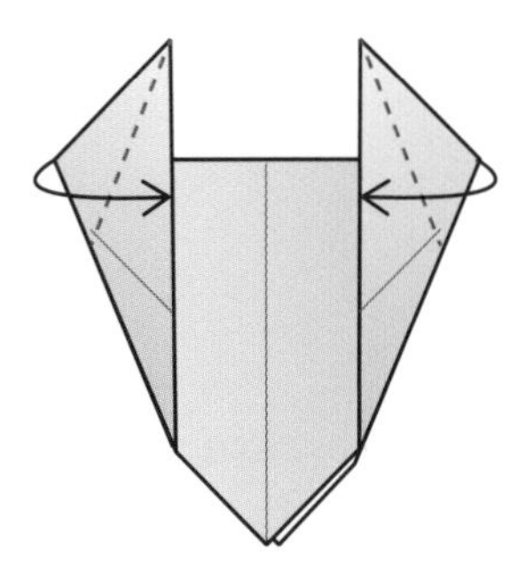

Narrow the corners by folding an angle bisector, bringing the outside corner in to meet the inside edge.

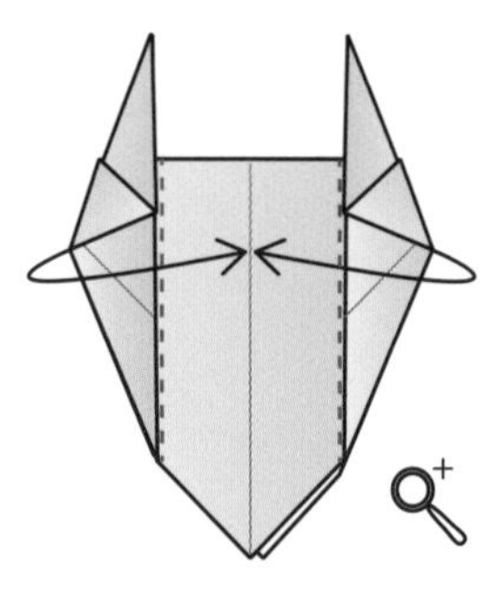

Fold the sides into the existing pre-crease. (Note: The next step is a magnified view.)

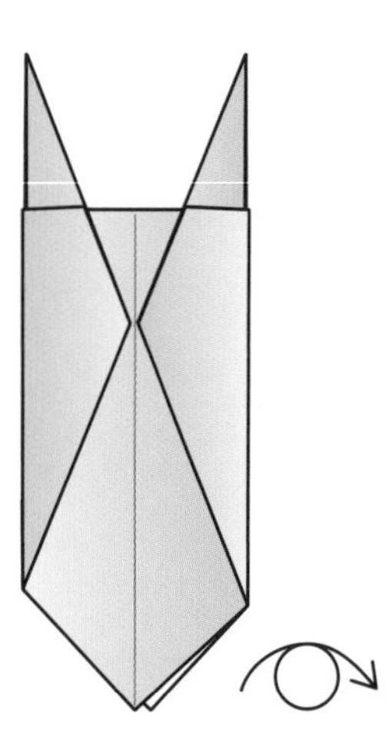

Turn the paper over.

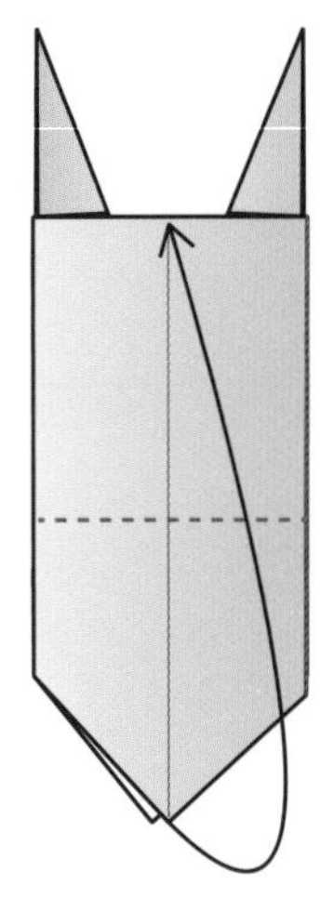

Fold the bottom corner up to the top edge.

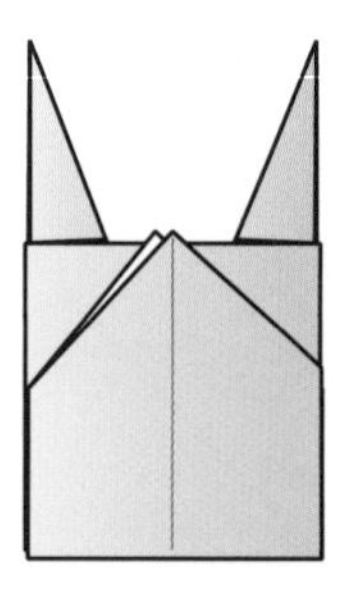

Turn the paper over.

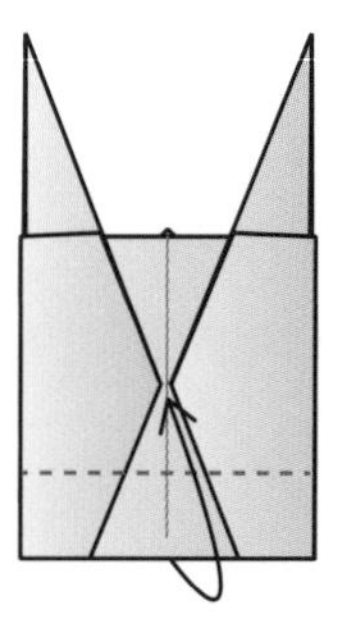

Fold the bottom edge up to where the corners meet in the center, flipping the back section to the front while doing so. This will create a pleat fold. (See the next step for reference.)

13

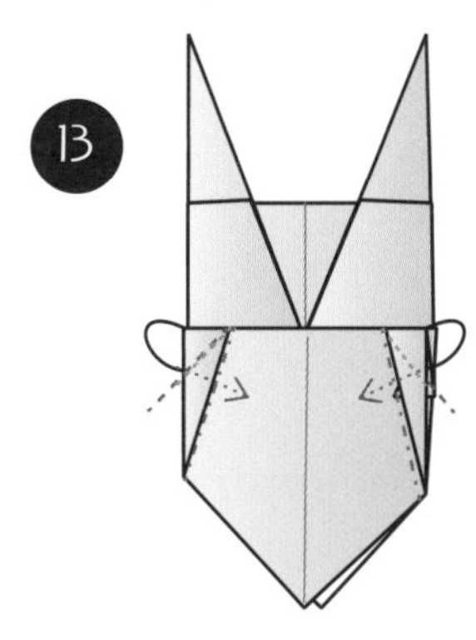

Inside reverse to tuck the bottom triangles in on the sides to shape the bottom of the swimsuit.

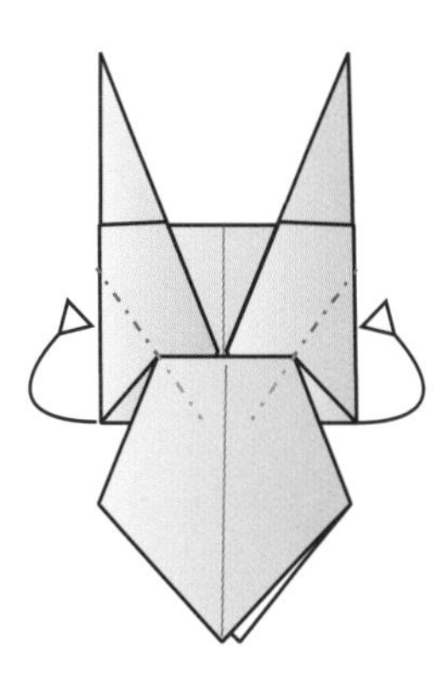

Mountain fold the corners to the back to shape the top section of the swimsuit.

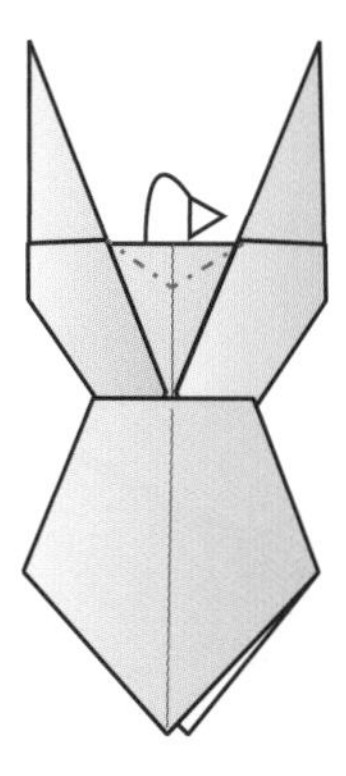

Optional: Mountain fold the top of the swimsuit to make a V-neck.

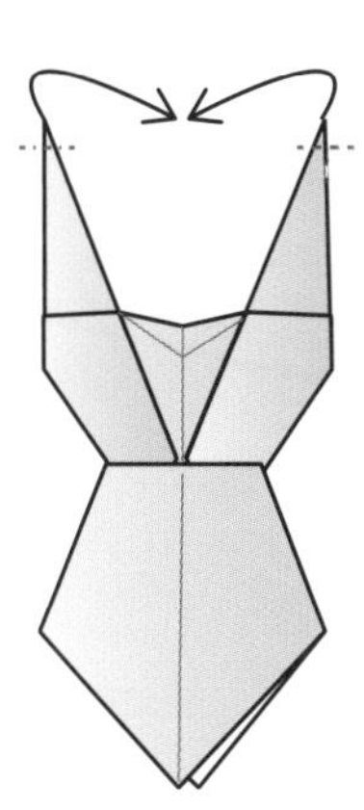

Optional: Bring the two top points together and gently fasten them with a mountain and valley fold to create a halter top. (Note: This will not be a strong lock but rather a suggestion to help shape the top of the swimsuit.)

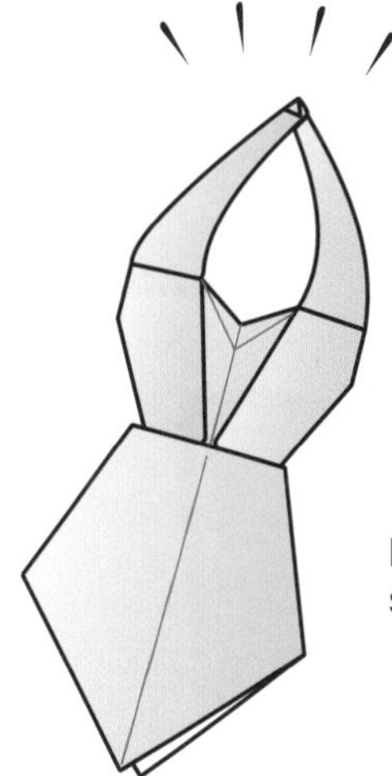

Enjoy your finished swimsuit!

Jacket

Jackets don't have be formal! This origami version can be customized with different patterns or minor folding adjustments. Use a denim pattern to create a jean jacket, or choose a solid brown or black pattern for a leather jacket. You can also narrow the sleeves or leave out the cuffs depending on your personal preference. Draw in your own stitching details and pockets, or add patches and stickers to make it a one-of-a-kind closet must-have.

STYLE TIPS

- A leather jacket looks great with jeans, while a denim jacket can be the perfect piece to pair with skinny pants.
- Layer your jacket over different tops to create different looks—a T-shirt, blouse, or sweater will each produce a unique outfit.

HOW TO FOLD

1

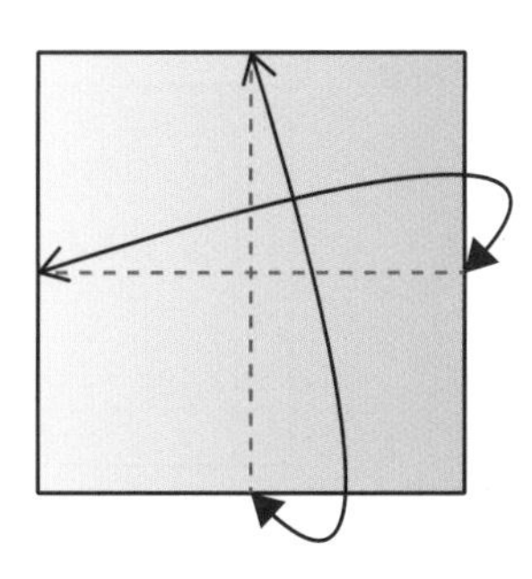

Fold your paper in half in both directions and then unfold. (Note: The side facing up will become the exterior of your jacket; the side facing down will become the interior lining and cuffs.)

2

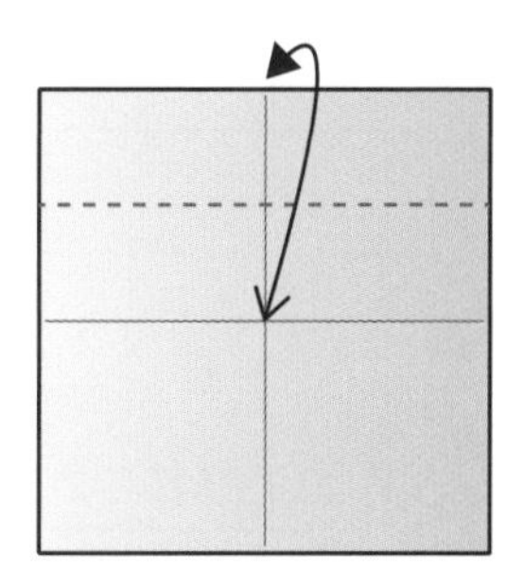

Fold the top edge down to the center crease and then unfold.

3

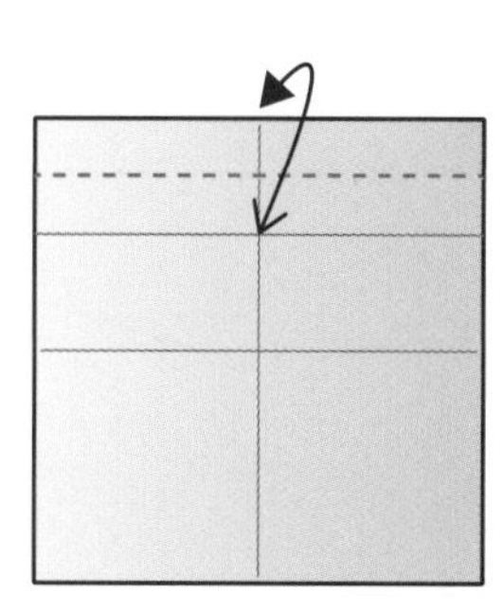

Fold the top edge down to the new crease created in the previous step and then unfold.

4

Fold the top edge down to the new crease created in the previous step.

5

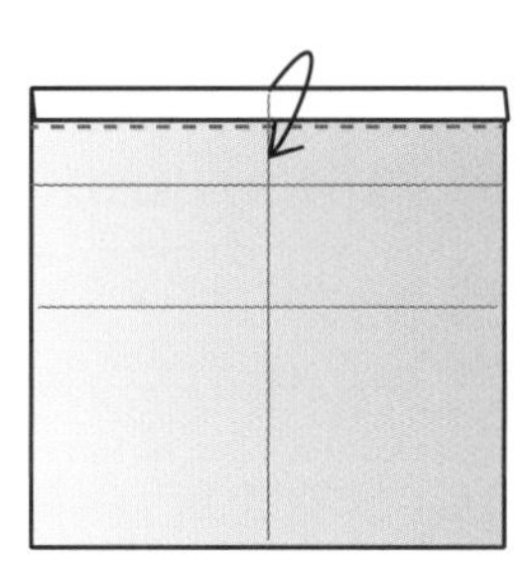

Fold the top edge down again on the existing pre-crease. This will become the jacket cuffs.

6

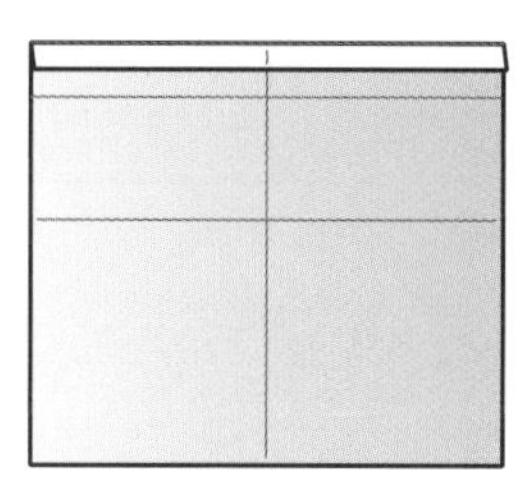

Turn the paper over.

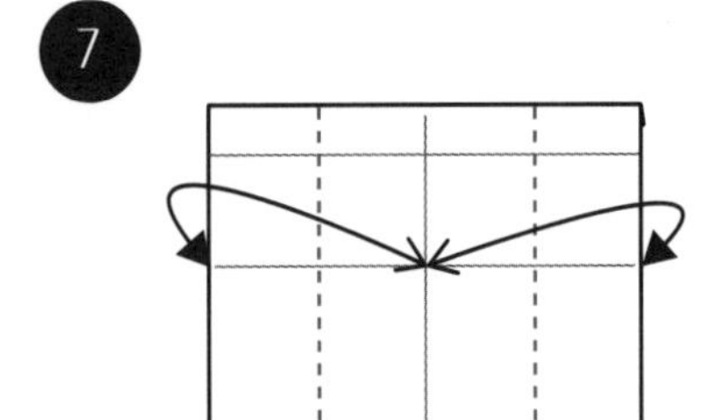

Fold the sides into the center and then unfold.

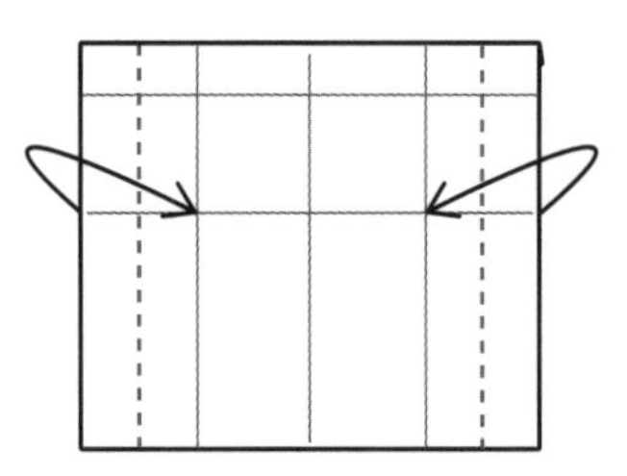

Fold both sides into the new creases created in the previous step.

9

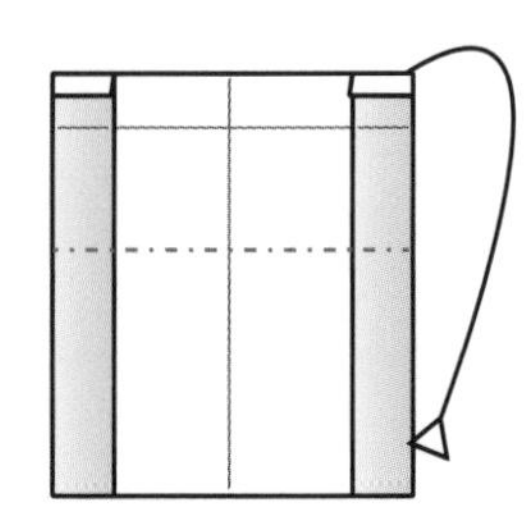

Mountain fold the top section to the back on the existing pre-crease.

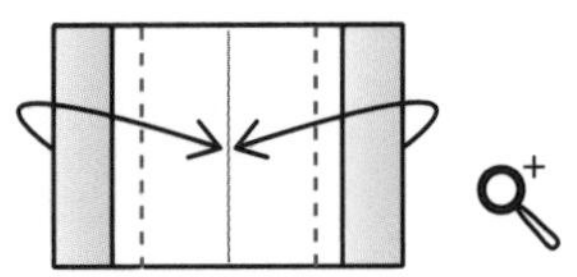

Fold the sides into the center crease. (Note: The next step is a magnified view.)

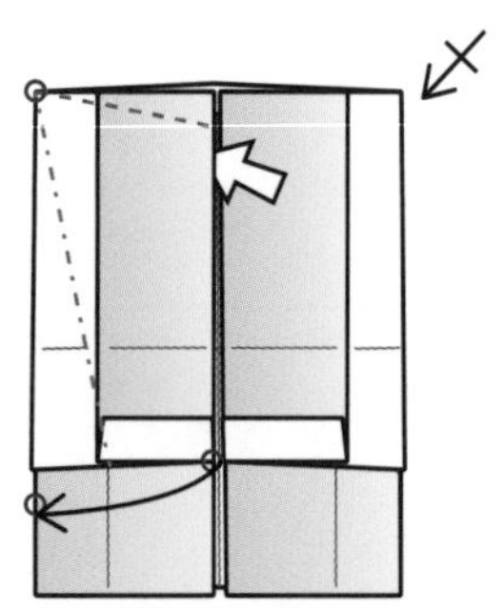

Working from the center, open up the pocket on the front layer and squash to form the sleeves. The creases will start at the top corner (as shown by the reference circle). Slide the front layers to the outside so the sleeve corner matches up with the side of the jacket. Repeat on the opposite side.

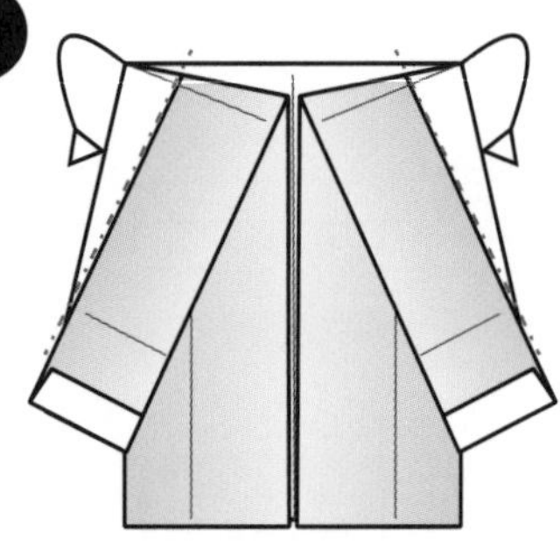

Mountain fold the contrasting triangles to the back to shape the sleeves.

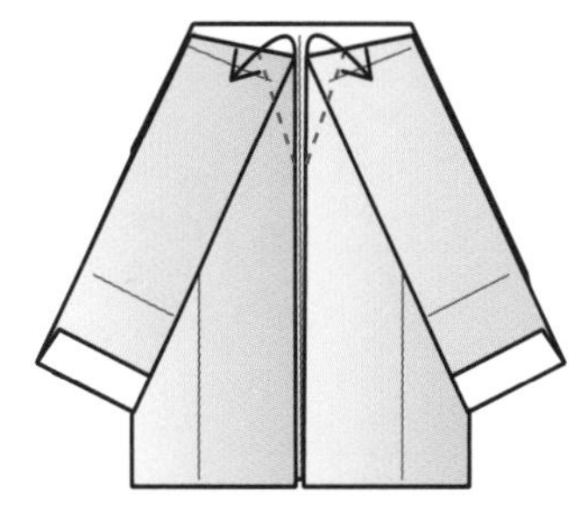

Fold down the lapels. (Note: You can make the lapels shorter or longer. Play around with some different styles and options.)

Mountain fold the top section to the back to shape the collar.

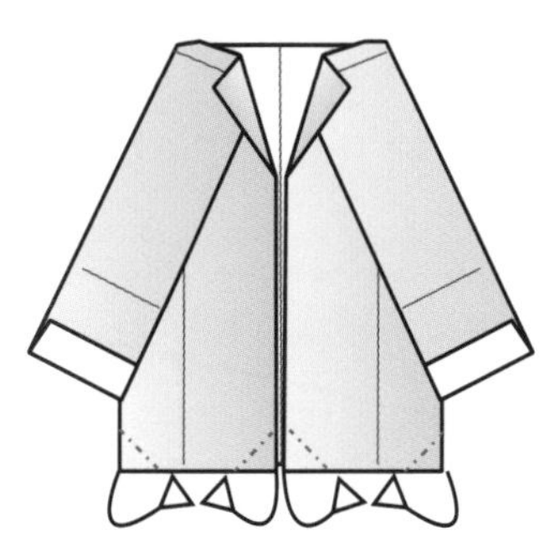

Mountain fold and tuck the bottom corners under to add detail to the bottom of the jacket. (Note: You can also alter the length of the jacket by leaving the bottom long or mountain folding it to the back.)

Enjoy your finished jacket!

Raincoat

Raincoats make it easy to stand out, even in the midst of bad weather. Choose a raincoat with fun details to make sure your jacket is part of your outfit, not just covering it up. This paper version pops in a bright, bold red and has a leopard-print lining for extra pizazz. You can reverse the paper for an even bolder animal-print look, or choose a different paper and pattern altogether.

STYLE TIPS

- Toss your raincoat on over your sundress or shift dress to stay dry and stylish in gloomy weather.
- Don't forget to grab a tote bag to throw your umbrella in!

HOW TO FOLD

1

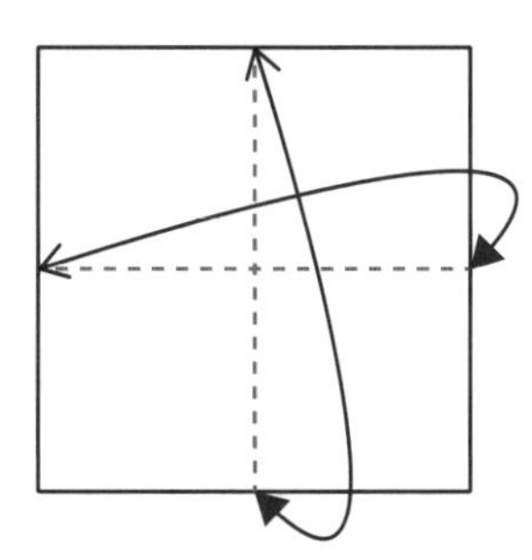

Fold the paper in half in both directions and then unfold. (Note: The side facing down will become the outside of the raincoat; the side facing up will become the lining.)

2

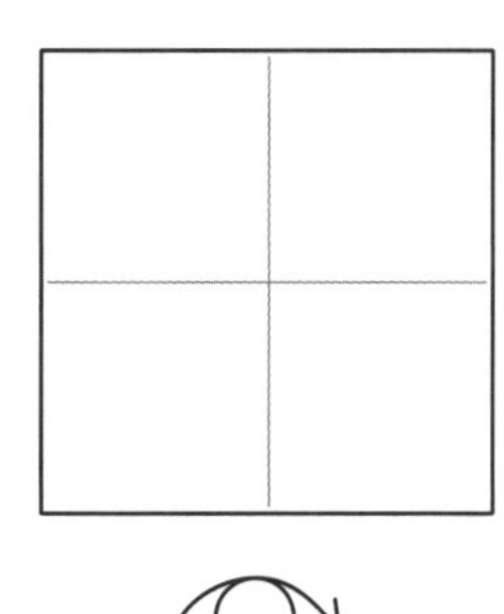

Turn the paper over.

3

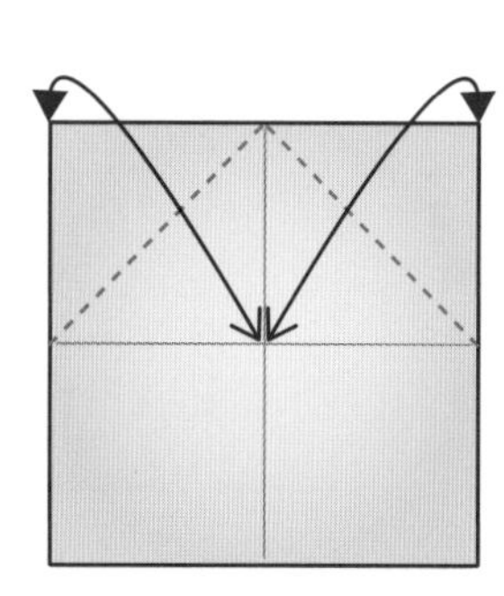

Fold the top corners down and into the center and then unfold.

4

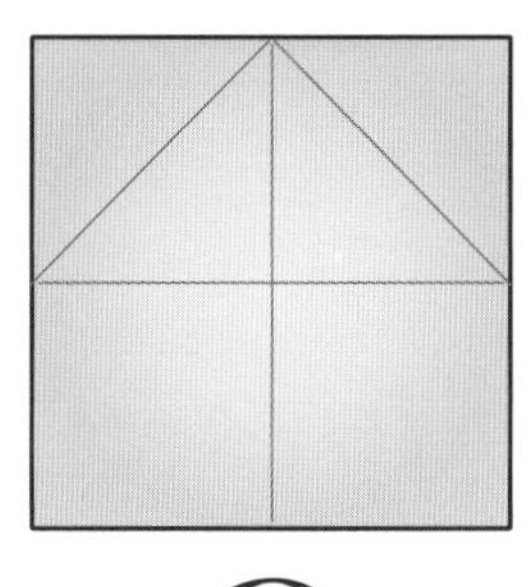

Turn the paper over.

5

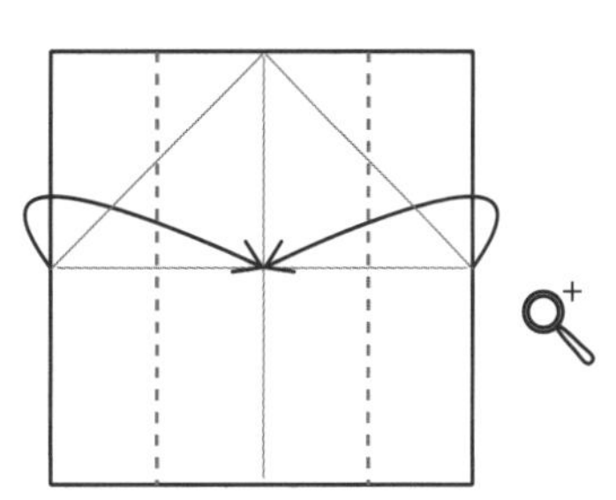

Fold the sides into the center crease. (Note: The next step is a magnified view.)

6

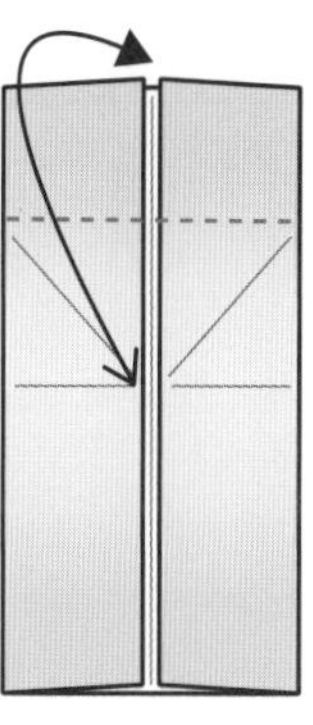

Fold the top edge down to the center crease and then unfold.

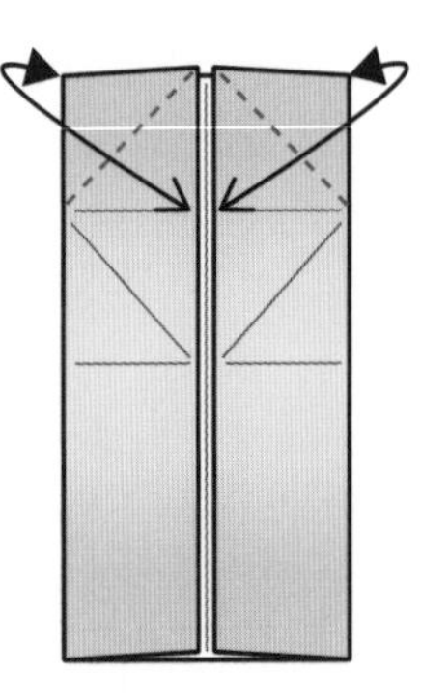

Fold the top corners down to the new crease made in the previous step and then unfold.

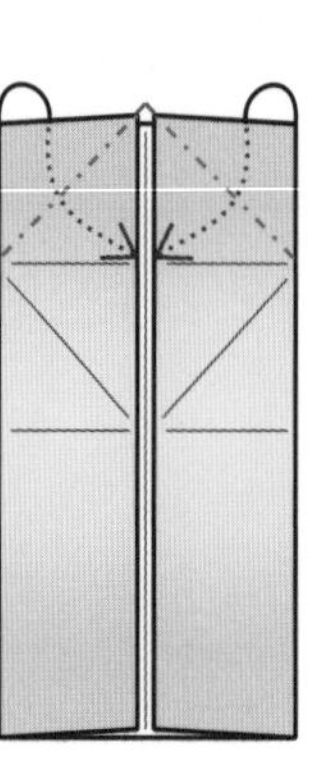

Inside reverse the corners using the pre-crease from the previous step.

9

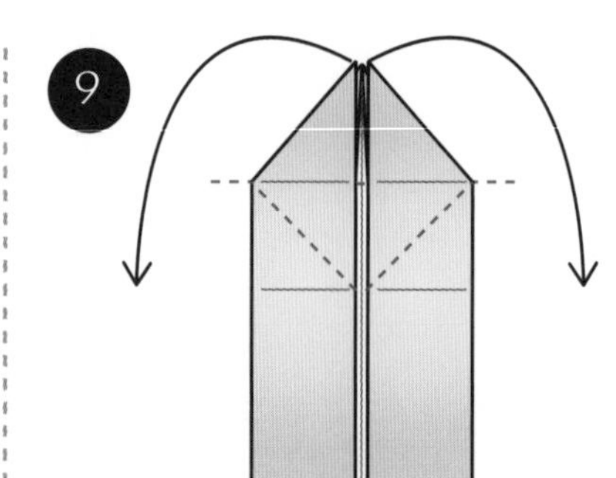

Pinch the top two corners in the front and pull out to the sides to make an upside-down boat shape. (See the next step for reference.)

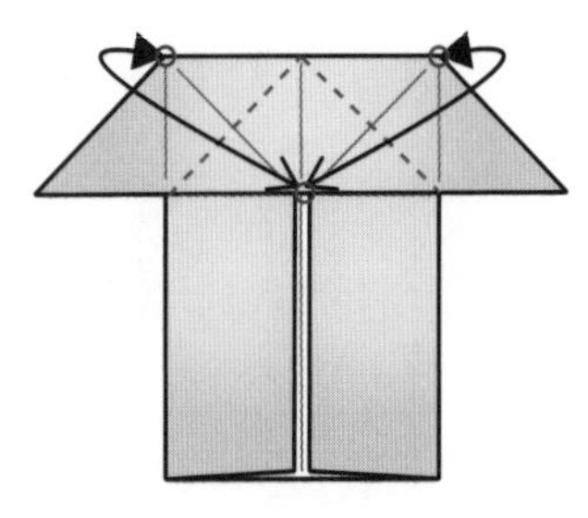

Fold the top corners down using the indicated circle points as a reference and then unfold.

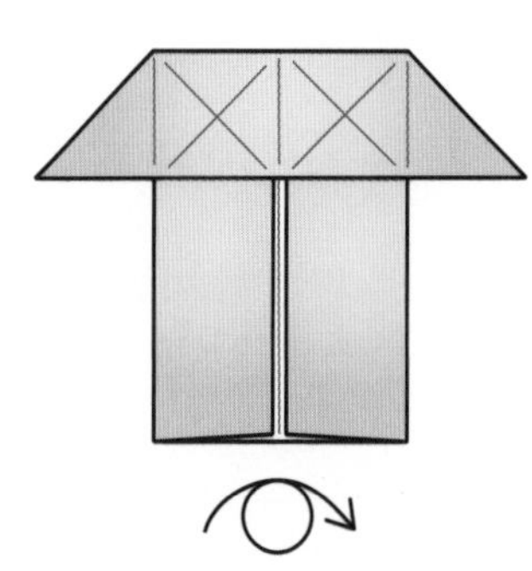

Turn the paper over.

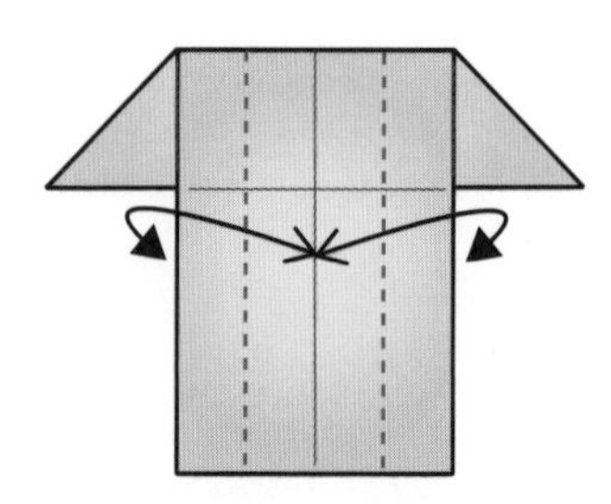

Fold the sides into the center crease and then unfold.

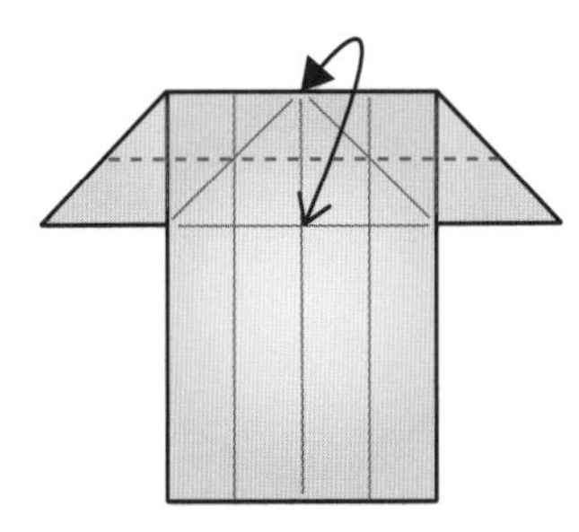

Fold the top edge down to the existing pre-crease and then unfold.

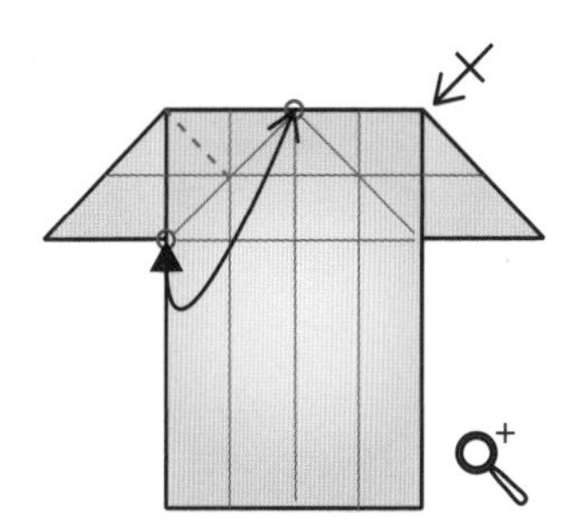

Fold a small diagonal crease on the upper, outside corner by bringing the circled points together and then unfold. Repeat on the opposite side. (Note: The next step is a magnified view.)

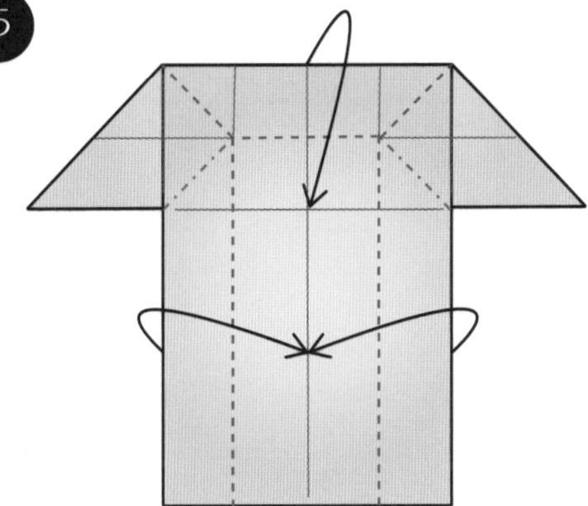

Collapse the model using the pre-creases. (Note: The next two steps are a detailed breakdown of this collapse.)

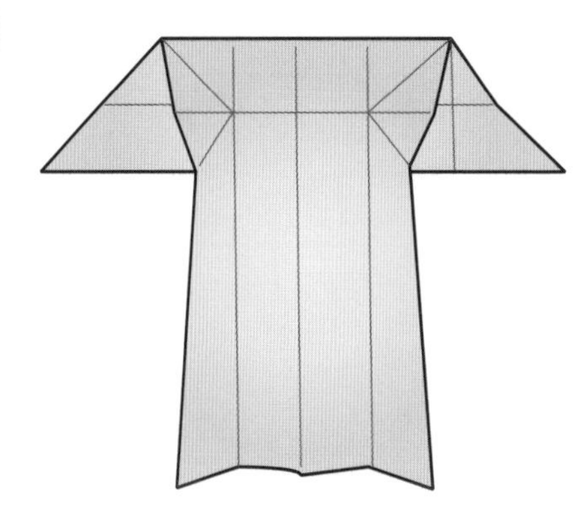

Fold the side edges in first, leaving the top section open. (See the next step for reference.)

17

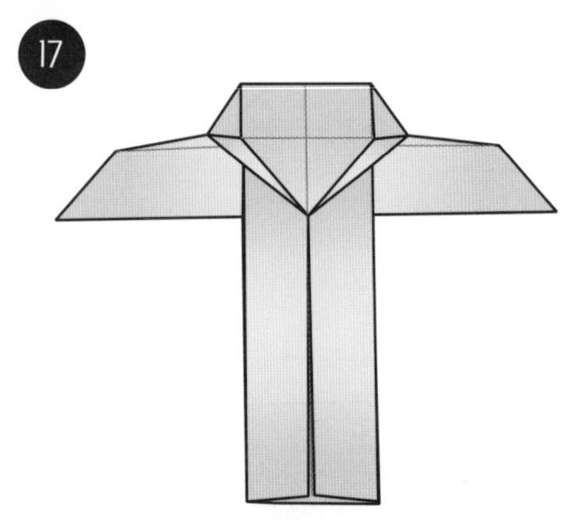

Fold the top edge down to make a long, narrow rectangle. (See the next step for reference.)

18

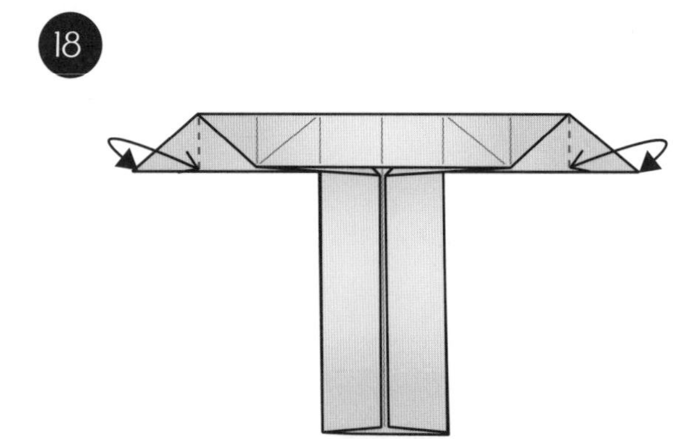

Fold the outside points in, folding the triangle in half, and then unfold.

19

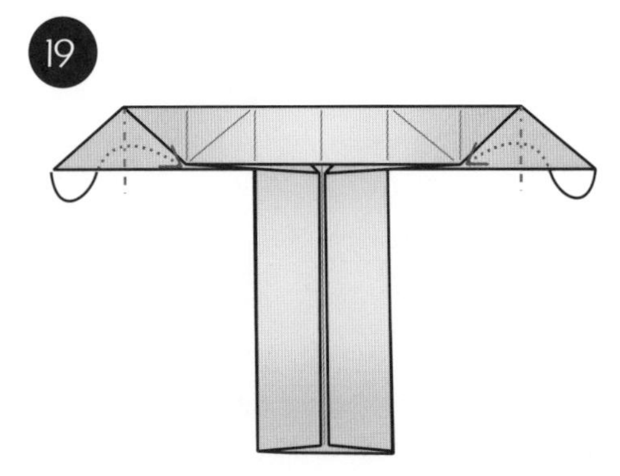

Inside reverse to tuck in the outside points using the pre-crease made in the previous step.

20

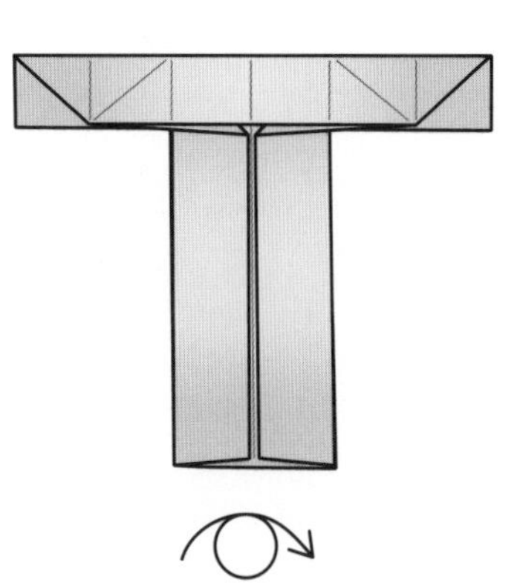

Turn the paper over.

21

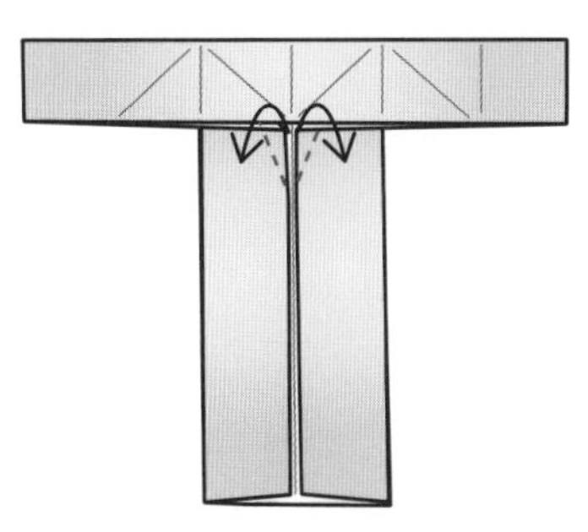

Lift up the top front layer and fold narrow triangles along the center opening to create the lapels of the coat. (Note: The top of the triangles will be underneath the front layer. See the next step for reference.)

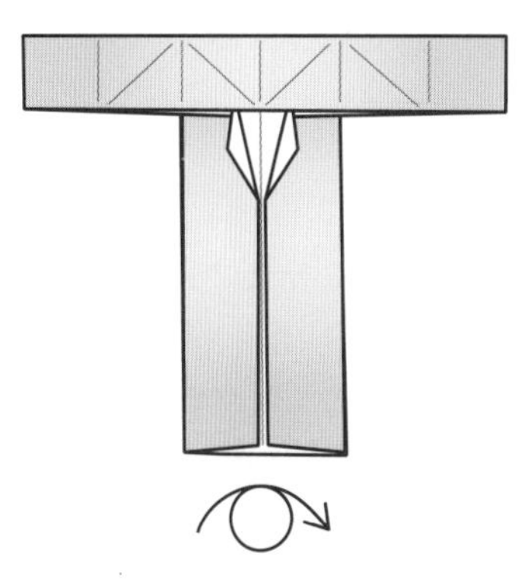

Turn the paper over.

23

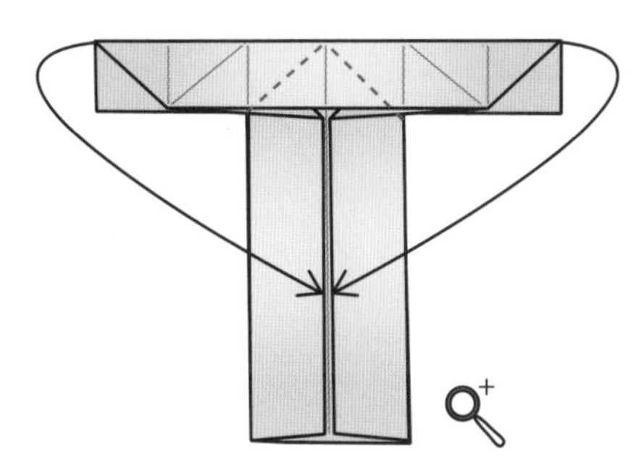

Fold down the sleeves. (Note: The next step is a magnified view.)

24

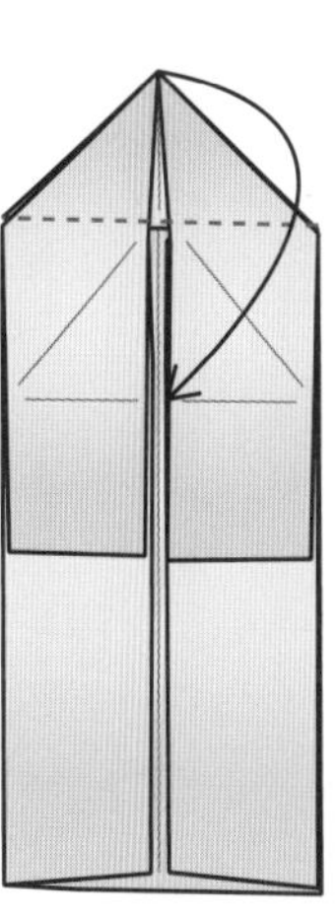

Fold the top triangle down to the front to create the hood of the raincoat.

25

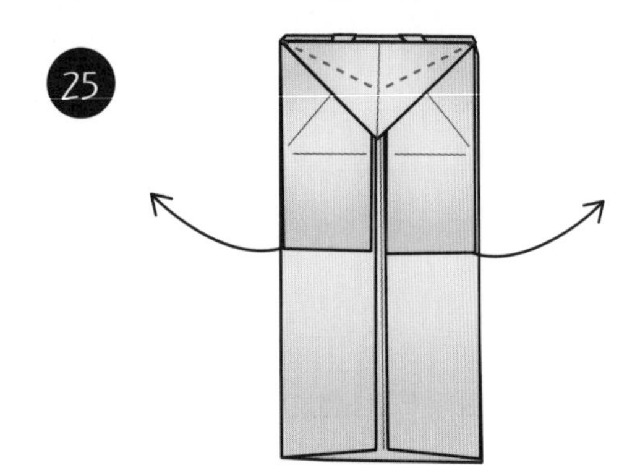

Keeping the top triangle folded, gently slide the sleeves out to the sides underneath. (See the next step for reference.)

26

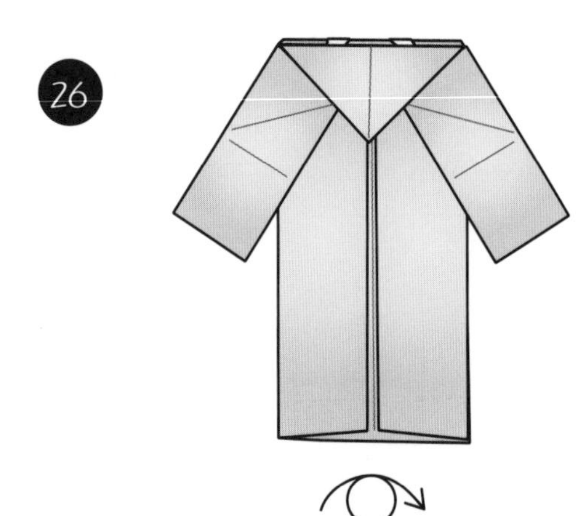

Turn the paper over.

27

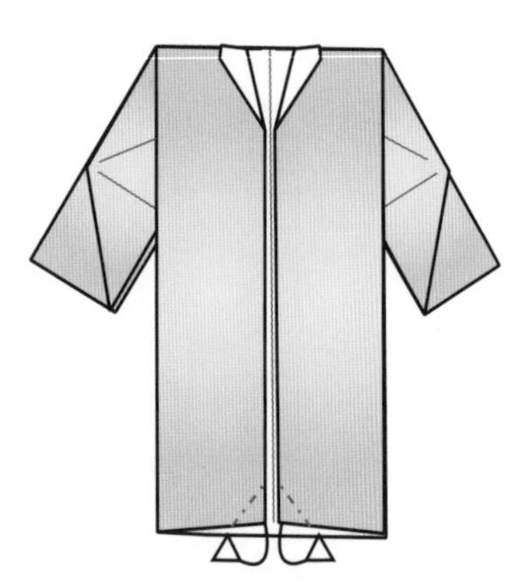

Optional: Mountain fold the bottom corners under for a more detailed look.

Enjoy your finished raincoat!

Accessories

Tote Bag

The right bag can make a statement while still being functional. This two-toned paper **tote bag** even has a pocket to store things, which makes it a great alternative to an everyday purse—toss in all your essentials and you're ready to go!

HOW TO USE

- Fold this tote bag in a variety of colors to match your different outfits.
- Try folding it with larger, heavier paper to carry around some of your lightweight belongings, like origami paper!

HOW TO FOLD

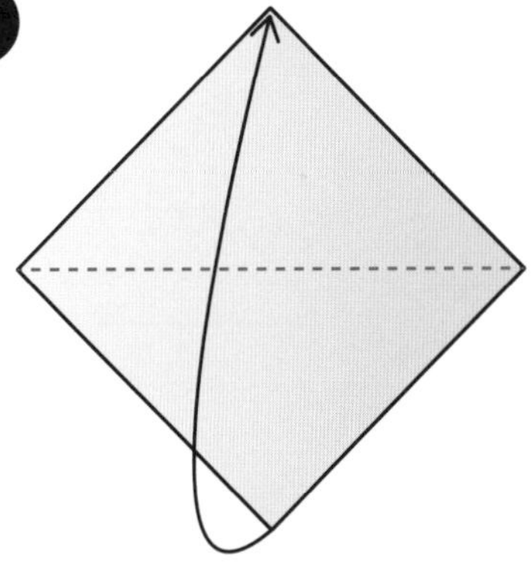

Fold the paper in half diagonally (Note: The side facing up will become the body of the tote; the side facing down will become the handle and bottom of the tote.)

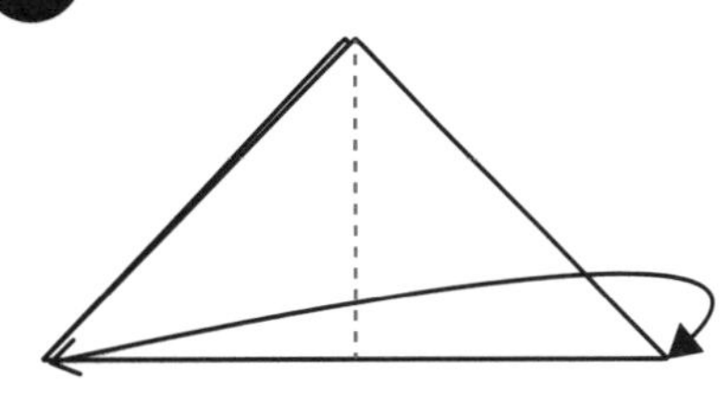

Fold the paper in half horizontally and then unfold.

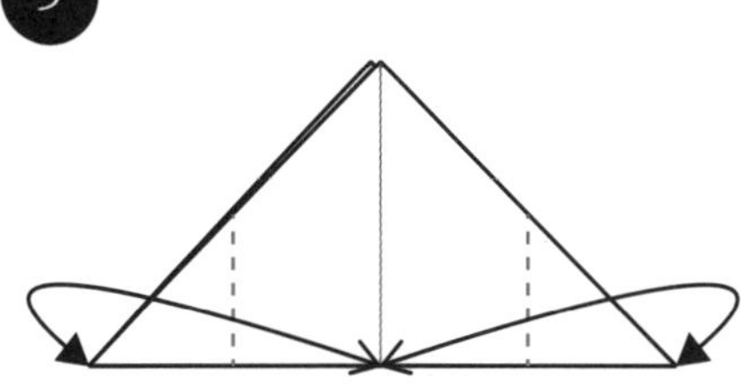

Fold both side corners into the center crease and then unfold.

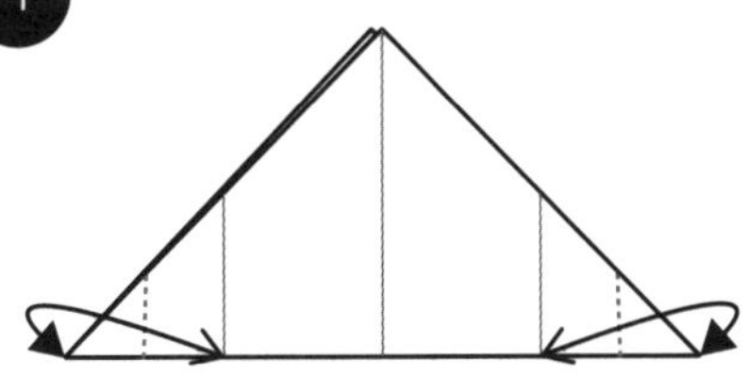

Fold the side corners into the creases made in the previous step and then unfold.

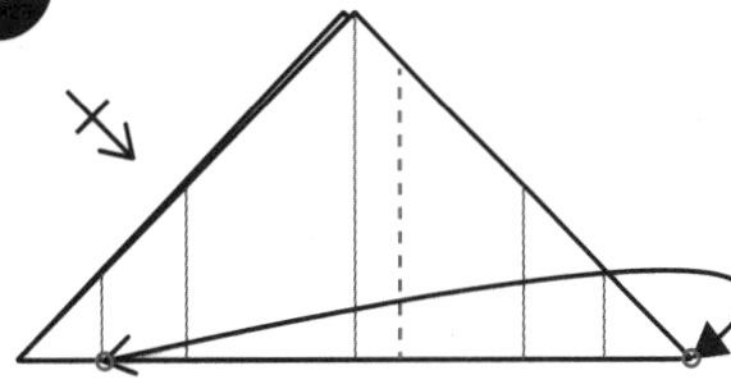

Fold the right corner to the farthest crease on the left side and then unfold. Repeat on the opposite side.

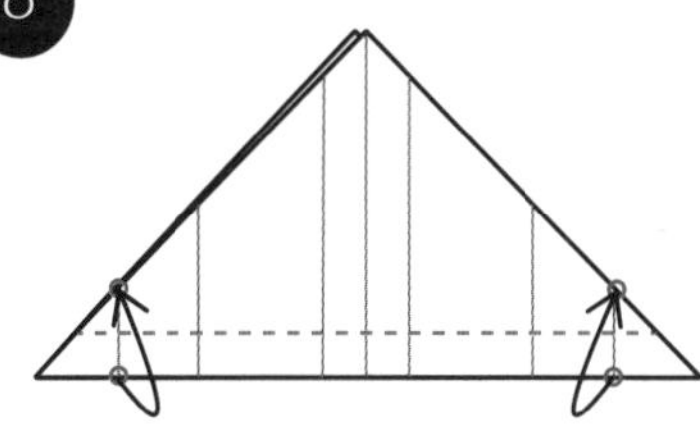

Fold the bottom edge up to the top of the creases made in step #4. Use the circled points as references.

7

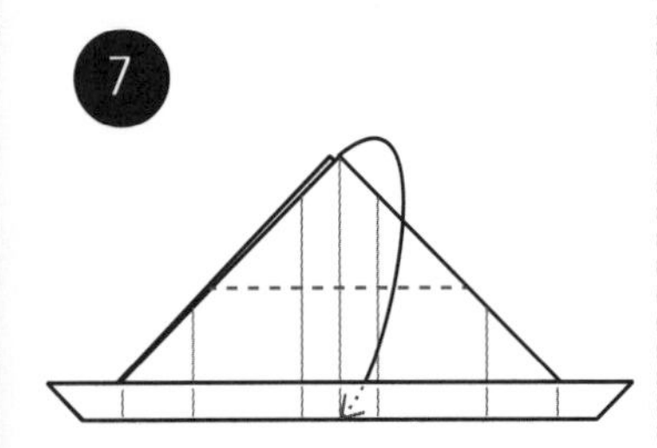

Fold the front corner flap down to the bottom and tuck it beneath the long strip from the previous step. (See the next step for reference.)

8

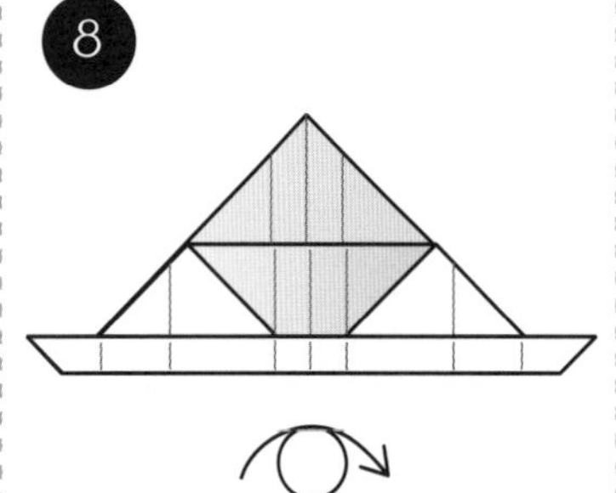

Turn the paper over.

9

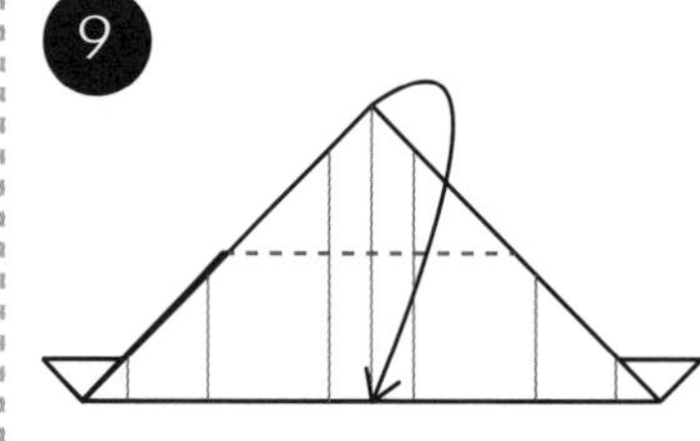

Fold the top corner down to the bottom edge.

10

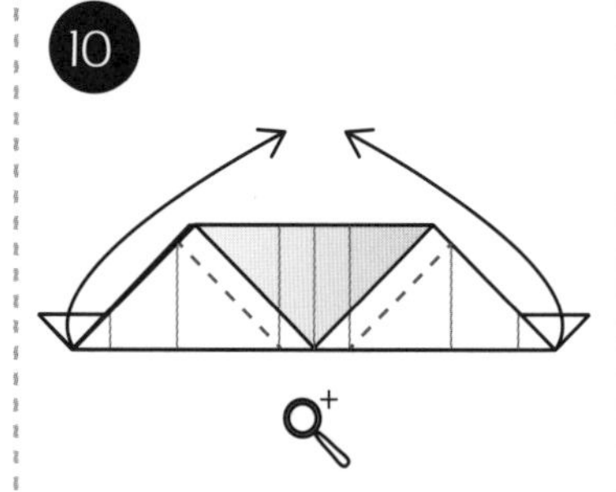

Fold the sides up at an angle so they line up with the creases made in step #5. (Note: The next step is a magnified view.)

11

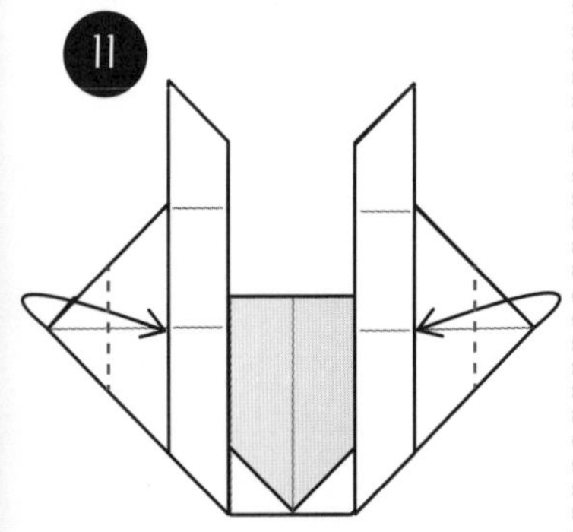

Fold the side corners into the outside folded edge.

12

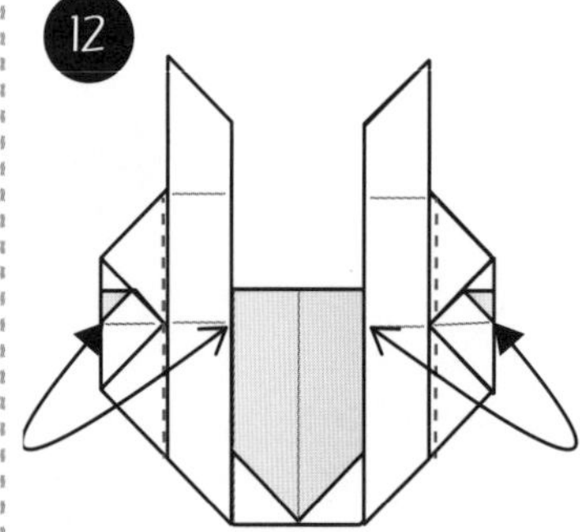

Fold the side flaps in and then unfold.

13

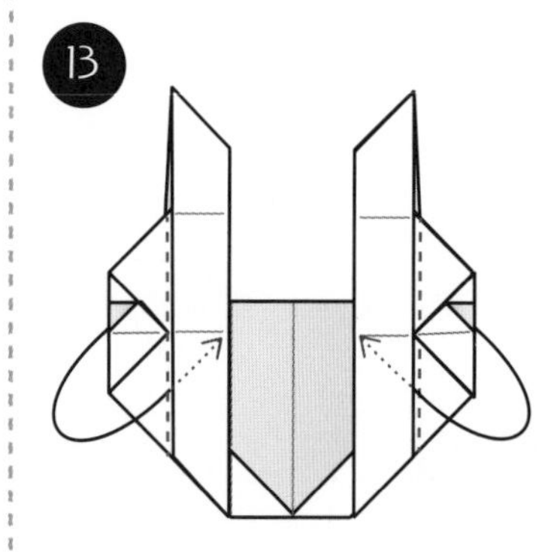

Tuck the side flaps inside and hide them underneath the long straps using the crease made in step #12. (See the next step for reference.)

14

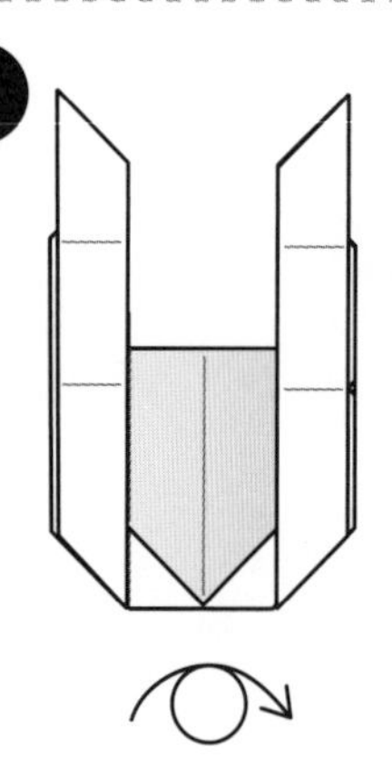

Turn the paper over.

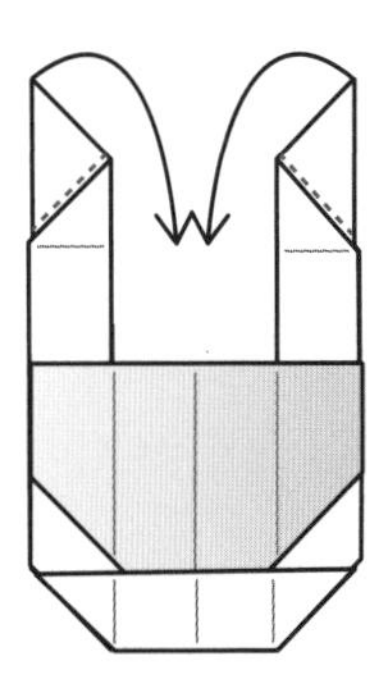

Fold the triangles at the top of the handles down.

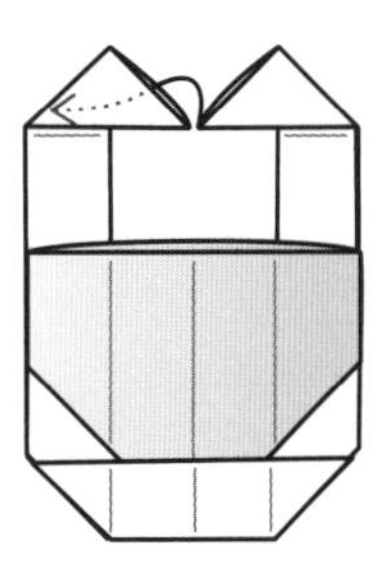

Slide one of the triangles inside the other triangle on the top. (Note: The tote section will become curved and 3-D.)

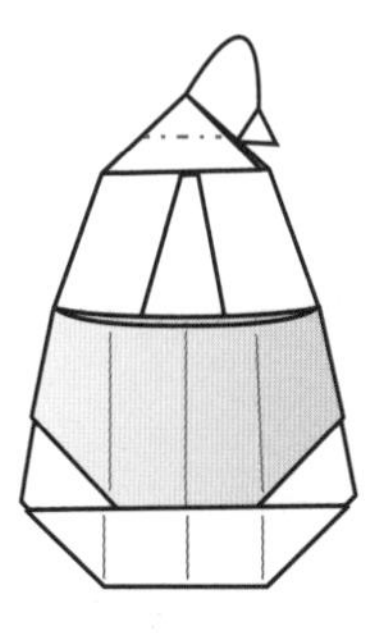

While holding the triangle flaps together, one inside the other, mountain fold the top corner to the back to lock the handle in place.

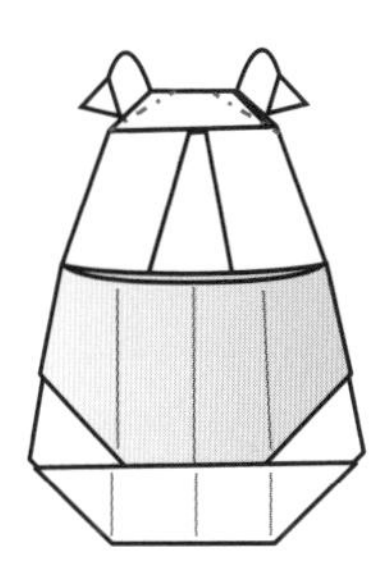

Mountain fold the corners on the top to shape the handle and create a stronger paper lock.

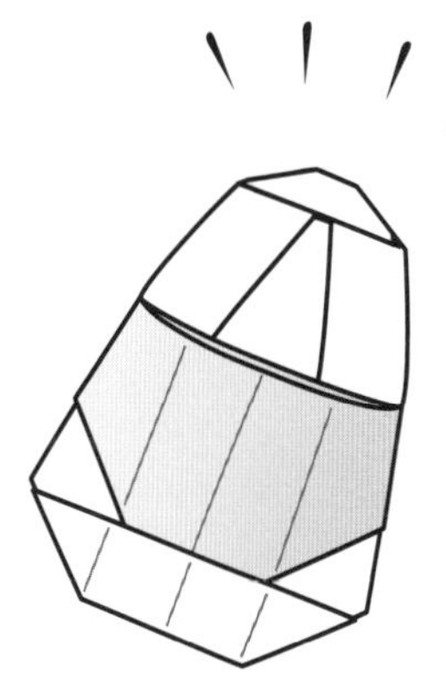

Enjoy your finished tote bag!

Scarf

Scarves have always been a practical, yet fashionable accessory. You can tie a scarf around your neck to add a fun pop of color to an outfit. Or fold your scarf into a narrower shape and use it to hold your hair out of your face while making a chic style statement! Try folding this paper version with different patterns, or layer multiple sheets to add more colors.

HOW TO USE

- Fold with a 6- or 8-inch (15- or 20-cm) square of paper and your paper scarf is the perfect size to wrap it around a water bottle, making it easily identifiable as your own.
- Use your paper scarf as a napkin ring or hair tie.

HOW TO FOLD

1

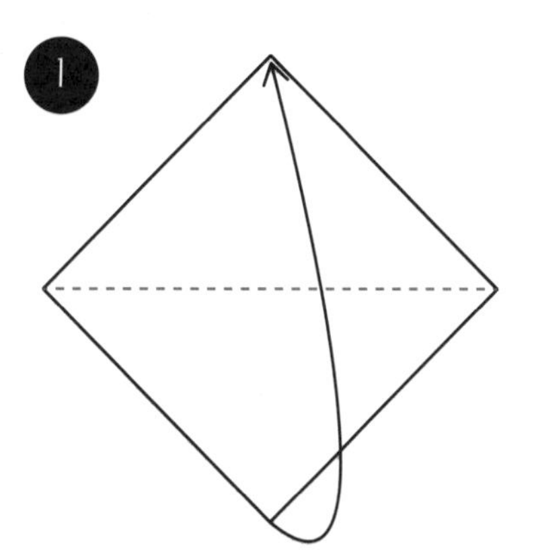

Fold the paper in half diagonally. (Note: The side facing down will become the majority of your scarf; the side facing up will become the contrasting trim.)

2

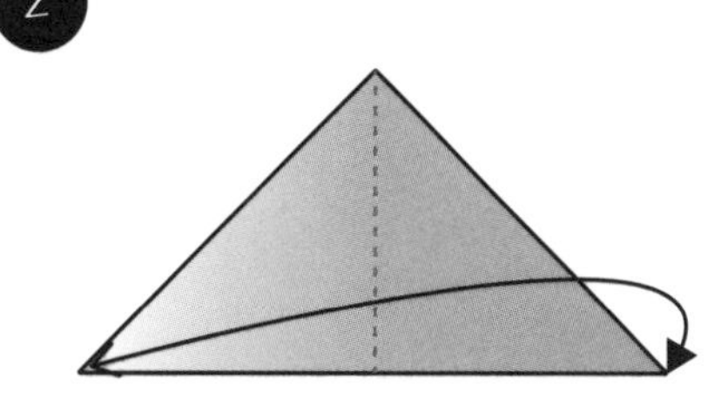

Fold the paper in half again, bringing one corner to the other corner, and then unfold.

3

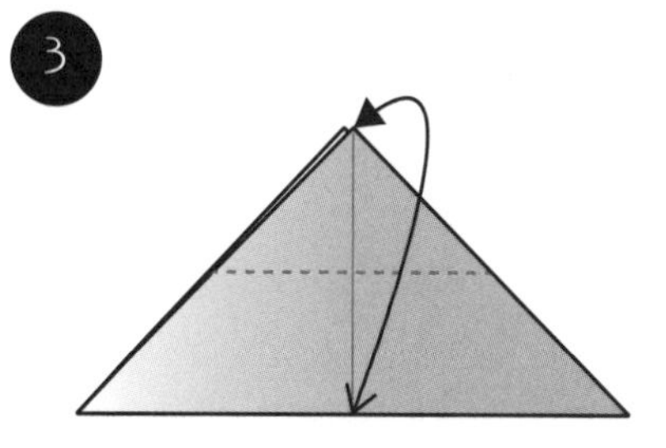

Using just the front layer of paper, fold the top corner down to the bottom edge and then unfold.

4

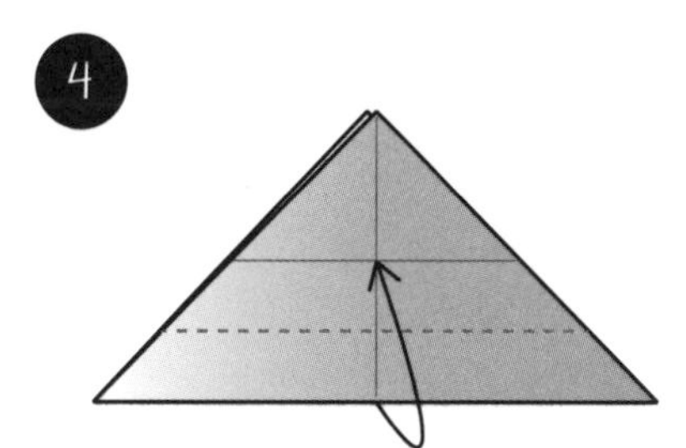

Fold the bottom edge up to the crease made in the previous step.

5

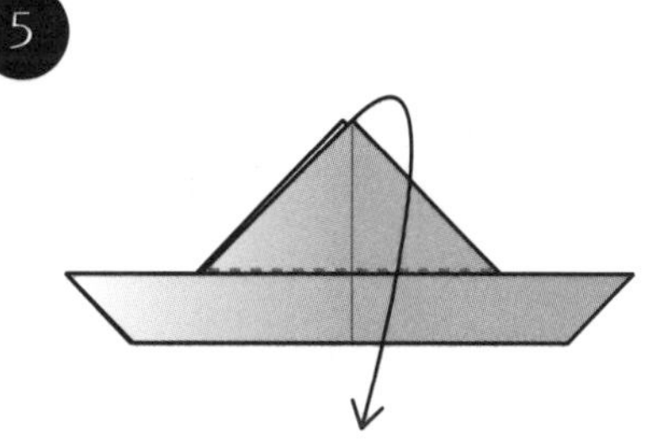

Fold the front flap down on the existing pre-crease.

6

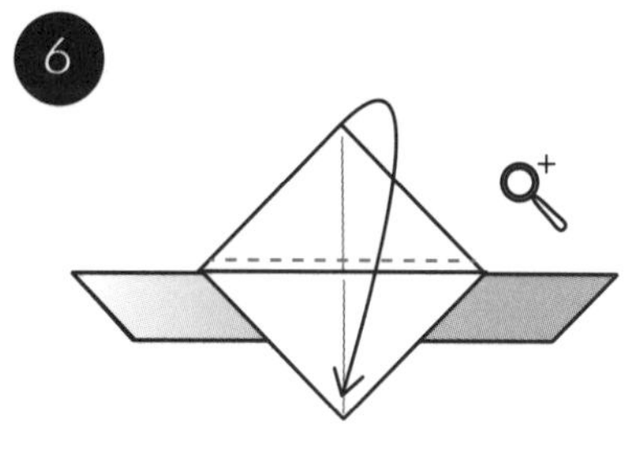

Fold the back flap down, making sure it's slightly higher than the previous flap to create a color-changed border. (See the next step—a magnified view—for reference.)

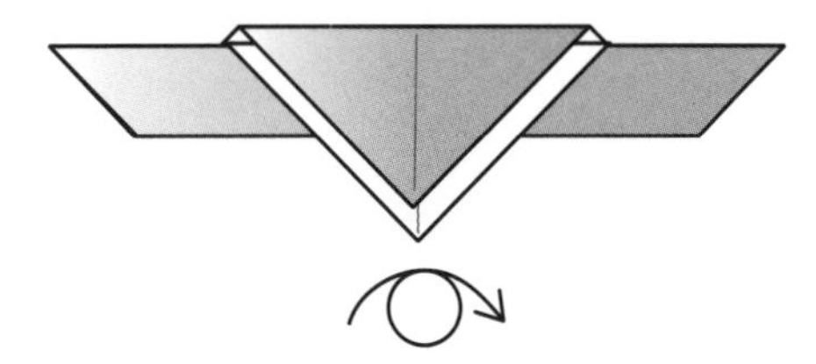

Turn the paper over.

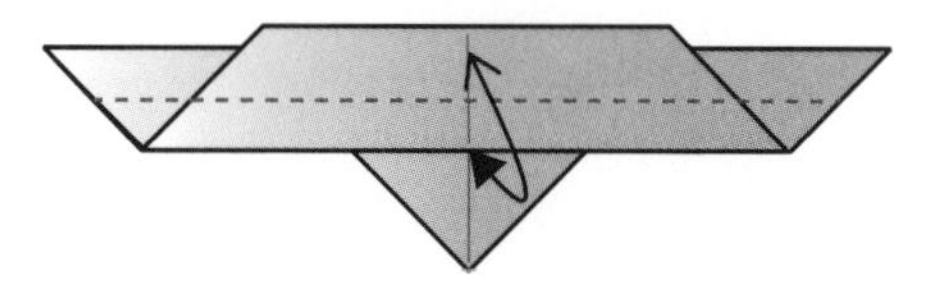

Fold the long folded edge up to the top and then unfold.

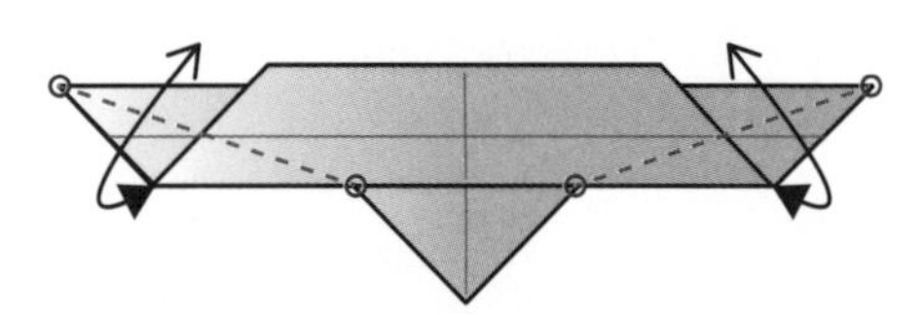

Fold a diagonal from the outside corners to where the bottom edge meets the triangle and then unfold. (Use the circled points for reference.)

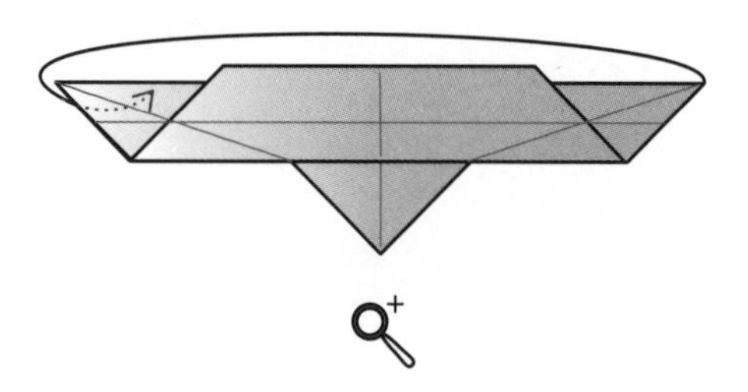

Wrap one corner around to the front and slide the tip into the opening on the opposite side. Leave a small triangle notch on the bottom. (Note: The next step is a magnified view.)

11

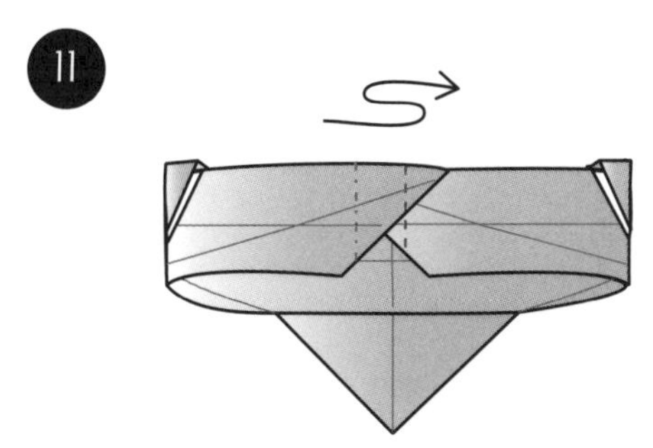

Make a small pleat in the center where the papers overlap inside.

12

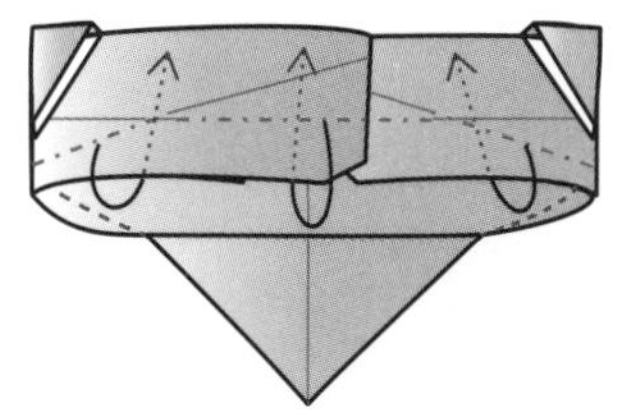

Mountain fold in on the existing pre-creases. (Note: The sides will be the angled creases from step #9 and the back edge will be a straight edge.)

13

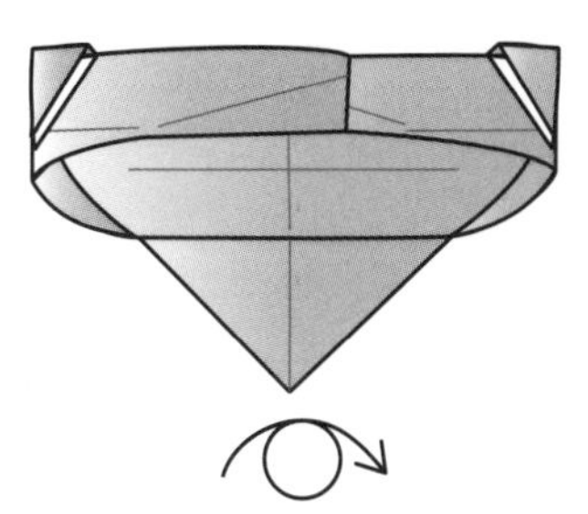

Turn the paper over.

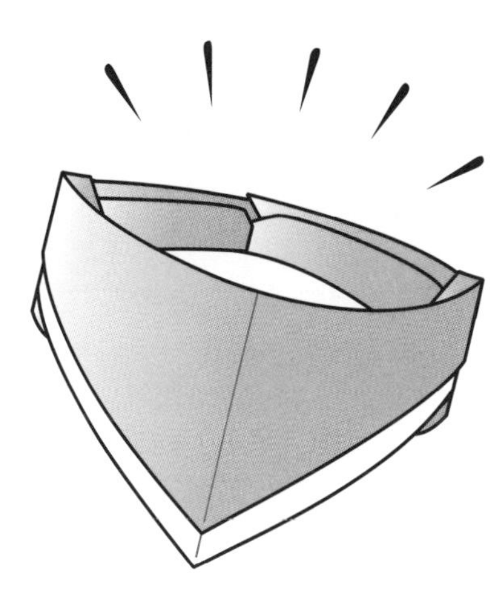

Enjoy your finished scarf!

Bow

Throughout history, **bows** have been a classic accessory for hair or clothing. The right bow can add a pop of color and surprise to an outfit or look. Try folding multiple bows in a variety of sizes and colors. You can attach these paper versions to your headbands and hairpins or to your outfit using pin-backs. You can also make this bow thinner and less bulky by using half a square of paper instead—just start from step #2.

HOW TO FOLD

1

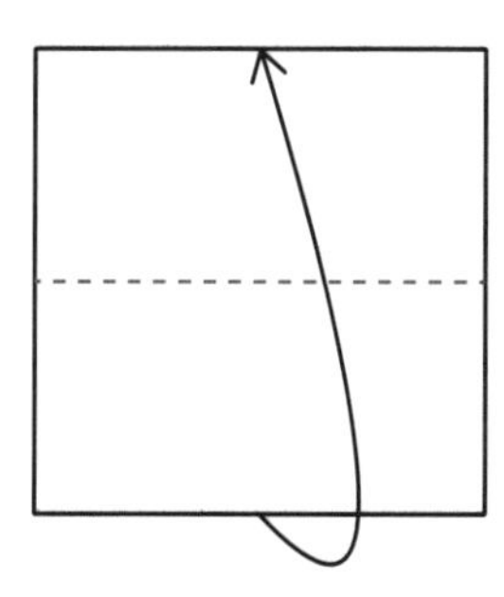

Fold the paper in half horizontally. (Note: The side facing down will become the pattern of the bow.)

2

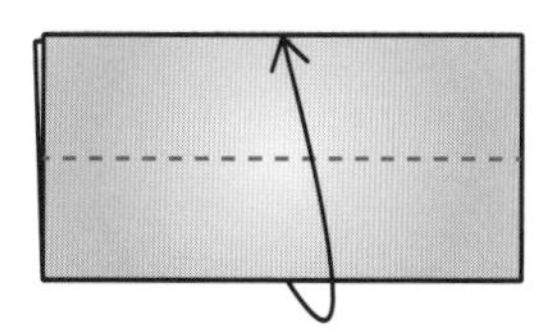

Fold the paper up and in half again.

3

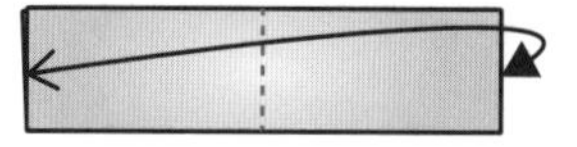

Fold the paper in half vertically and then unfold.

4

Fold the sides into the center and then unfold.

5

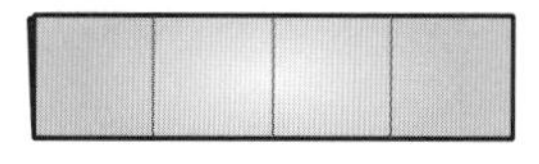

Turn the paper over.

6

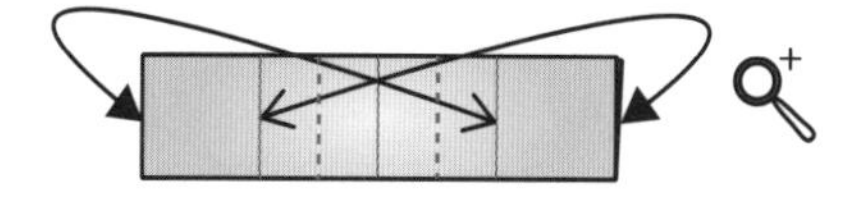

Fold the right side across to the crease on the opposite side and then unfold. Repeat on the left side. (Note: The next step is a magnified view.)

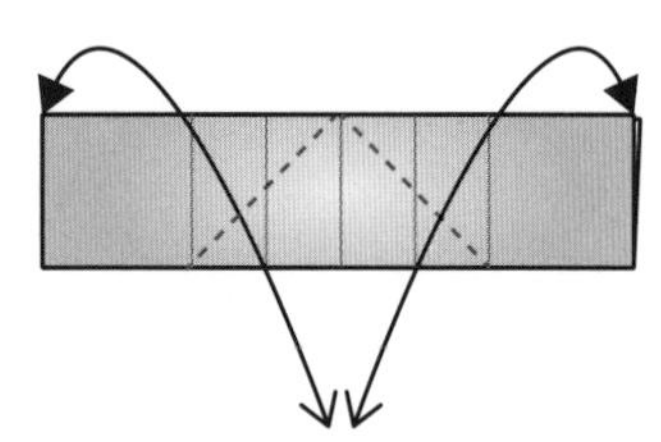

Fold the sides down diagonally along the center crease and then unfold.

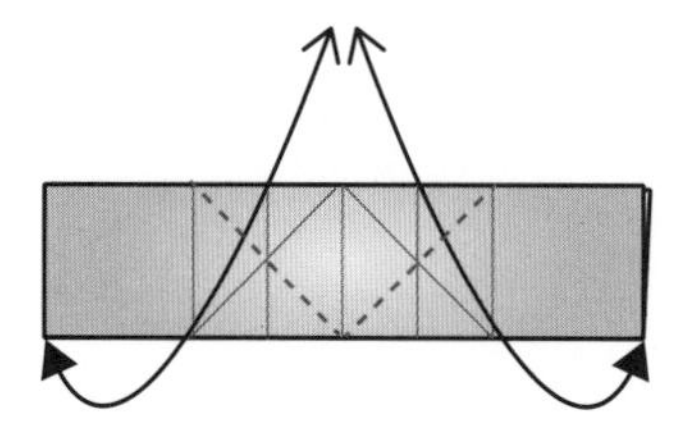

Fold the sides up diagonally along the center crease and then unfold.

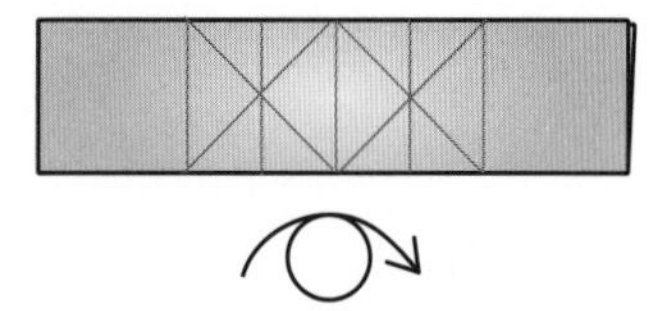

Turn the paper over.

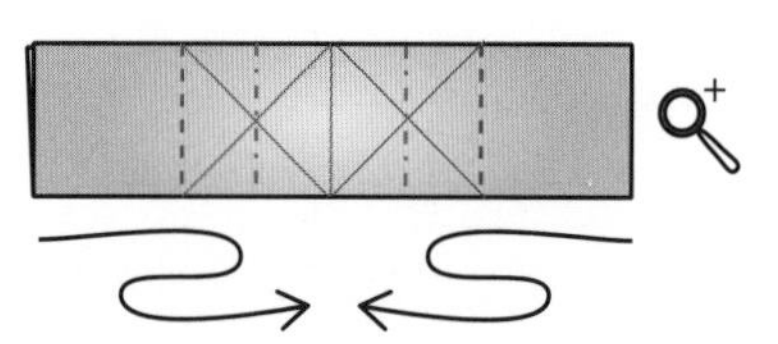

Using the existing vertical pre-creases, pleat the sides into the center. (See the next step—a magnified view—for reference.)

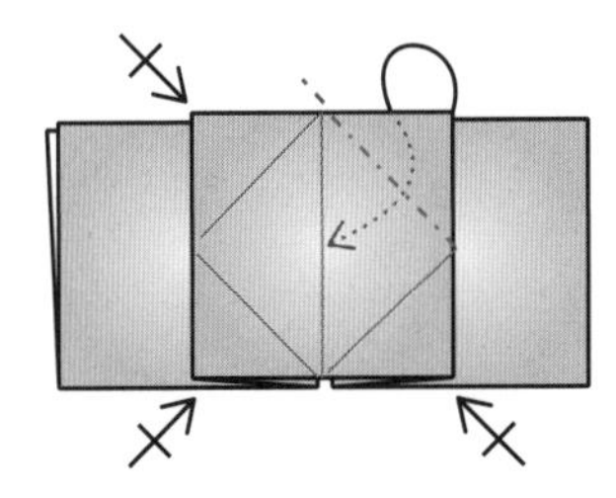

Inside reverse the upper right corner using the angled pre-creases. Repeat on all the other corners of the center square.

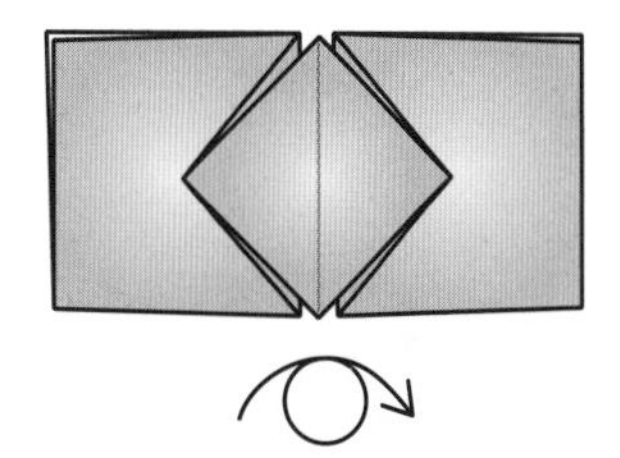

Turn the paper over.

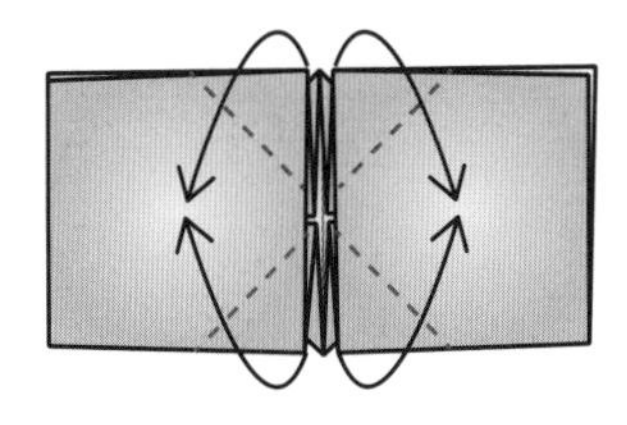

Fold the corner tips down to shape the bow. (See the next step for reference.)

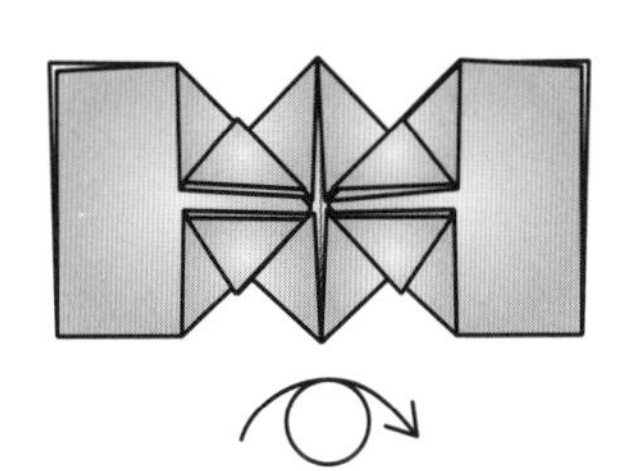

Turn the paper over.

Enjoy your finished paper bow!

Ballet Flats

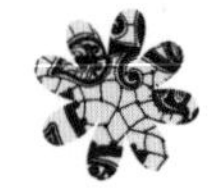

Ballet flats are a fashion classic, dating all the way back to the 16th century. They can be dressed up or down depending on the occasion. Pair them with skinny pants or leggings for a comfy, casual look or fold them in a sparkly paper and pair them with your prom dress or ball gown for a classier ensemble!

STYLE TIPS

- Ballet flats are the perfect shoes to choose when you're going to be on your feet; they're both comfortable and stylish!
- Toss a pair of ballet flats in your tote bag; they're easy to take on the go, and you'll be grateful to have them if your high heels start hurting!

HOW TO FOLD

1

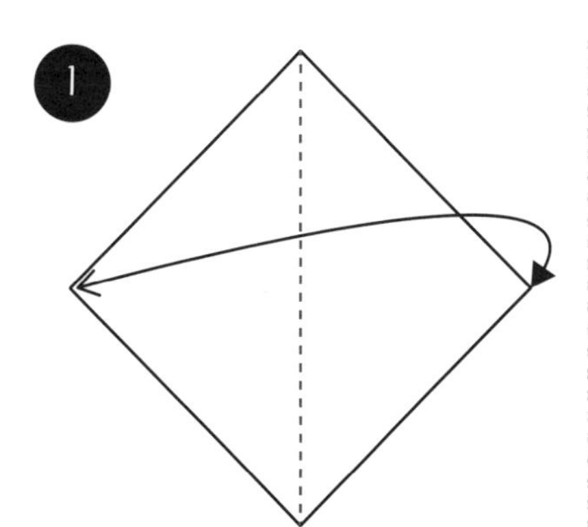

Fold the paper in half diagonally and then unfold. (Note: The side facing down will become the outside of the ballet flats.)

2

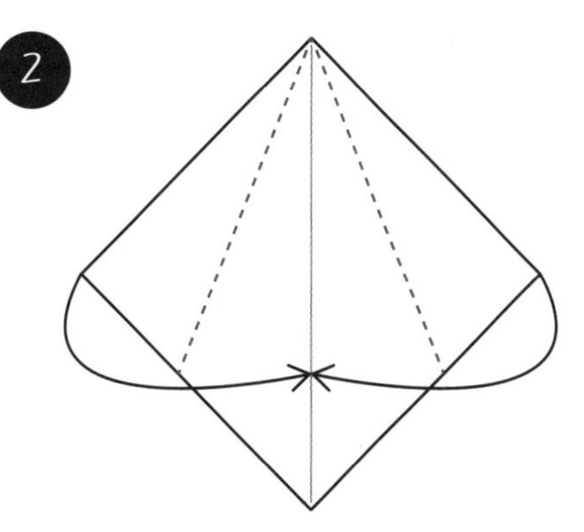

Fold the side edges into the center crease.

3

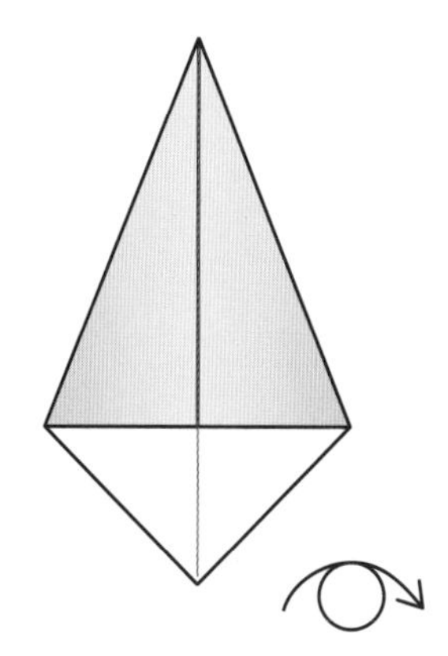

Turn the paper over.

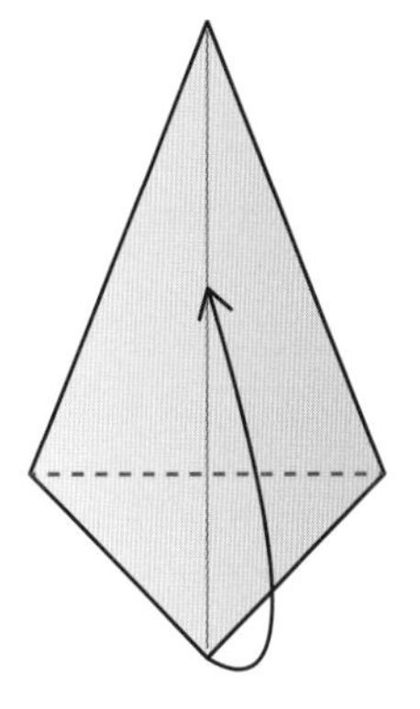

Fold the bottom triangle up at the lower edge of the side creases.

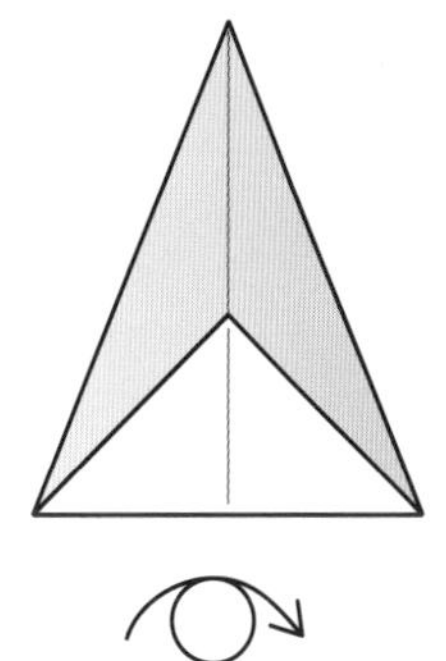

Turn the paper over.

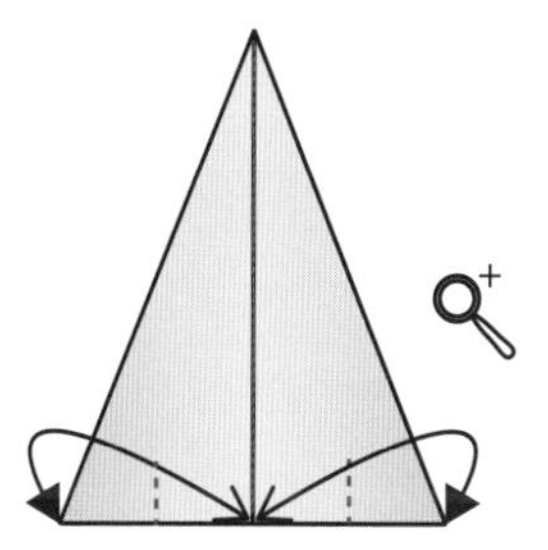

Pinch two reference points along the bottom edge by bringing both corners into the center crease and then unfold. (Note: The next step is a magnified view.)

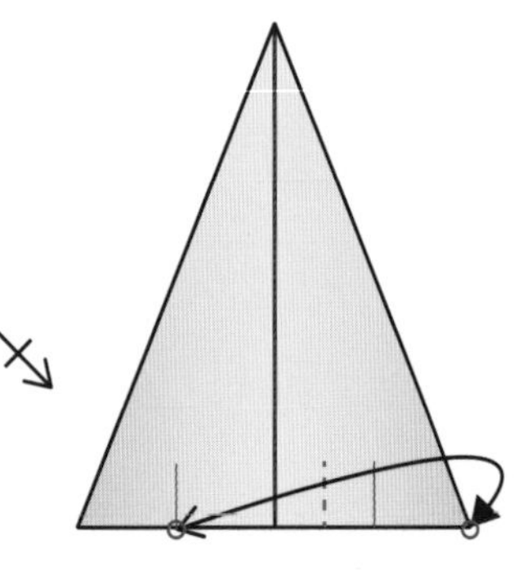

Pinch another reference crease by bringing the right corner across to the pinch on the left side and then unfold. Repeat on the opposite side.

8

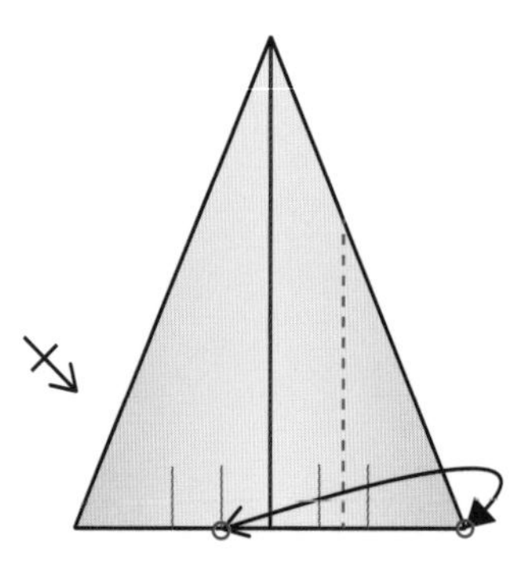

Fold the right corner across to the pinch closest to the center on the left side and then unfold. Repeat on the opposite side.

9

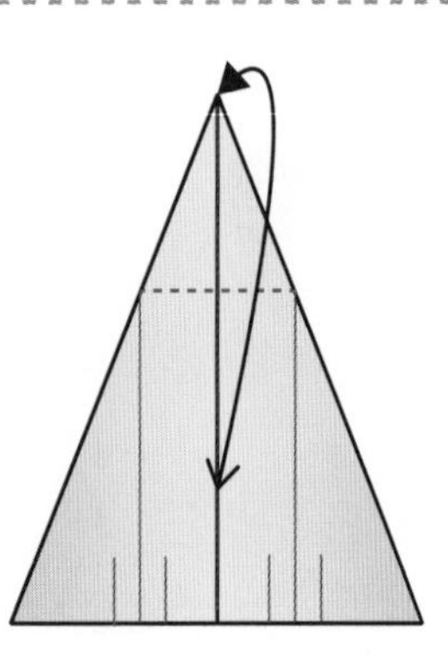

Fold the top corner down at the top edge of the creases made in the previous step and then unfold.

10

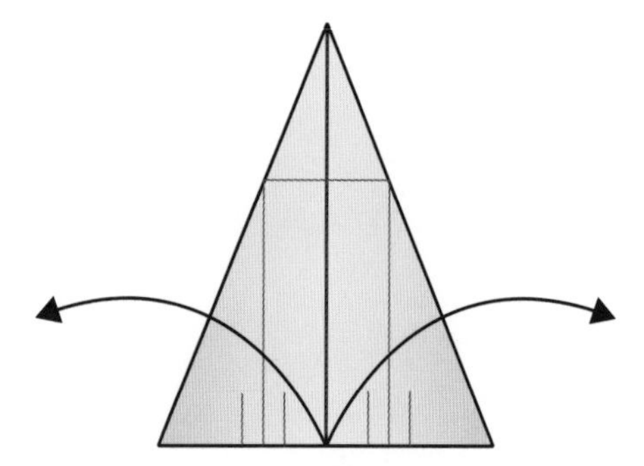

Open the flaps back out to the sides.

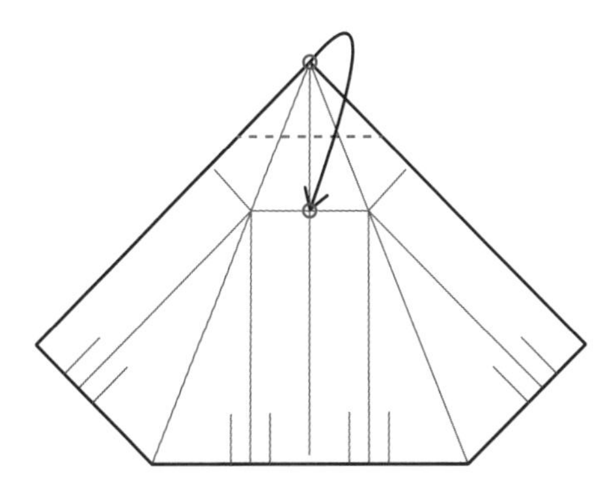

Fold the top corner down to the crease made in step #9.

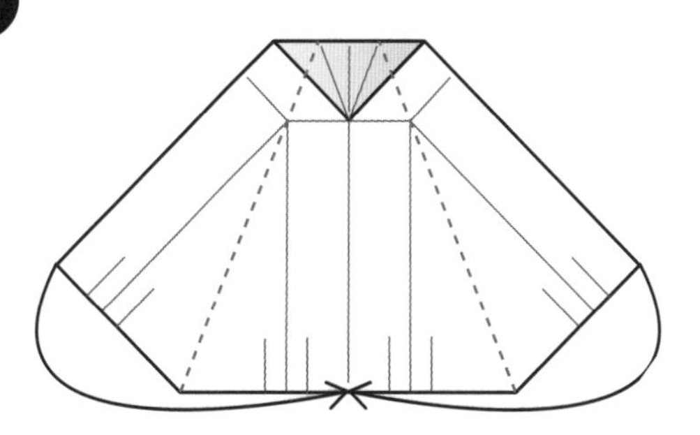

Fold the side flaps back into the center on the existing pre-creases.

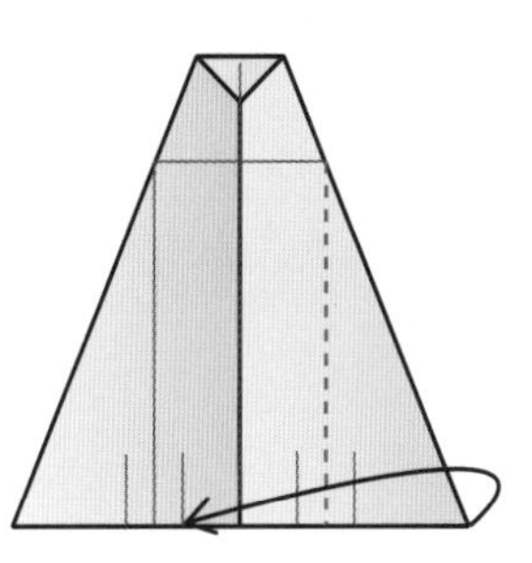

Fold the right side across on the existing pre-crease made in step #8.

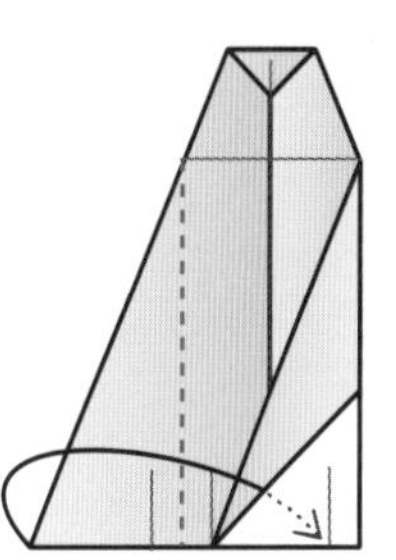

Fold the opposite side across on the existing pre-crease and insert it into the pocket of the other flap. (Note: The next step is a magnified view.)

15

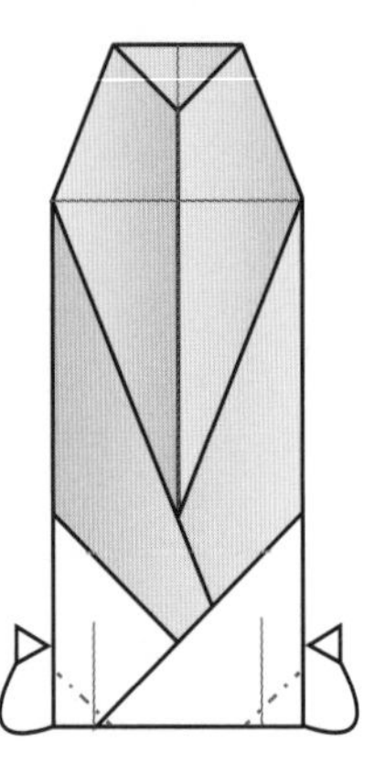

Mountain fold the bottom corners to the back to shape the front of the shoe.

16

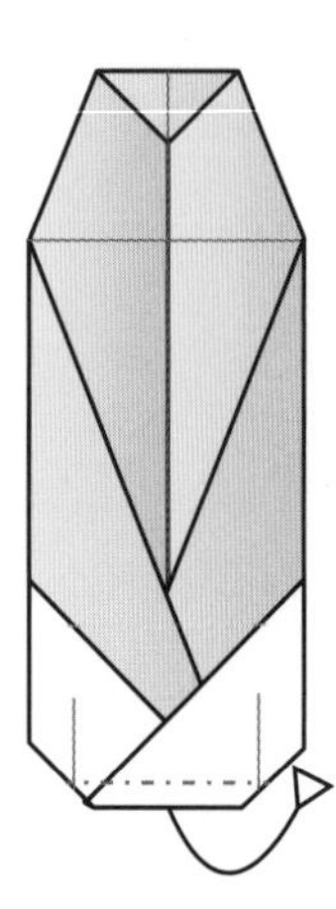

Mountain fold the bottom edge to the back to further shape the front of the shoe.

17

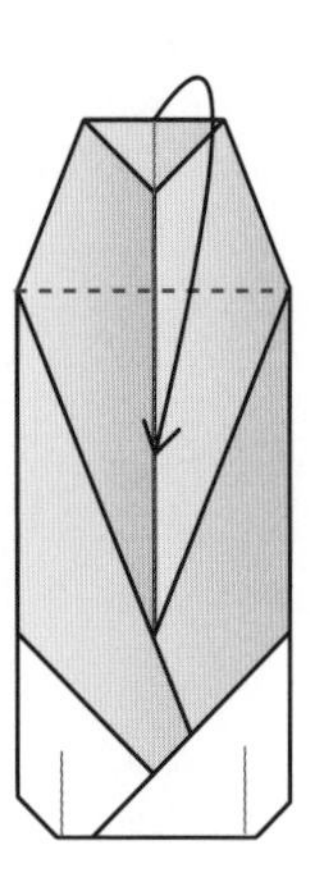

Fold the top section down on the existing pre-crease.

18

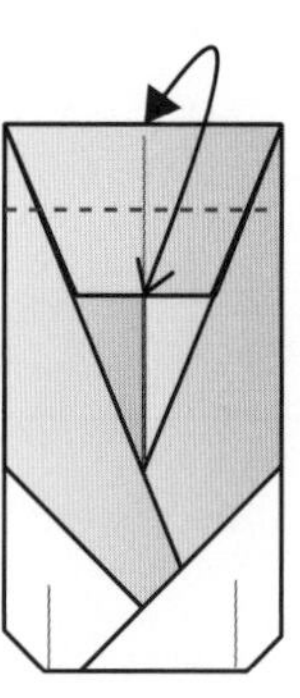

Fold the top edge down to the bottom edge of the flap from the previous step and then unfold.

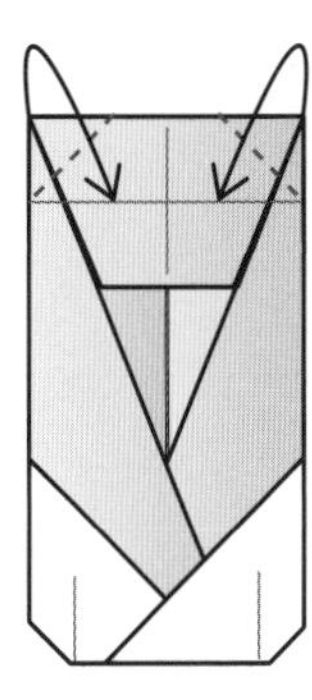

Fold the top corners down to line up with the crease made in the previous step.

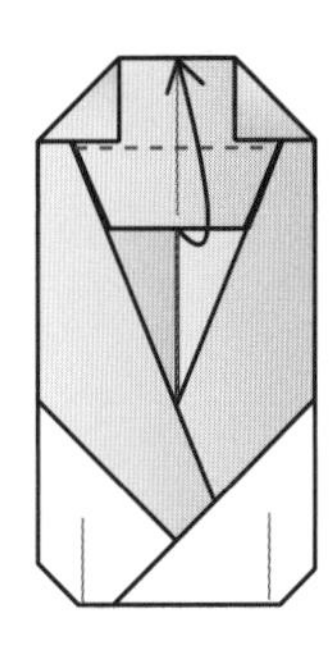

Fold the flap back up, hiding the folded corners from previous step. This will create a paper lock.

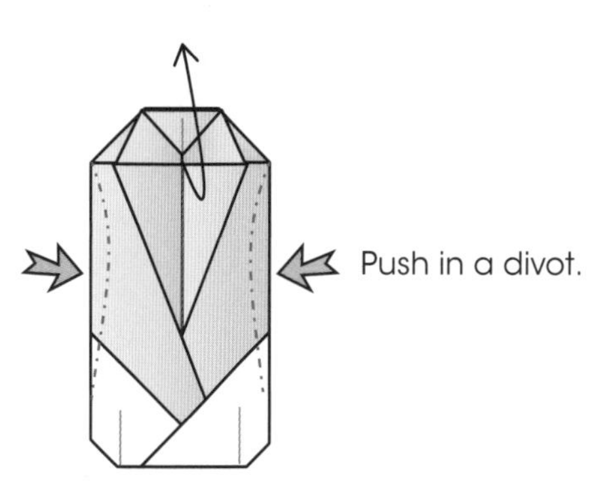

Gently lift the back section from inside the pocket to open and shape the shoe. (Note: Hold the paper lock you creased in the previous step while lifting the back up—the triangles need to remain locked underneath the flap.) Lift the sides and push them in slightly to further shape the shoe. This will make the shoe 3-D .

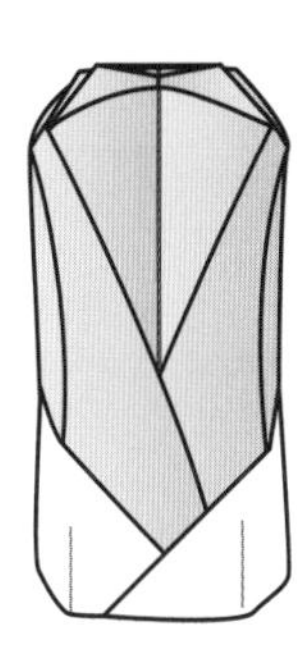

Enjoy your finished ballet flats!

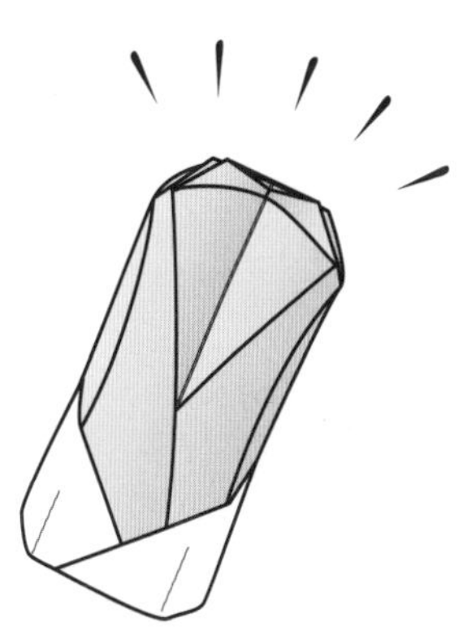

*These instructions will make one finished ballet flat. Fold another one to make a pair! You can vary the shape of each model—creating a left and right shoe—by folding the corners in different sizes in step #15 and by shaping in step #21.)

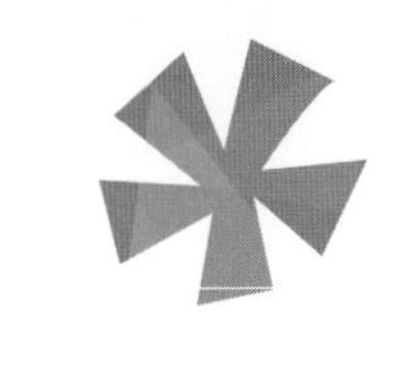

High Heels

Formal and elegant, the right **high heels** can take your outfit to new heights—literally! This simple paper version has a color-change geometric bow shape in the front and can be folded with many different patterns and colors. After all, you can never have too many pairs of fabulous shoes!

STYLE TIPS

- Pair your heels with jeans or skinny pants and a dressy blouse for a fun night out. Just make sure to choose heels that are comfortable!
- High heels are the perfect choice to wear with a ball gown, prom dress, or little black dress for a formal occasion.

HOW TO FOLD

1

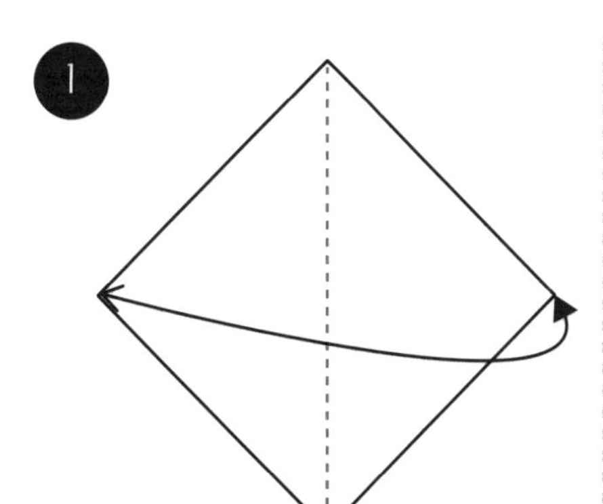

Fold the paper in half diagonally and then unfold. (Note: The side facing down will become the outside of the heels; the side facing up will become the contrasting bow.)

2

Fold the side edges into the center crease.

3

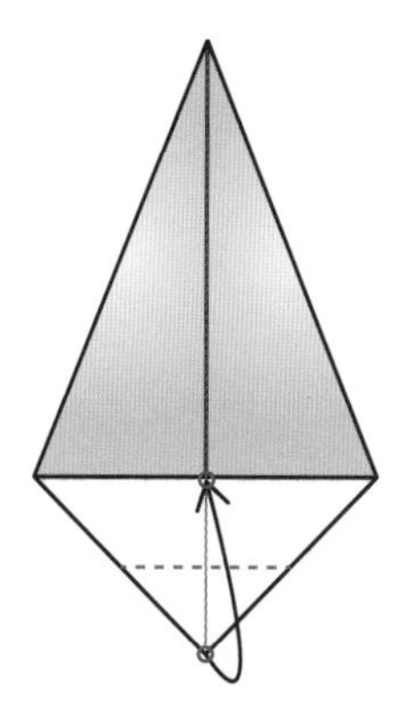

Fold the tip of the bottom triangle up to the contrasting edge.

4

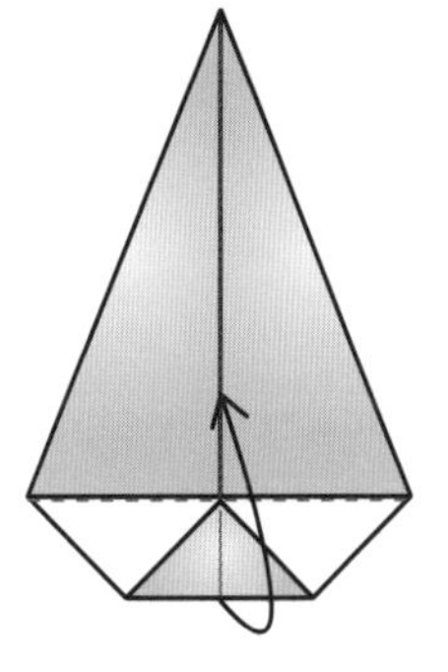

Fold the bottom section up at the contrasting edge.

5

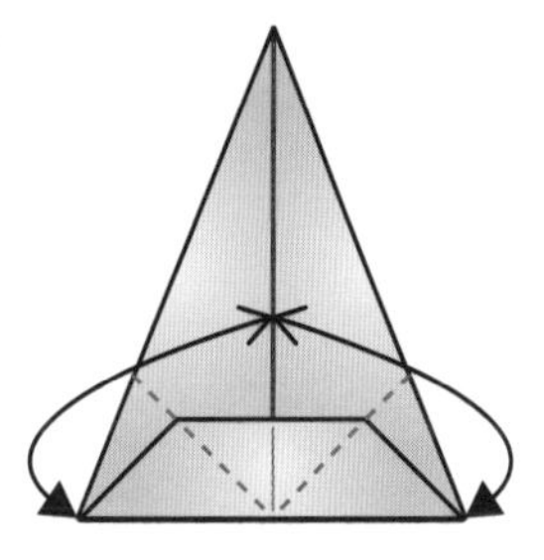

Fold the bottom corners up and into the center crease and then unfold.

6

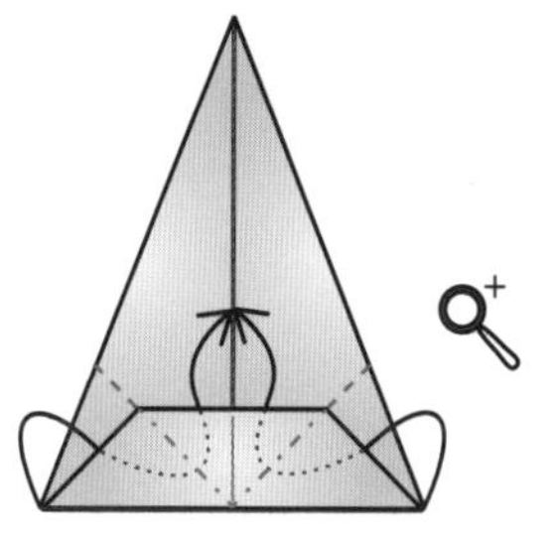

Inside reverse the corners. (Note: The next step is a magnified view.)

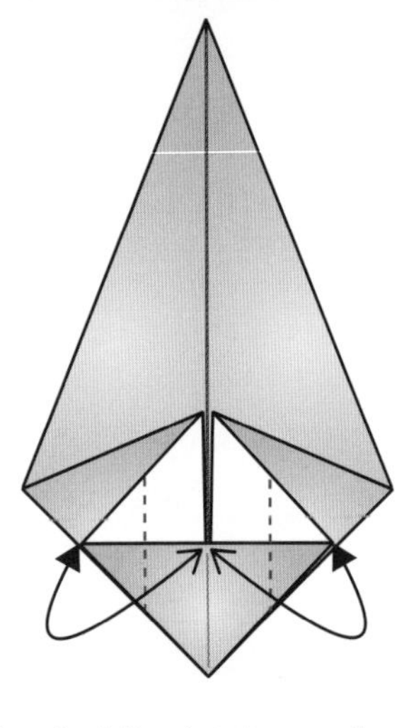

Using just the top layer of paper, fold the side corners into the center and then unfold.

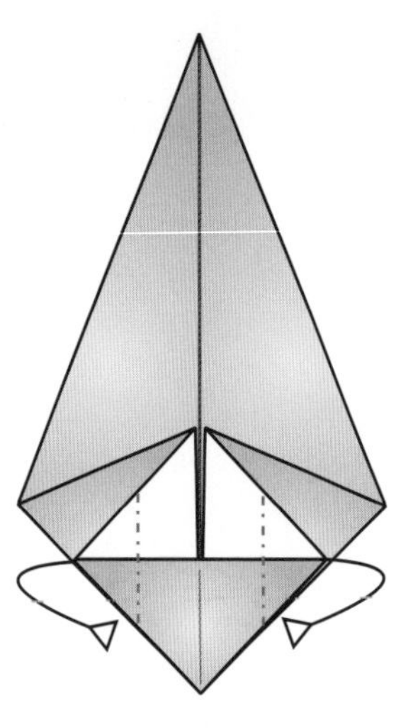

Mountain fold the corners to the back on the crease made in the previous step. (Note: This is not an inside reverse. Just fold and tuck to the back.)

9

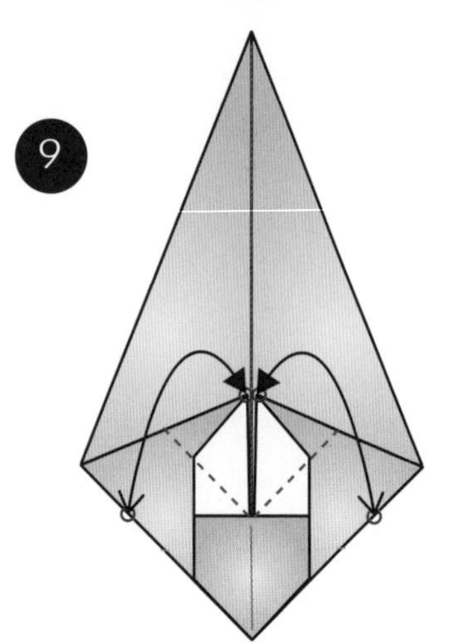

Fold the corners down and then unfold. (Note: Use the circled points for reference.)

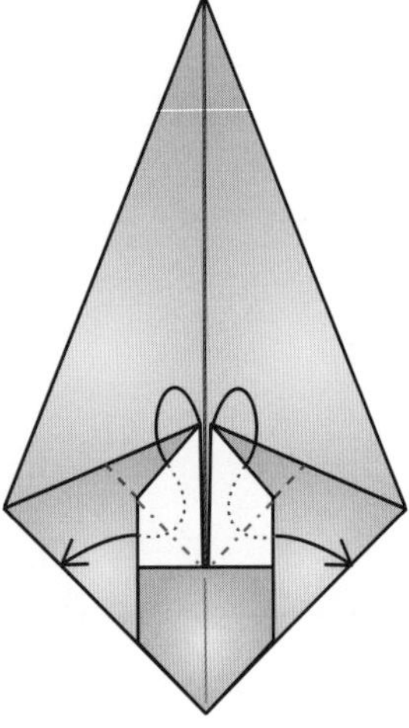

Inside reverse the points on the existing pre-creases.

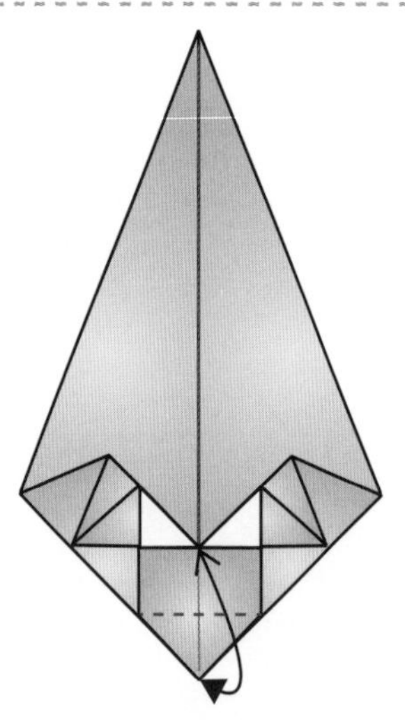

Fold the bottom corner up and then unfold.

12

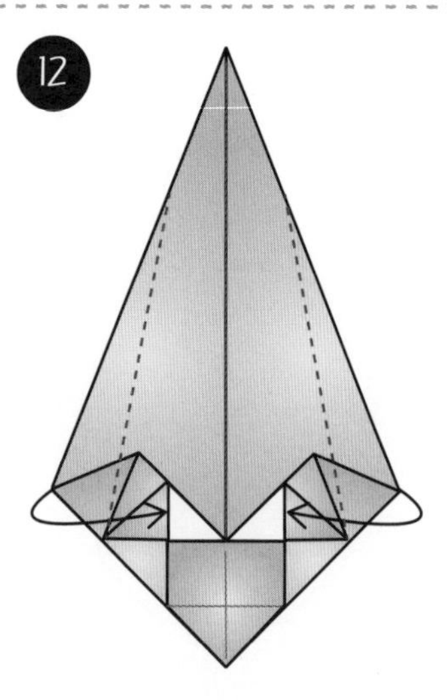

Fold the sides in. The side corners will align with the outside edges of the contrasting triangles. (See the next step for reference.)

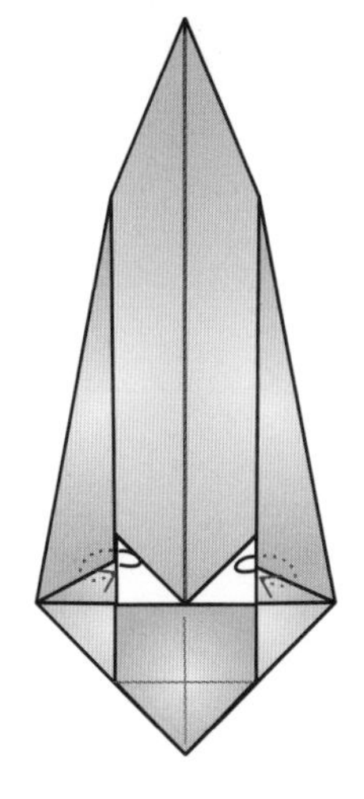

Tuck the bottom corners underneath the bi-colored triangular flaps.

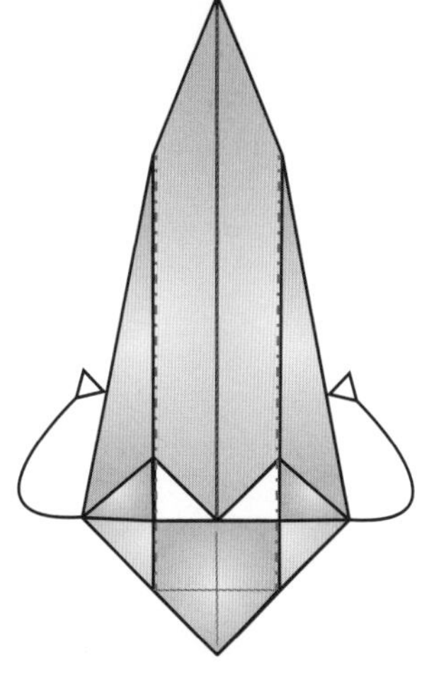

Mountain fold the sides to the back.

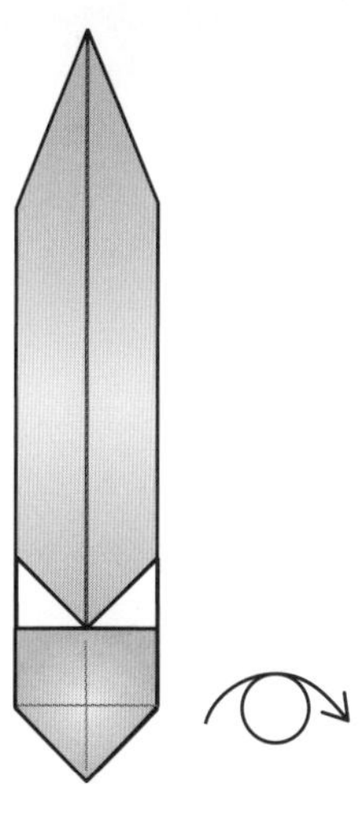

Turn the paper over.

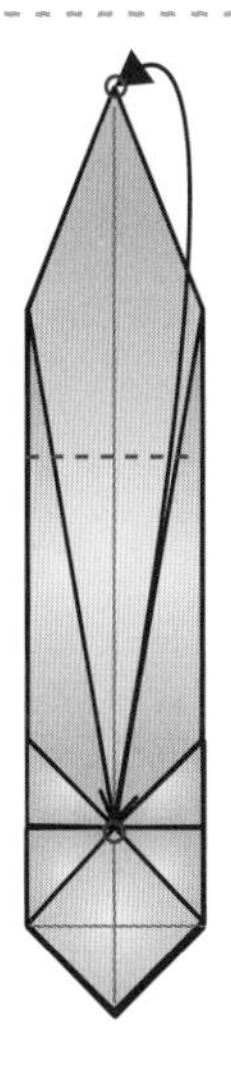

Fold the top corner down to the indicated point and then unfold.

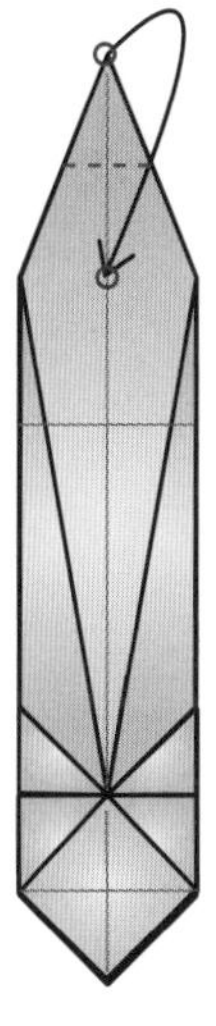

Fold the top corner down, halfway between the crease made in the previous step and the top of the paper. (Use the circled points for reference.)

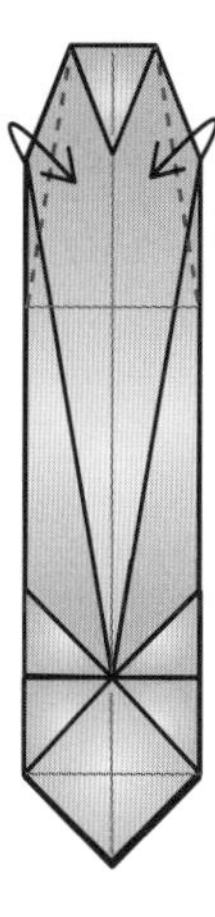

Narrow the sides of the top section.

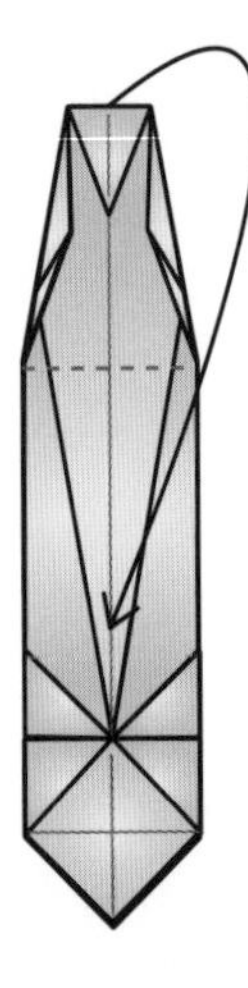

Fold the top down on the existing pre-crease.

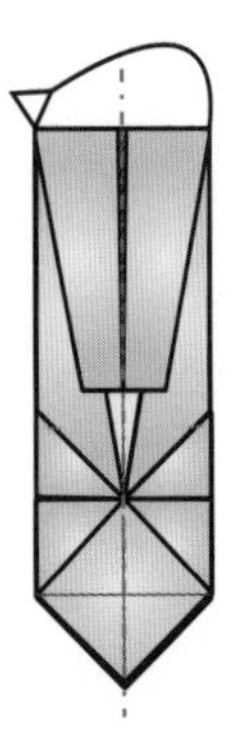

Mountain fold all the layers in half vertically on the existing pre-crease in the center.

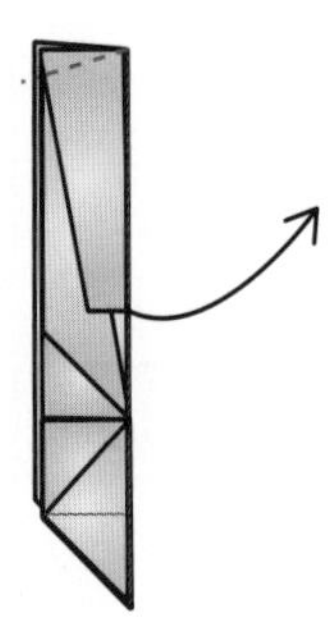

Pull the heel of the shoe out at an angle. You can change the angle depending on how high you want the heel to be. (See the next step for reference.)

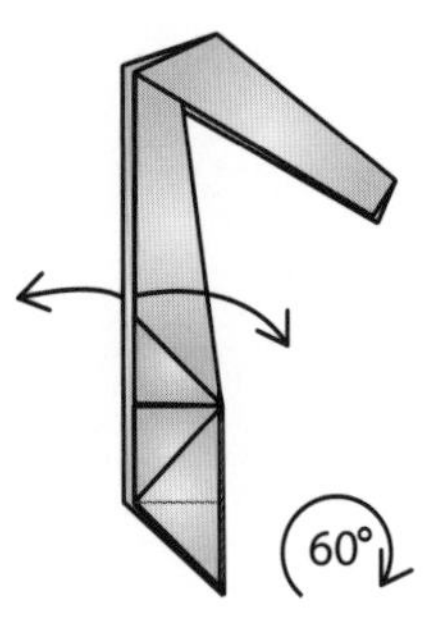

Gently pull the sides open to shape the front of the shoe and rotate the model 60°.

23

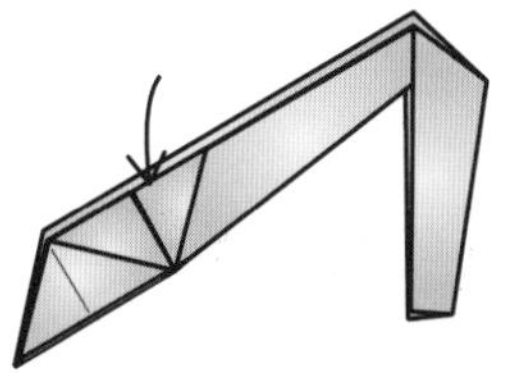

Open the inside of the shoe in the front and pull the side edges down to shape the shoe. (See the next step for reference.)

24

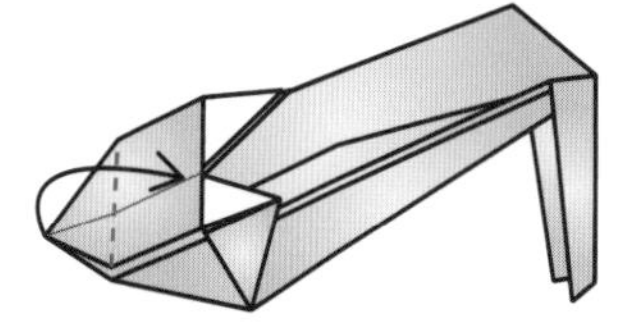

Using the existing pre-crease, fold the small triangle at the tip back slightly to help shape the front of the shoe.

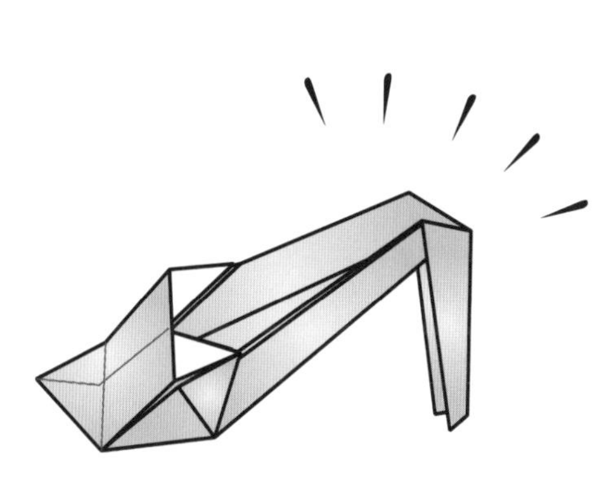

Enjoy your finished high heel!

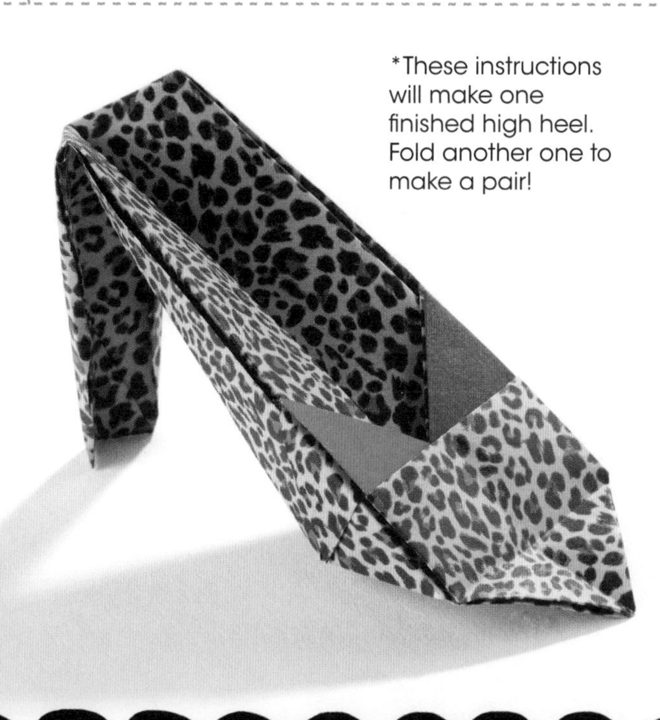

*These instructions will make one finished high heel. Fold another one to make a pair!

Bracelet

Origami lends itself very easily to becoming jewelry. You can turn almost any origami model into pieces of jewelry that you can wear. This simple paper **bracelet** uses the same paper lock as a few of the other designs in this book. Try playing with proportions and different colors to make it your own accessory. Coordinate your bracelet with your other jewelry by choosing complementary colors, but don't make it too matchy-matchy.

HOW TO USE

- Try folding this bracelet in a variety of colors and patterns. Then stack several bracelets in unique patterns and textures for a wrist full of fun bangles.
- Fold this paper bracelet model with smaller paper, and it can function as a ring instead of a bracelet.

HOW TO FOLD

1

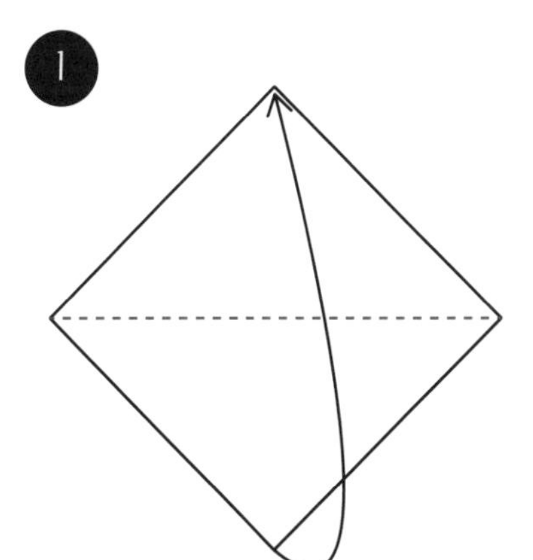

Fold the paper in half diagonally.

2

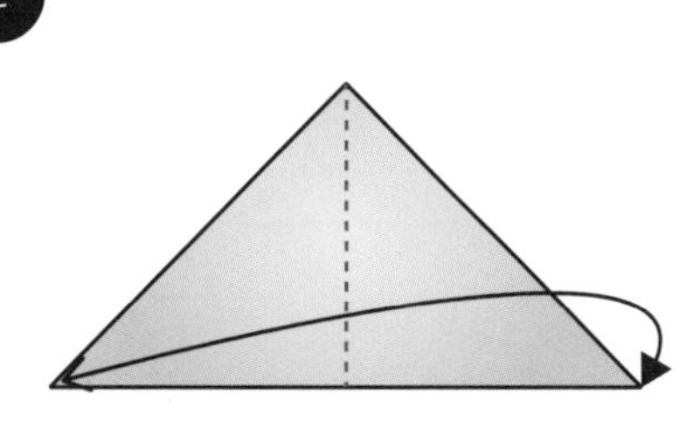

Fold the paper in half again and then unfold.

3

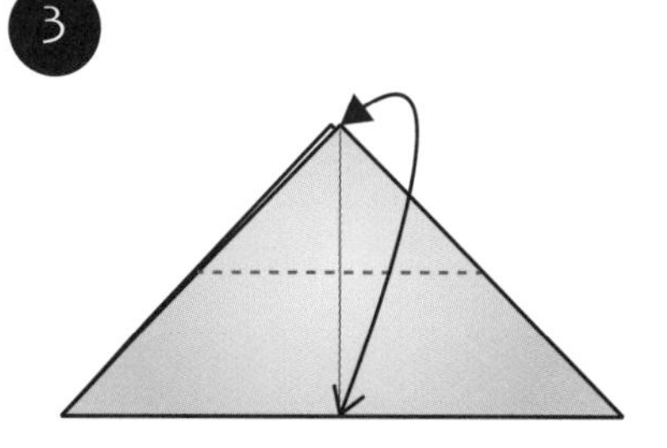

Fold the top corner (through both layers of paper) down to the bottom edge and then unfold.

4

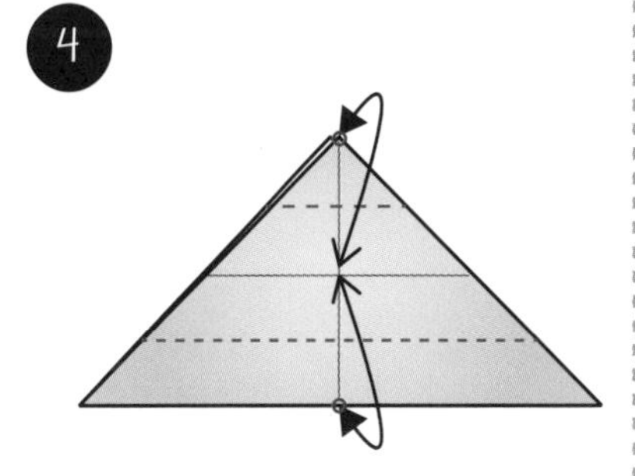

Fold both the top corner and bottom edge to the center crease and then unfold.

5

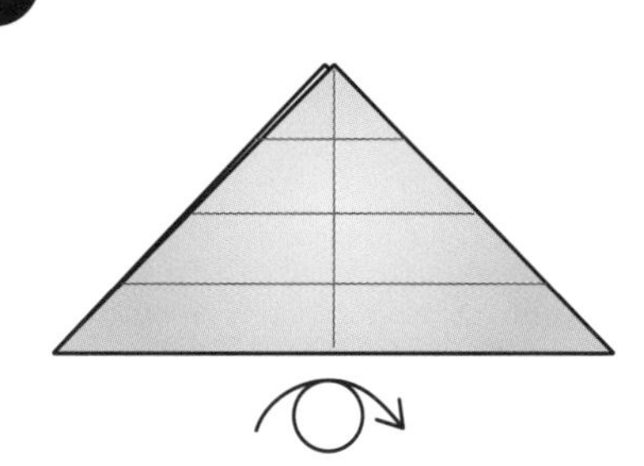

Turn the paper over.

6

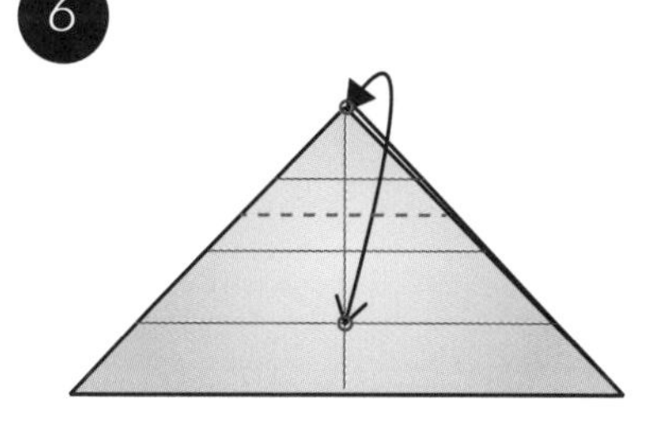

Fold the top corner down to the bottom crease made in step #4 and then unfold.

7

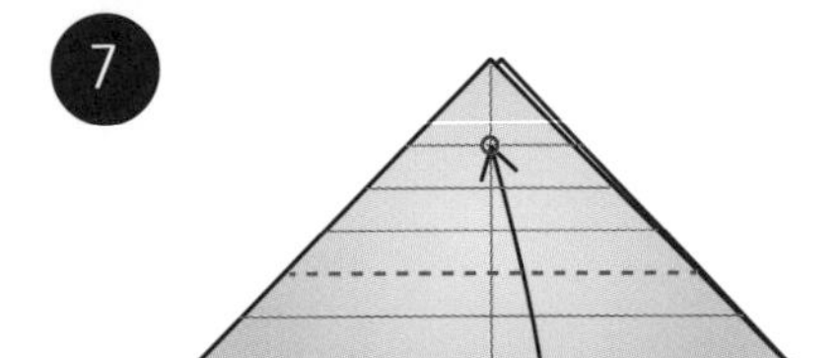

Fold the bottom edge up to the top crease made in step #4 and then unfold. (Note: You are dividing the paper diagonally into sixteenths.)

8

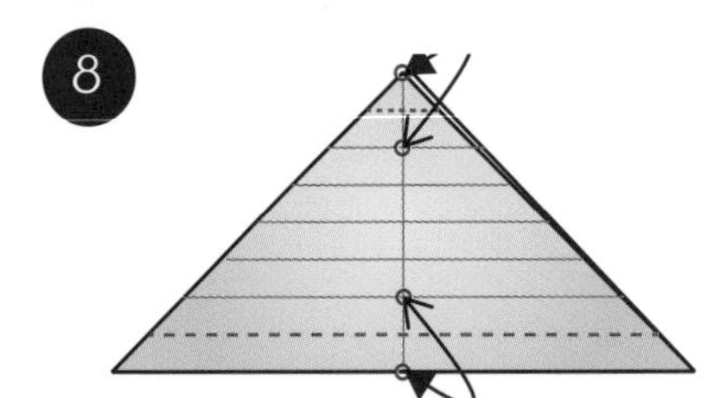

Fold the top corner down to the nearest crease and then unfold. Do the same with the bottom edge.

9

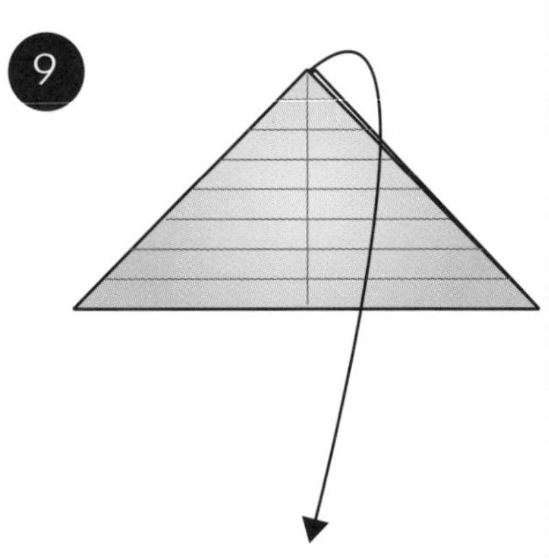

Open the paper back to the original square.

10

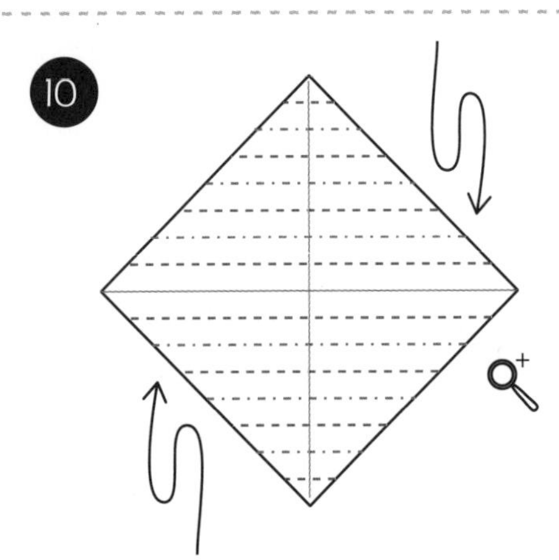

Working first from the top, then from the bottom, pleat the paper using the creases made in the previous steps. (Note: The top half will have all the creases going in the correct direction, but you will need to reverse the creases on the bottom half. See the next step—a magnified view—for reference.)

11

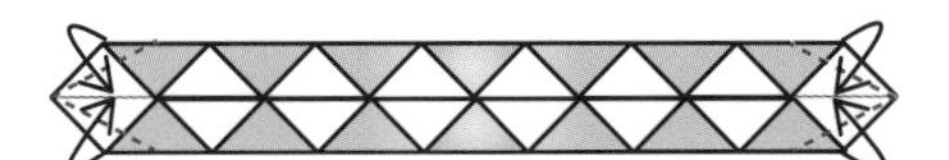

Fold the outer corners into the center crease.

12

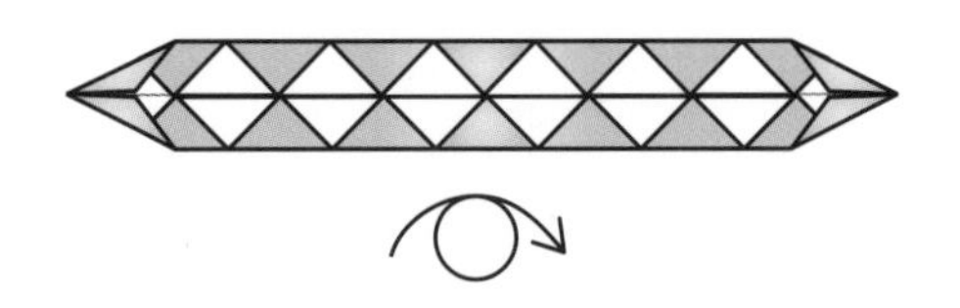

Turn the paper over.

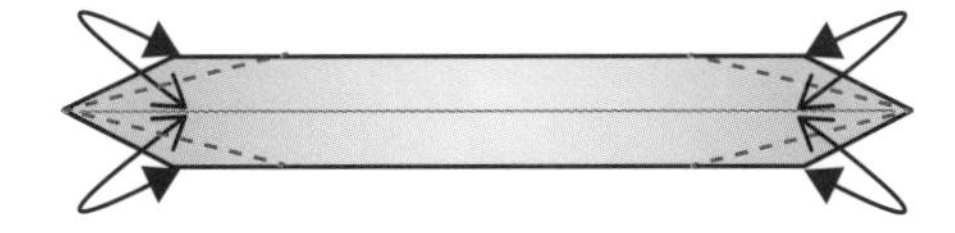

Fold the outer corners into the center crease again and then unfold. (Note: This fold will involve only the back layers of paper, not the front layers.)

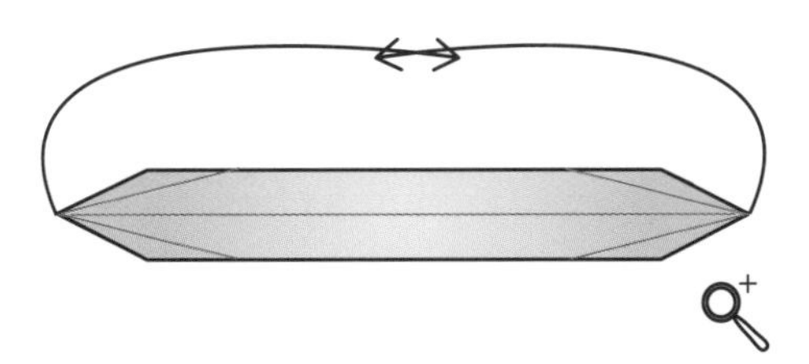

Wrap one corner around to the back and then insert it into the pocket on the opposite side. The pocket is the diagonal triangle flap folded in step #11. (Note: The next step is a magnified view.)

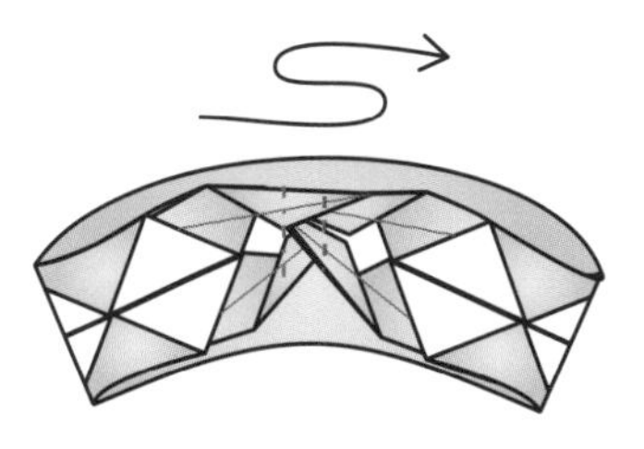

Pleat the back section where the corners overlap, creating a paper lock.

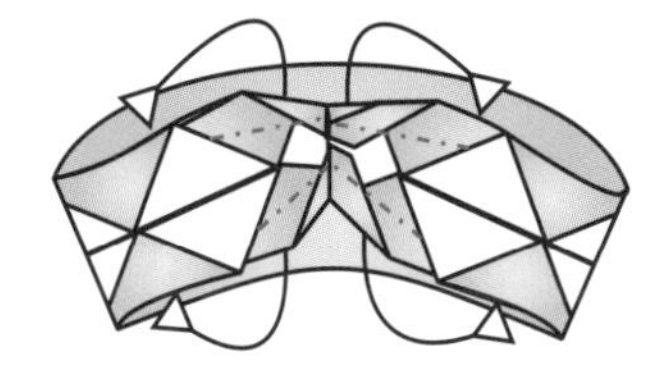

Mountain fold the paper to the inside along the diagonals folded in step #13 to complete the paper lock.

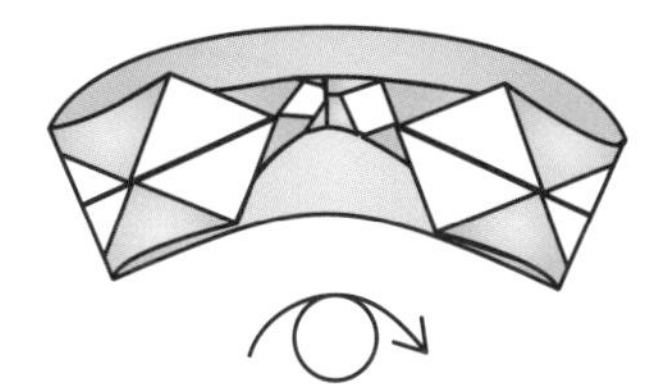

Turn the paper over.

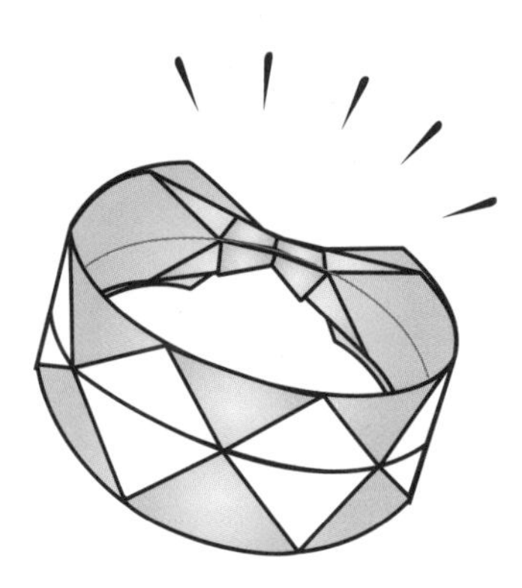

Enjoy your finished bracelet!

Backpack

Practical and modern, this geometric **backpack** uses a simple paper lock to make the straps. A backpack can be used as a functional school accessory or in place of a purse to hold your belongings and keep you looking smart and stylish.

STYLE TIPS

- Pair with jeans or skinny pants and an easy top—like a T-shirt or sweater—for a casual look.
- Backpacks make great travel bags—just throw yours over your shoulder and go!

HOW TO FOLD

1

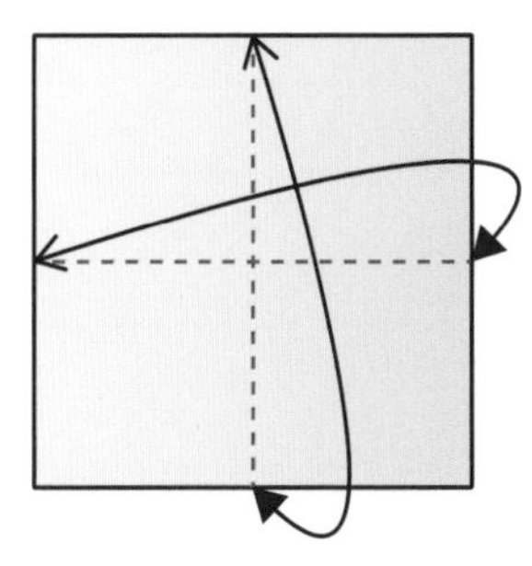

Fold the paper in half in both directions and then unfold. (Note: The side facing up will become the pattern of the backpack.)

2

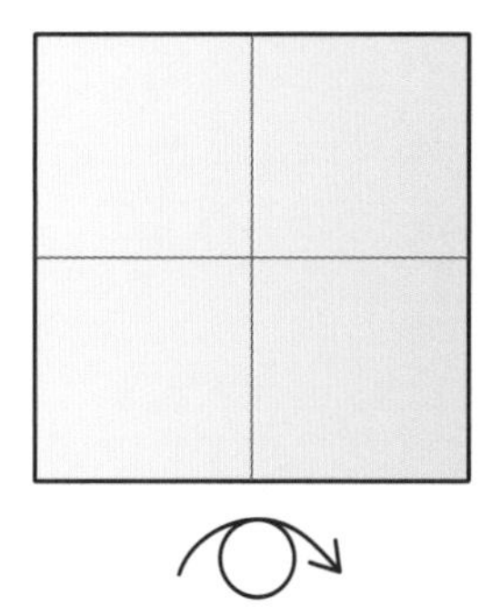

Turn the paper over.

3

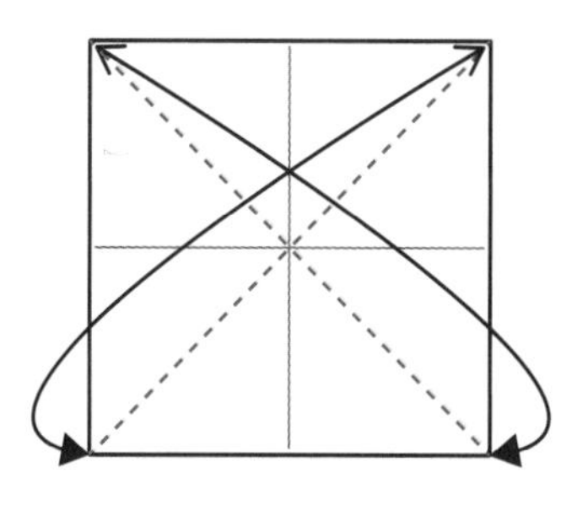

Fold the paper in half diagonally in both directions and then unfold.

4

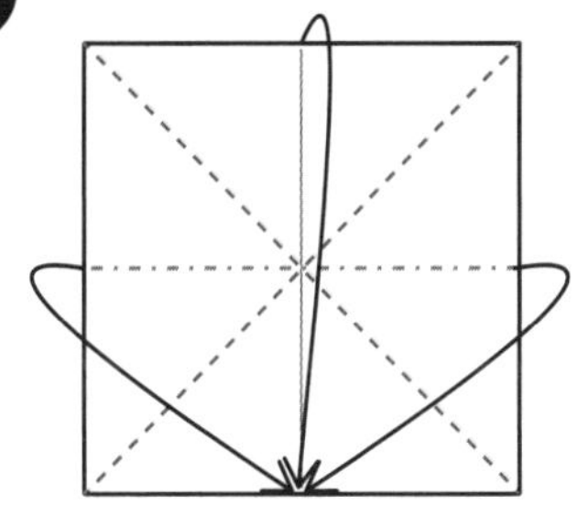

Bring the sides and top down to the bottom to collapse into a triangle with four loose flaps on the bottom. (See the next step for reference.)

5

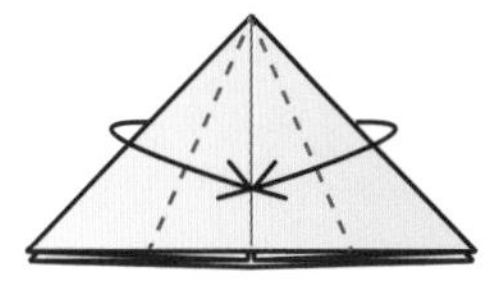

Using just the top layer, fold the side edges into the center crease.

6

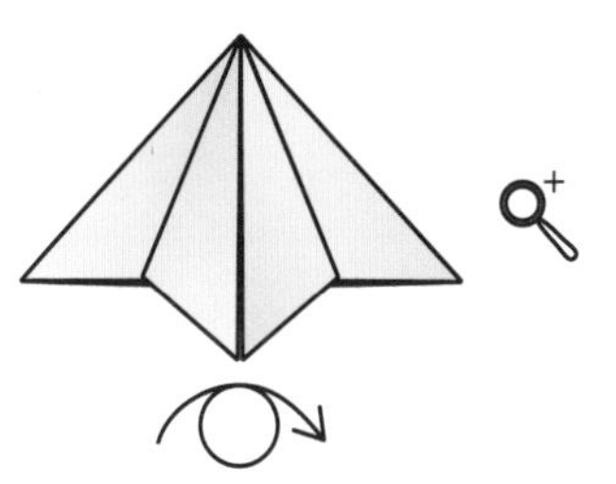

Turn the paper over. (Note: The next step is a magnified view.)

7

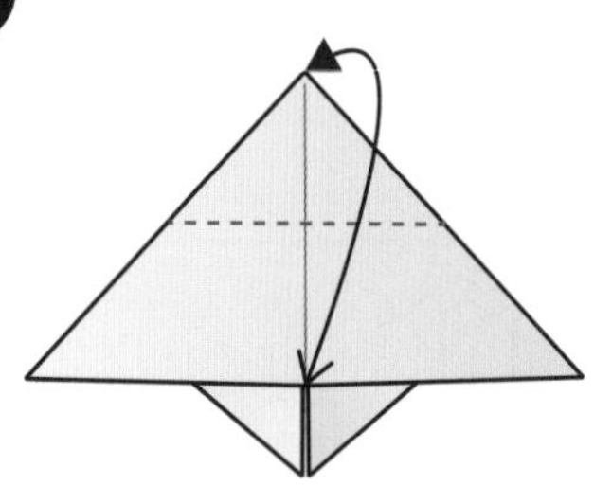

Fold the top corner down to the bottom edge and then unfold.

8

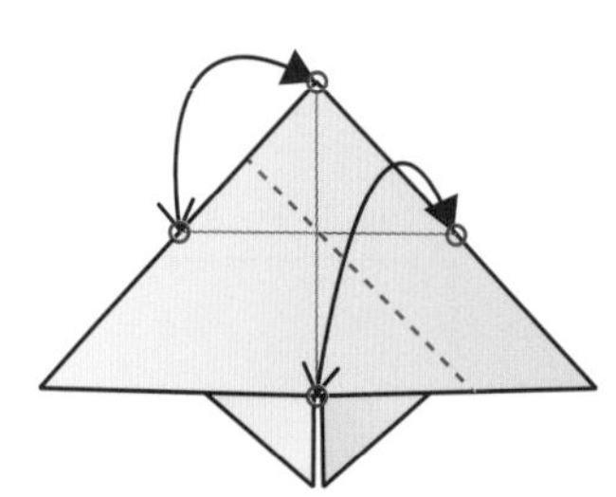

Fold the top corner down to the left edge (to the start of the crease made in the previous step) and then unfold. (Note: This diagonal fold will go through the center of the creases.)

9

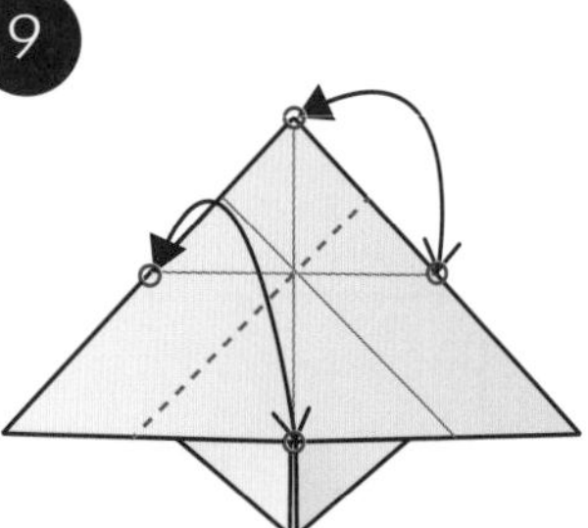

Repeat step #8 in the other direction and then unfold.

10

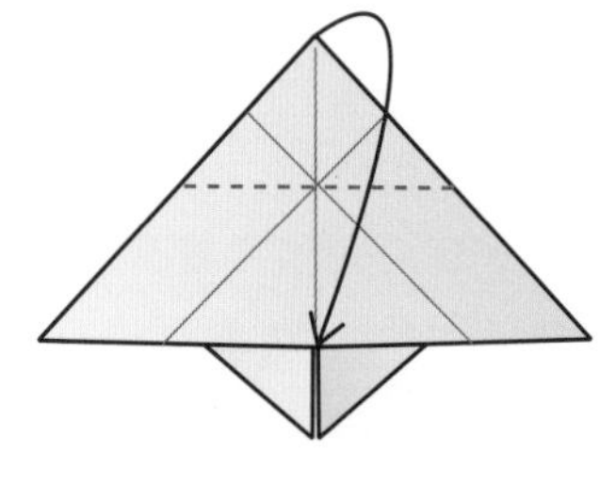

Fold the top corner down on the existing pre-crease.

11

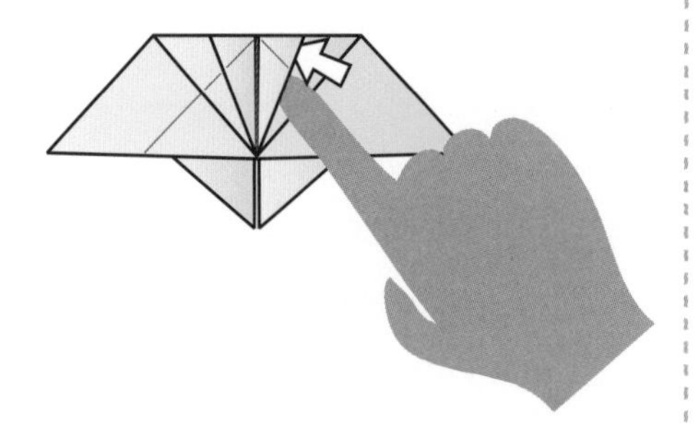

Find the pocket to the right of the center triangle. (Note: This is to help with the steps #12 and 13.)

12

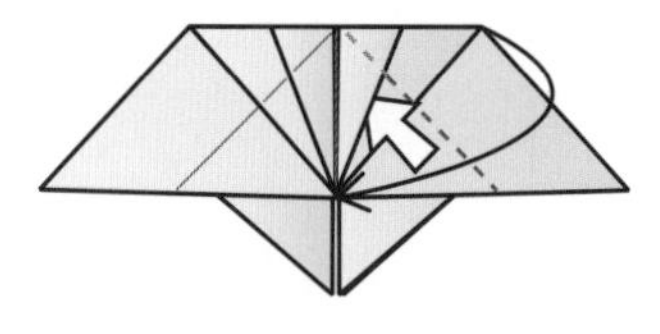

Using the pre-crease made in step #8, fold the flap down on the inside of the pocket.

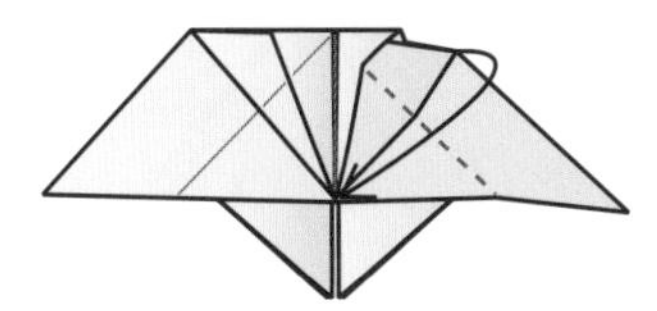

Fold in progress. (Note: Make sure to go all the way to the inside corner of the pocket to make this fold.)

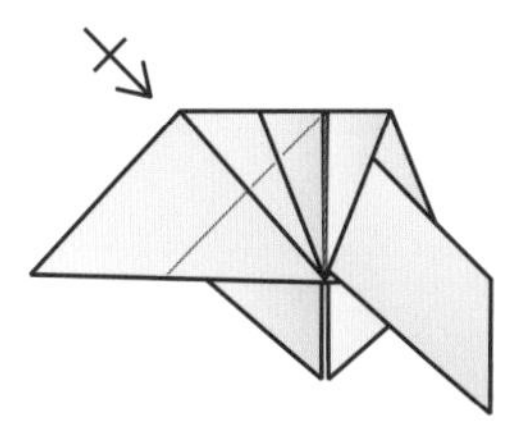

Repeat steps #11–13 on the opposite side.

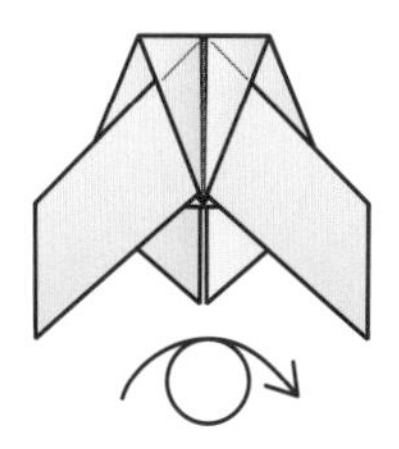

Turn the paper over.

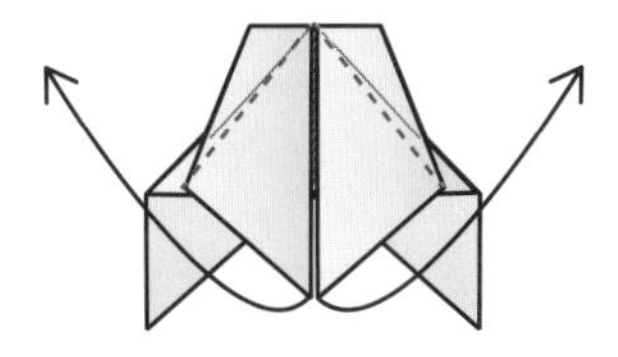

Fold the bottom center flaps up to the top and out to the sides as far as the paper will allow. (See the next step for reference.)

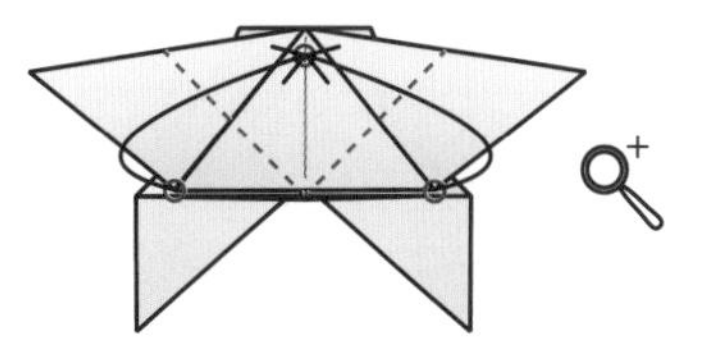

Fold the circled points into the center crease. The corners won't quite reach the top on this fold. (Note: The next step is a magnified view.)

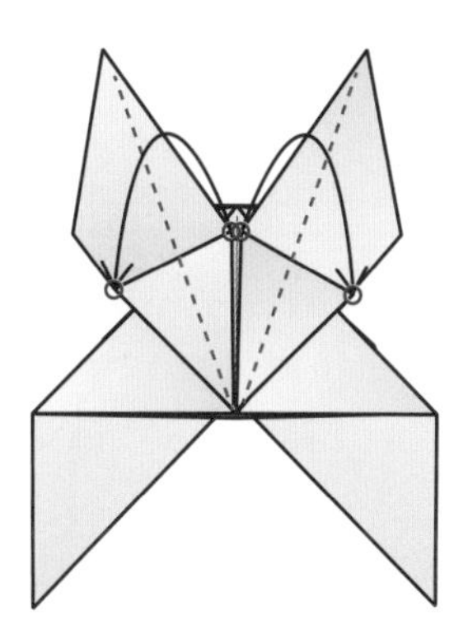

Narrow the flaps by folding in half. Use the circled points for reference.

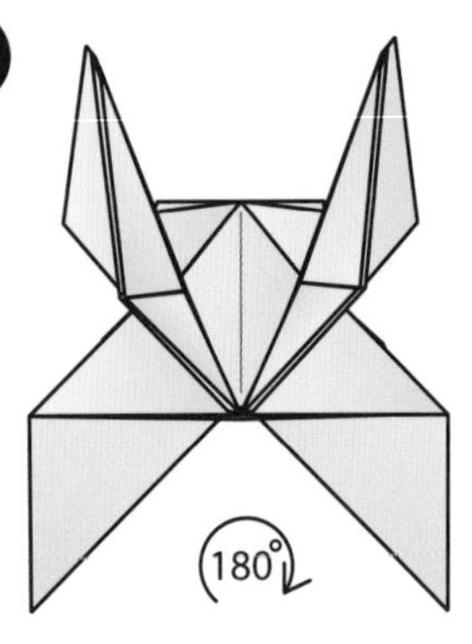

Rotate the paper 180°.

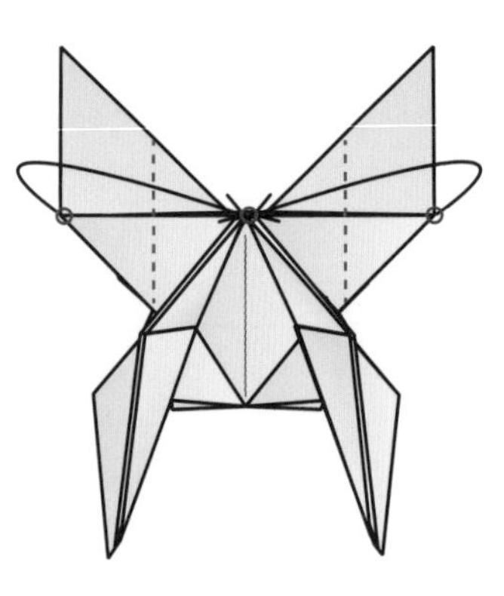

Fold the sides of the new top section into the center.

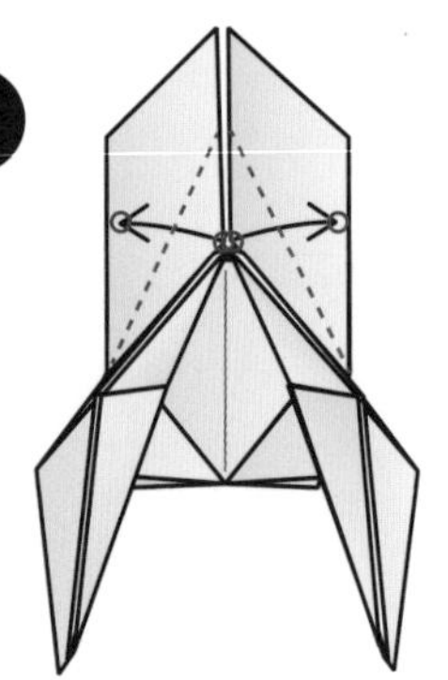

Fold the center corners toward the sides, making sure they don't quite reach the edges. (Note: This will create a pocket for the lower half of the backpack strap, locking the top and bottom straps together.)

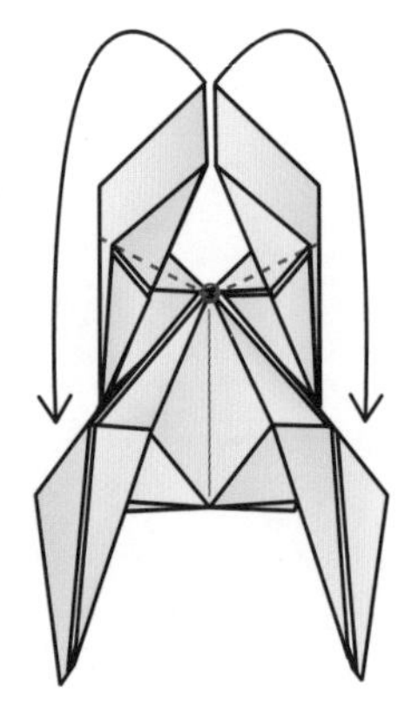

Valley fold the top flaps to the front, lining up the side edges so they are as perpendicular as possible. (See the next step for reference.)

23

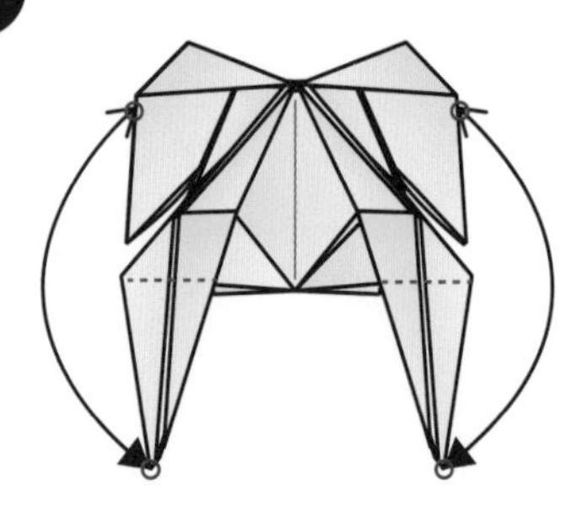

Fold the bottom flaps up to line up with the outside edges of the top flaps and then unfold. The side edges should align and be as parallel as possible to the center vertical line. (See the next step for reference.)

24

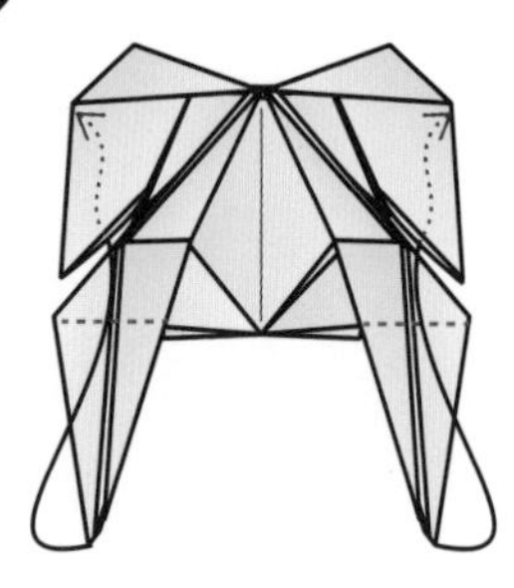

Using the existing pre-crease, insert the bottom flaps into the openings at the bottom of the top flaps.

25

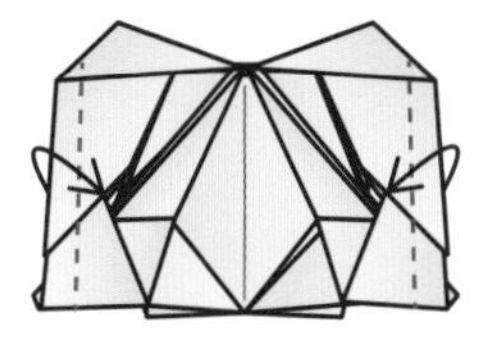

Fold the side edges
in to narrow the straps.

26

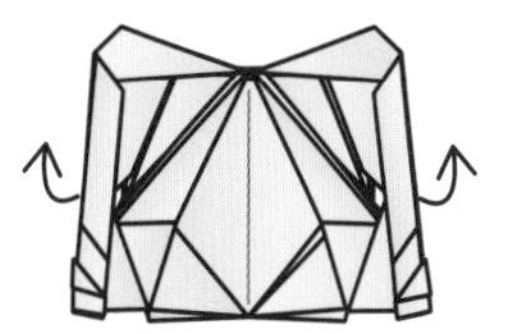

Holding the straps together in the center so they don't slip, gently pull and round the straps to shape the backpack. (Note: You can narrow the straps further to make a stronger paper lock.)

27

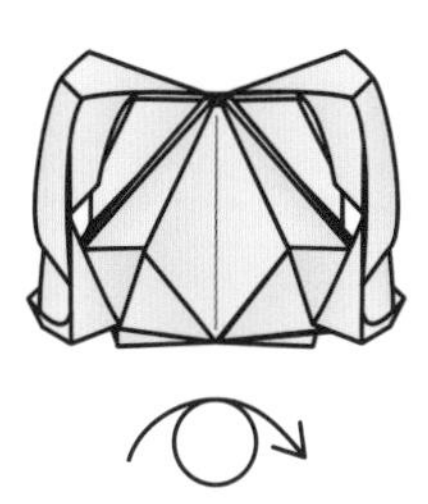

Turn the paper over.

Enjoy your finished backpack!

Sunglasses

Sunglasses are functional and can add unique flair to any outfit, whether it's a summery sundress or jeans and a T-shirt. Try folding these lenses into different shapes on the bottom. Don't forget to use different colors and patterns to coordinate your shades with a variety of outfits.

HOW TO USE

- Try folding these sunglasses out of clear or colored acetate to make your sunglasses functional rather simply decorative.
- Toss a pair of colorful shades in your life-size tote bag—along with your flip-flops!—for a day at the beach.

Pg. 144

HOW TO FOLD

1

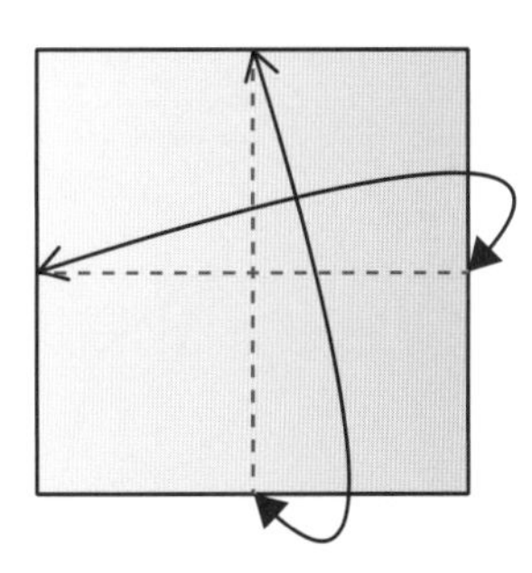

Fold the paper in half in both directions and then unfold. (Note: The side facing up will become the frame of the sunglasses; the side facing down will become the lenses.)

2

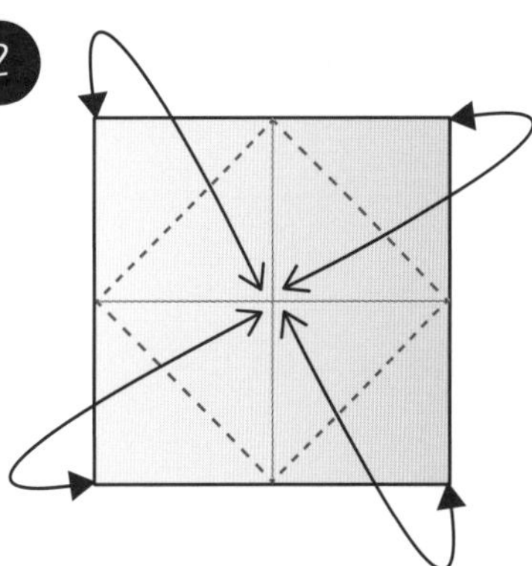

Fold all four corners into the center and then unfold.

3

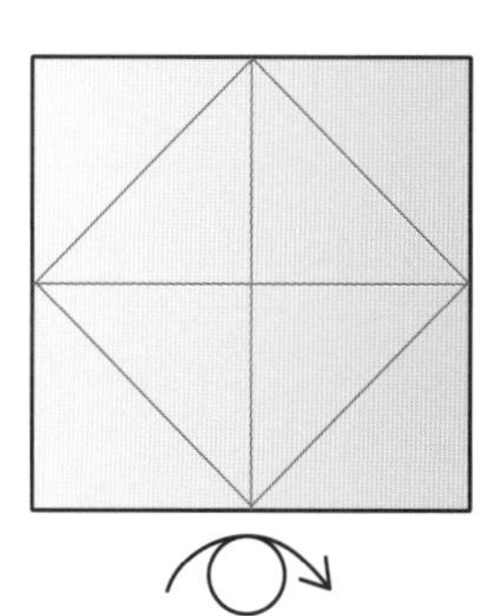

Turn the paper over.

4

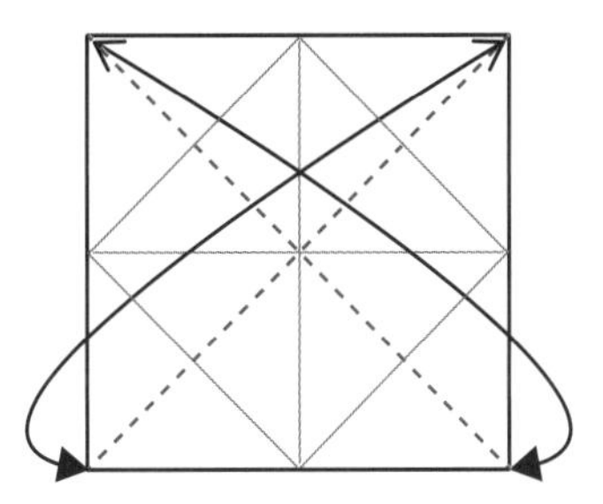

Fold the paper in half diagonally in both directions and then unfold.

5

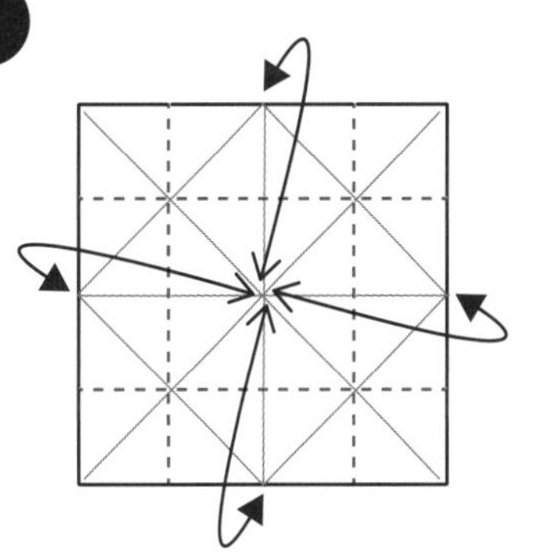

One at a time, fold all four side edges into the center crease and then unfold.

6

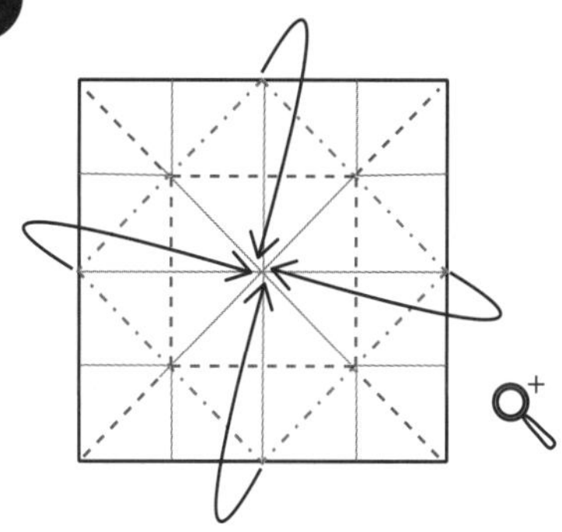

Fold each side of the square into the center at the same time while pinching the corners. (Note: The next step is a magnified view.)

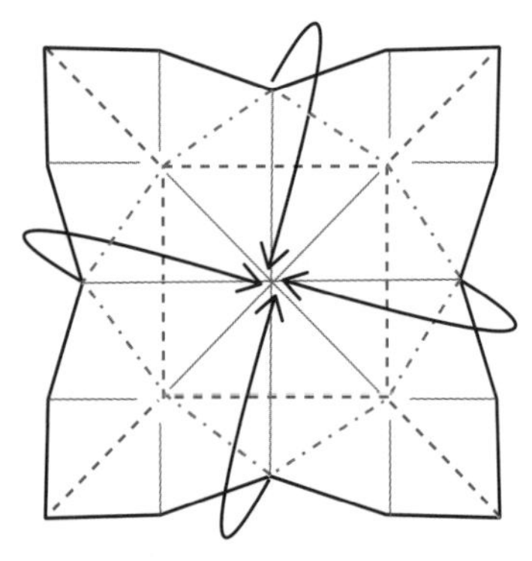

(Collapse in progress.) The existing pre-creases will help everything come together in the center.

8

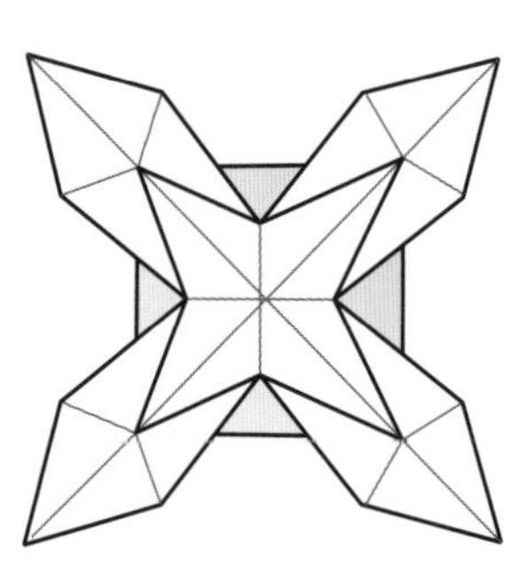

Collapse almost finished.

9

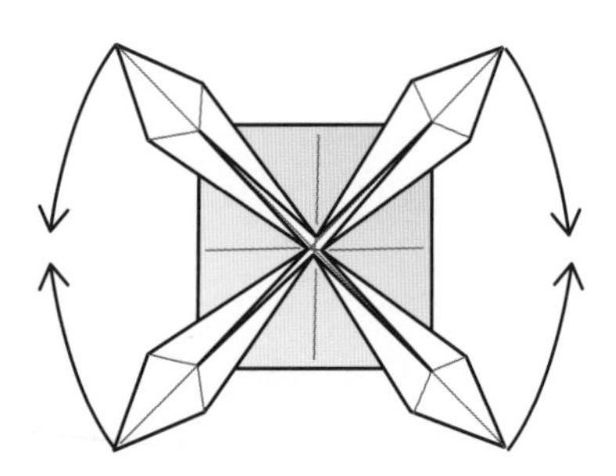

Fold the flaps down and in to make two trapezoid boat shapes. (See the next step for reference.)

10

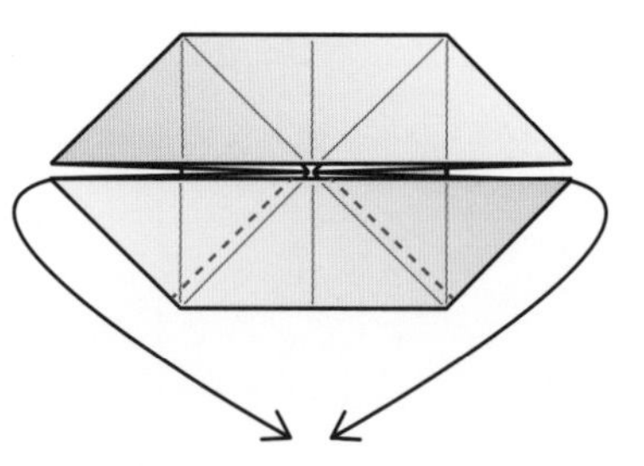

Fold the bottom corner flaps down so they don't quite meet in the center. The gap between the two sides will become the bridge of the glasses. (See the next step for reference.)

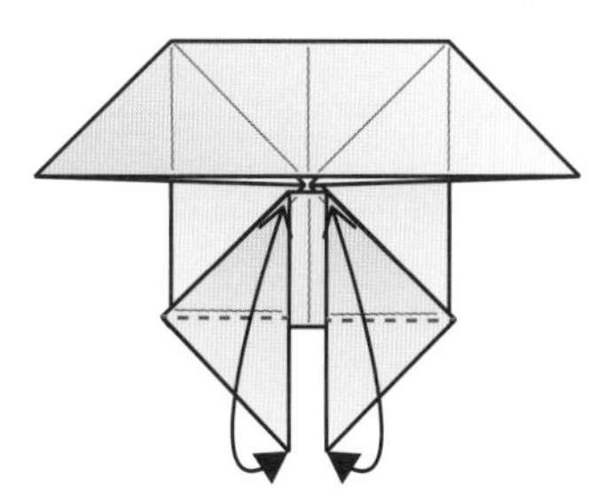

Fold the corners up and then unfold. (Note: This is a new crease.)

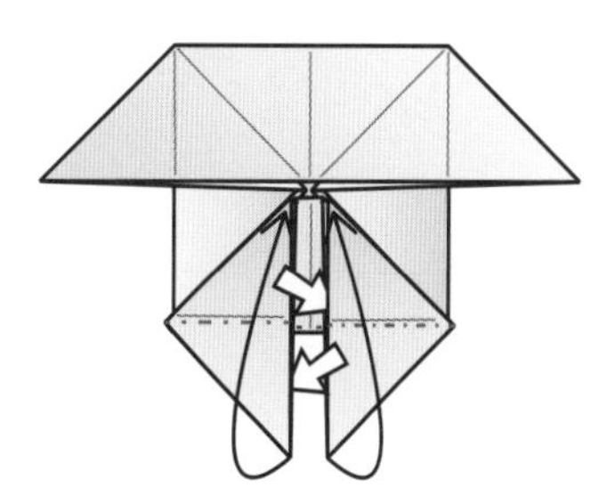

Open and squash the pockets on the creases made in the previous step to make flat squares.

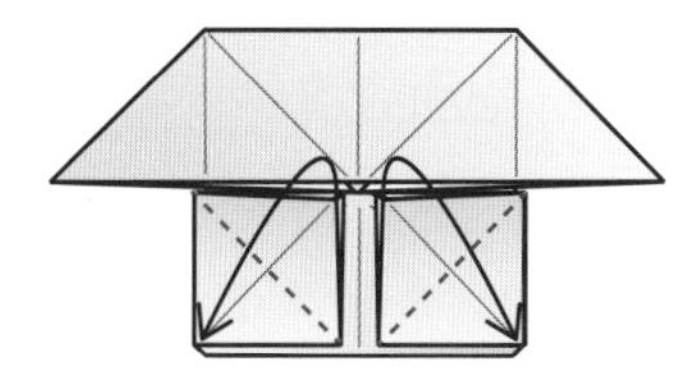

Fold the upper corners down to reveal the contrasting side of the paper. This will become the lenses of the sunglasses.

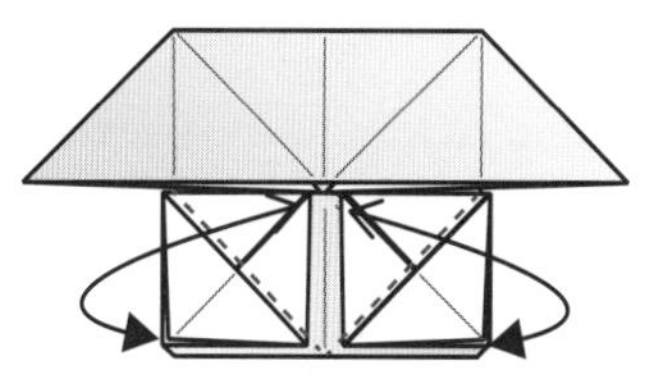

Fold the bottom corners up and then unfold. There will still be a small gap in the center.

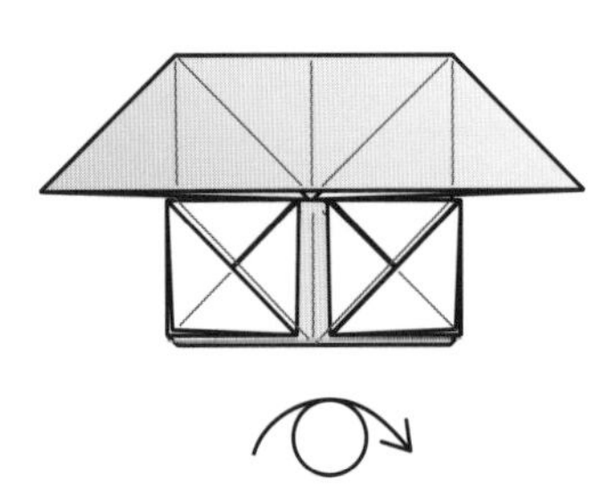

Turn the paper over.

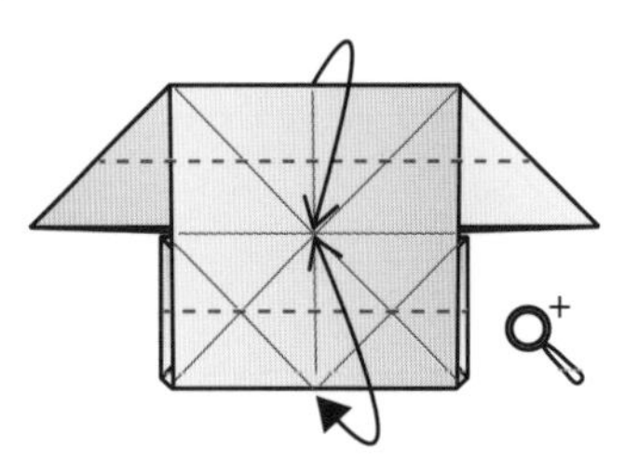

Fold the top and bottom edges into the center crease. Unfold only the bottom edge. (Note: The next step is a magnified view.)

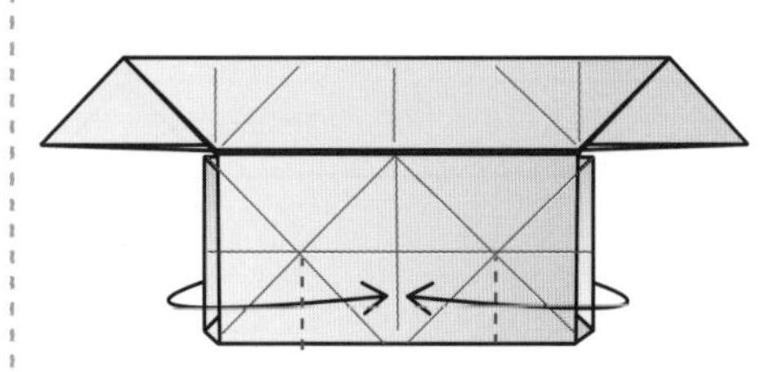

Fold the sides of the bottom section into the center and then unfold. (Note: This crease will be just a partial pinch and won't go all the way to the top.)

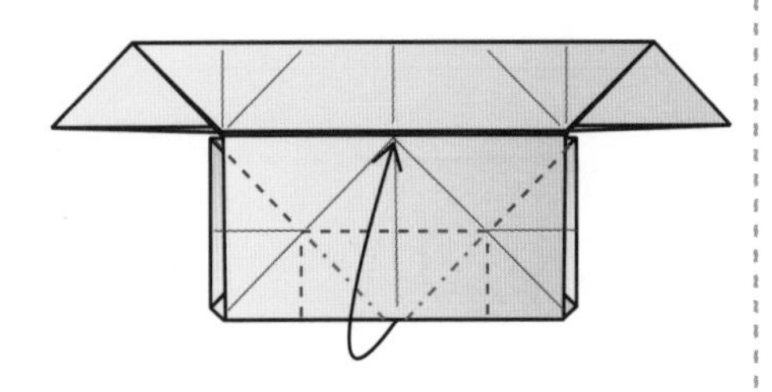

Bring the front layer of the bottom section up to the center and collapse using the pre-creases. These will help the bottom section lay flat. (See the next step for reference.)

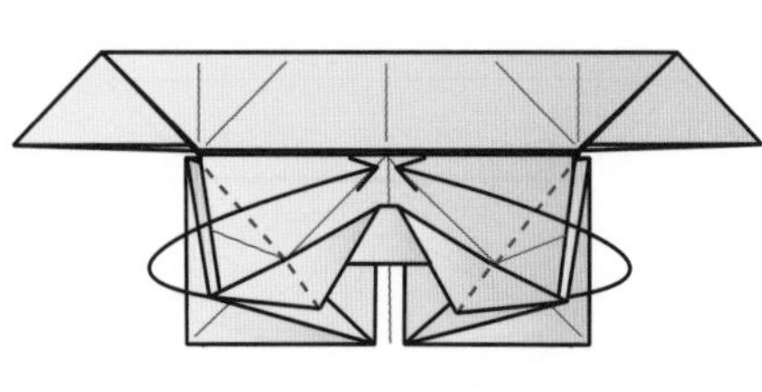

(Collapse in progress.) Push the blunted triangle section up along with the side corners and flatten. (See the next step for reference.)

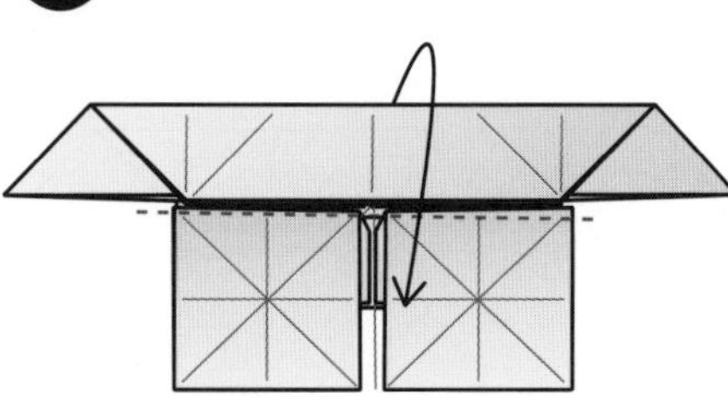

Fold down the top section.

21

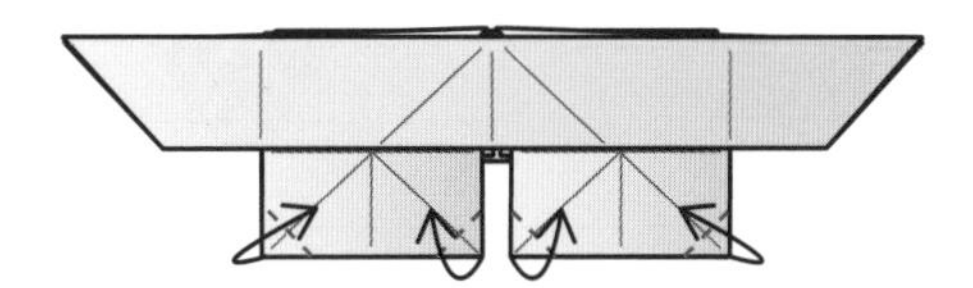

Shape the lenses by folding in small corners on the bottom sections of each side. (Note: You can try different angles and shapes to give your sunglasses a different look.)

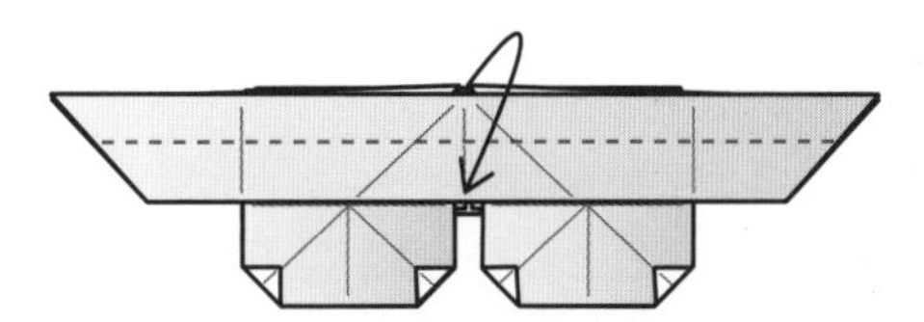

Fold the top section down and in half again. (Note: There are several layers of paper at the top. Fold all the layers together and press down to make a hard crease.)

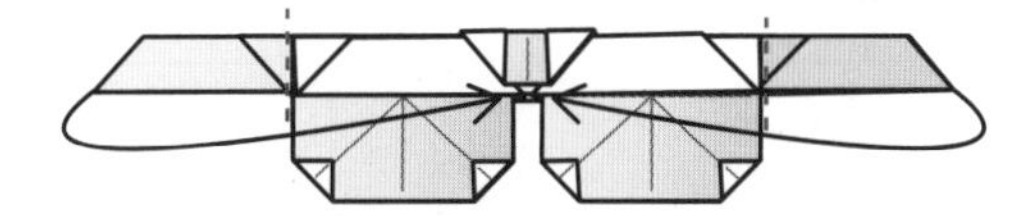

Fold the sides in to make the arms of the glasses. (Note: You can also put a soft crease in the bridge of the glasses or a bend to shape the glasses and help the layers stay together.)

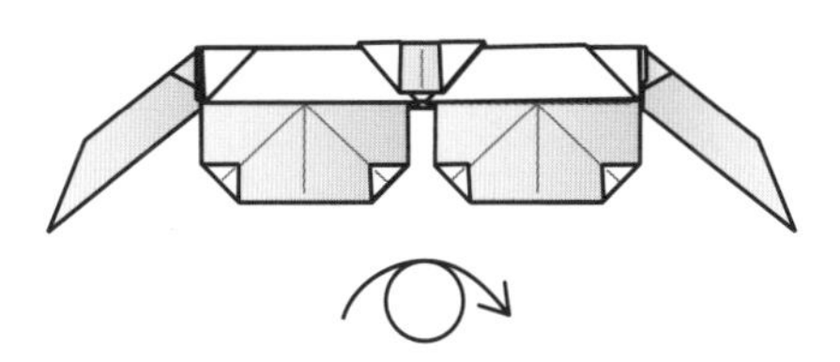

Turn the paper over.

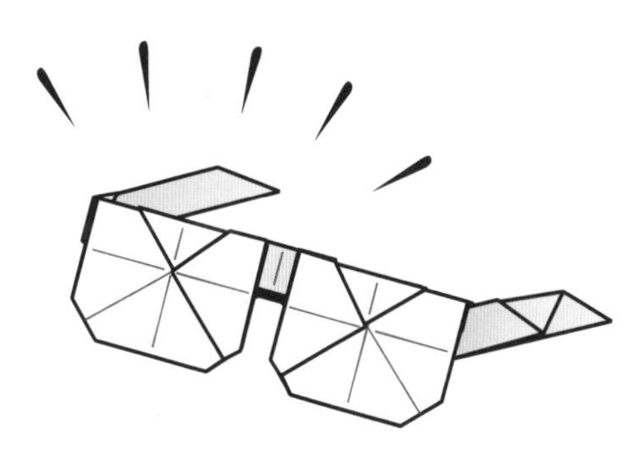

Enjoy your finished sunglasses!

Clutch

This easy-to-fold paper **clutch** was designed out of necessity. It's the perfect little pouch to hold all of your essentials for a night out—everything from a phone to lipstick to money. Fold it in a sophisticated pattern and pair your clutch with a ball gown, prom dress, or LBD.

HOW TO USE

- Fold this paper clutch in a variety of papers to coordinate with any outfit.
- Try folding using a paper-lined fabric, such as bookbinding paper, or a thicker card stock to make your own functional clutch.

HOW TO FOLD

1

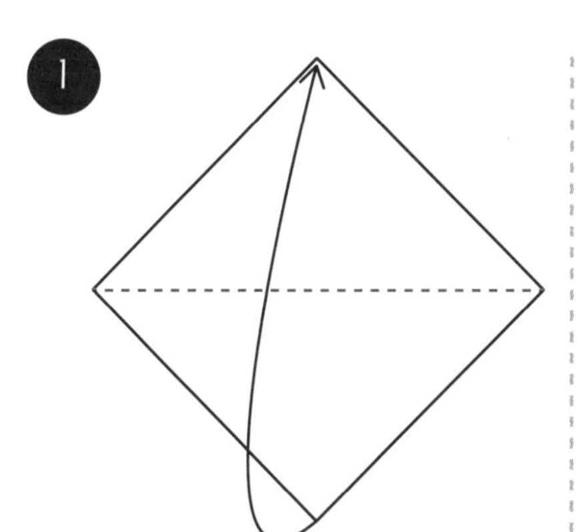

Fold the paper in half diagonally. (Note: The side facing down will become the outside of your clutch; the side facing up will be the lining.)

2

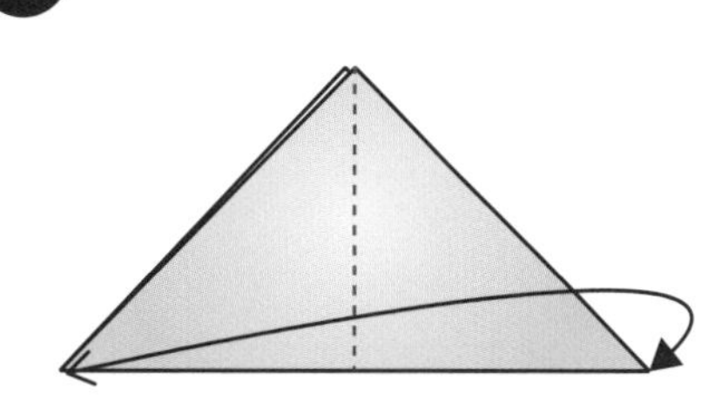

Fold the paper in half again and then unfold.

3

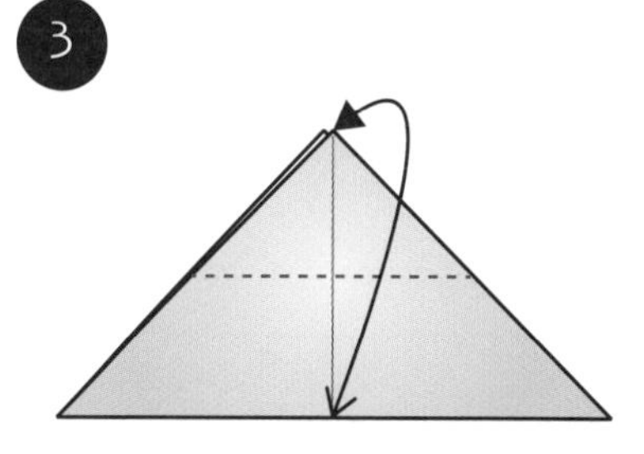

Using just the top layer of paper, fold the top corner down to the bottom edge and then unfold.

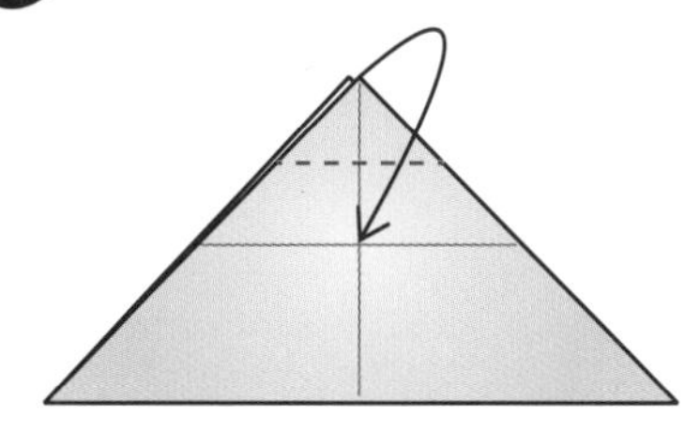

Still using just the top layer of paper, fold the top corner down to the crease made in the previous step.

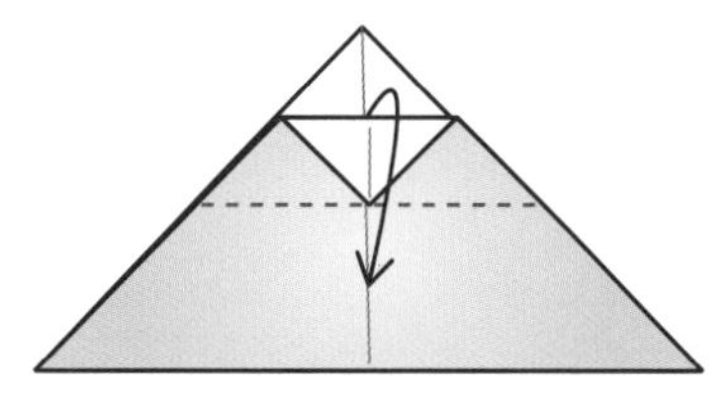

Fold the top layer down on the existing pre-crease.

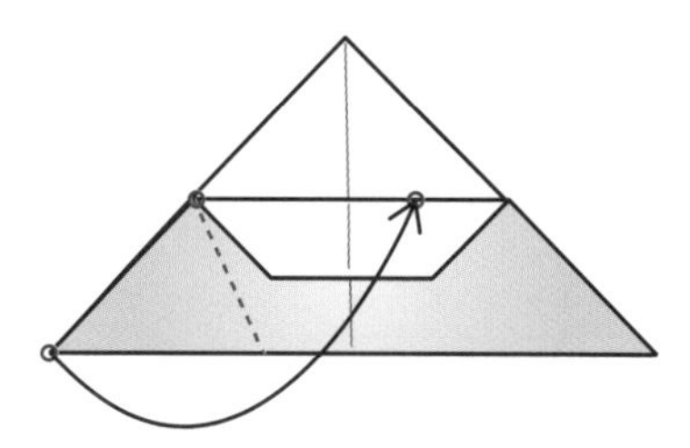

Fold the bottom left corner up and line it up along the folded edge. (Use the circled points for reference.)

7

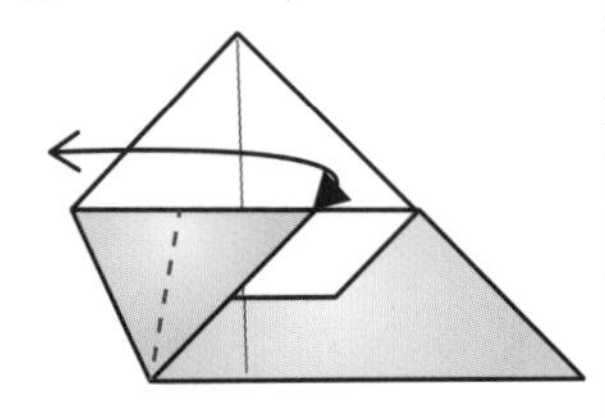

Using the bottom corner as a starting point, fold the top triangle in half and then unfold.

8

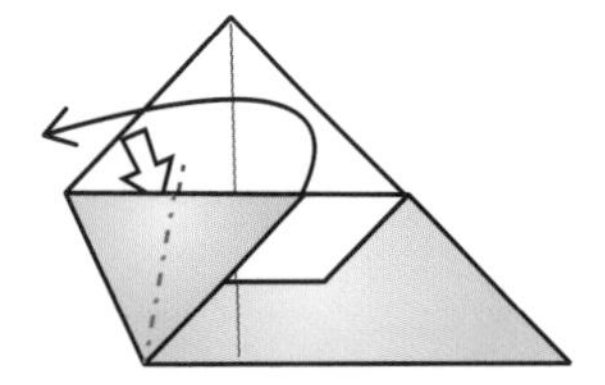

Open and squash fold the pocket on the existing pre-creases.

9

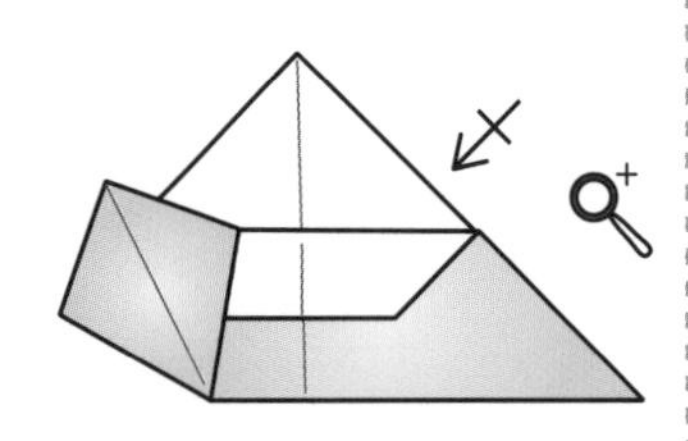

Repeat steps #6–8 on the opposite side. (Note: The next step is a magnified view.)

10

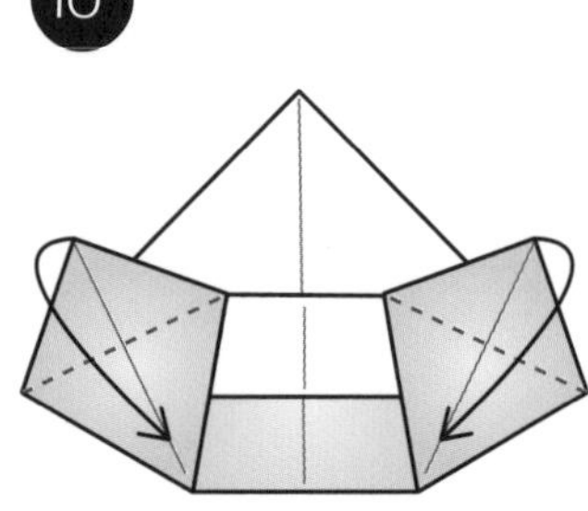

Fold the top triangle flaps down on each side.

11

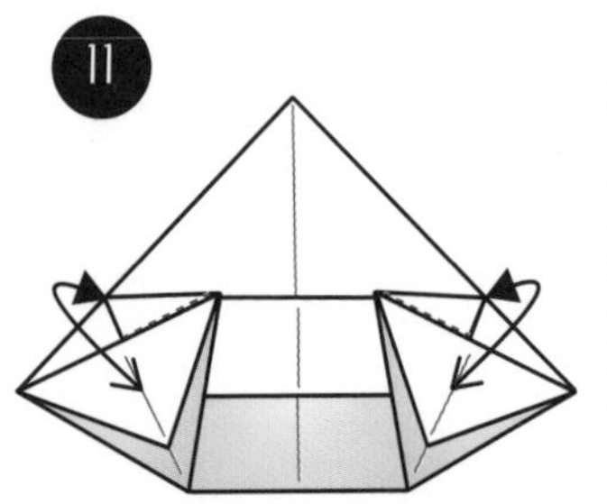

Fold the small triangle flaps still sticking out on top down and then unfold.

12

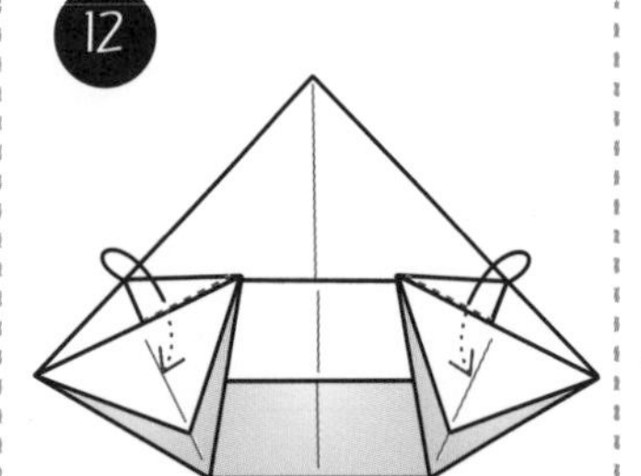

Tuck the small triangle flaps in. (Note: This is not an inside reverse. Just fold the flaps under the top layer to hold them in place.)

13

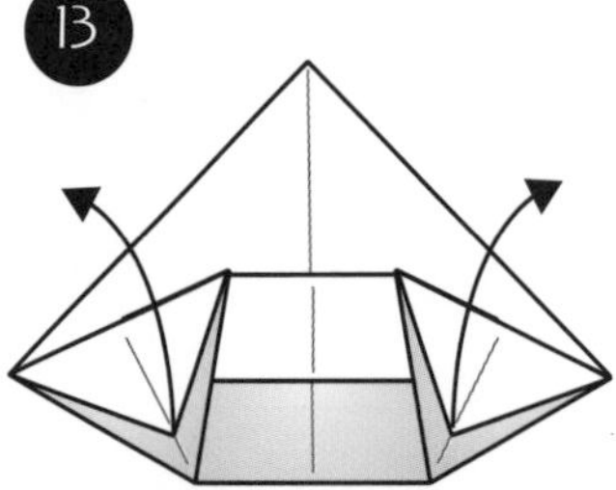

Unfold the front triangles back up to the top.

14

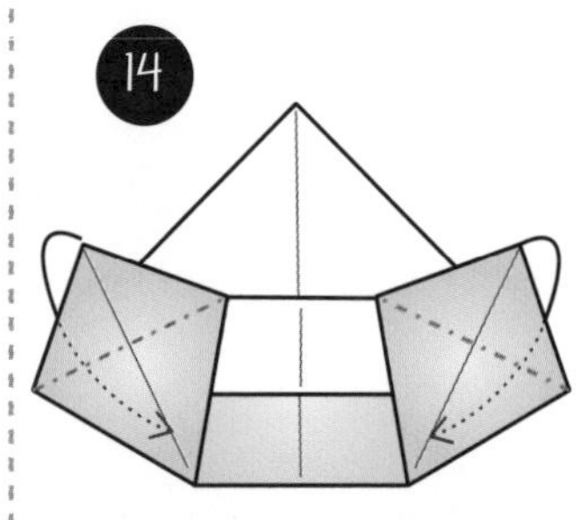

Mountain fold and tuck the flaps in on the existing pre-creases. (Note: This fold will cover up the paper lock made in step #12.) Don't tuck the triangles in between layers, just fold them to the back.

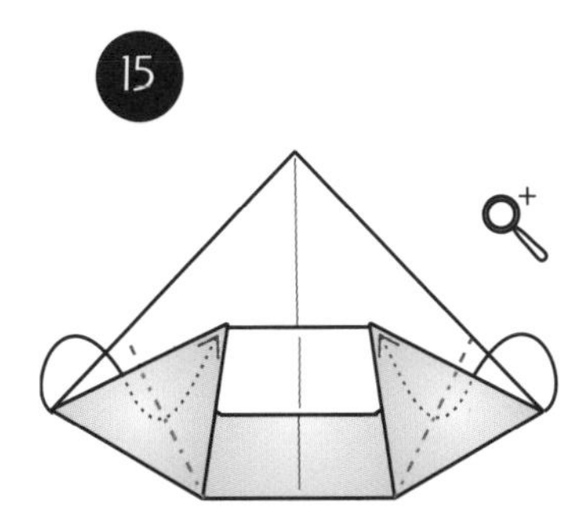

Inside reverse the outer corners on the existing pre-creases. (Note: The next step is a magnified view.)

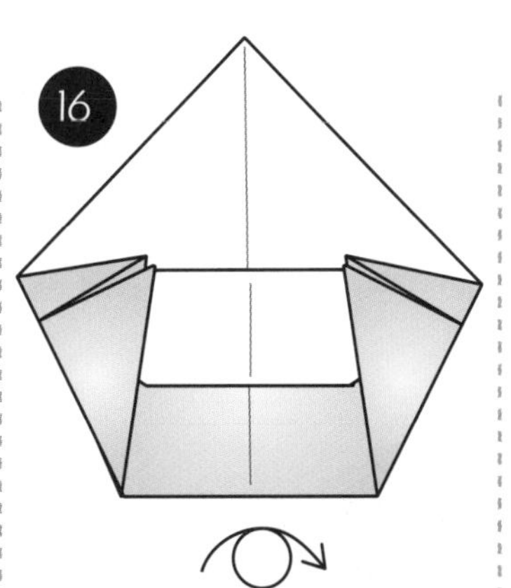

Turn the paper over.

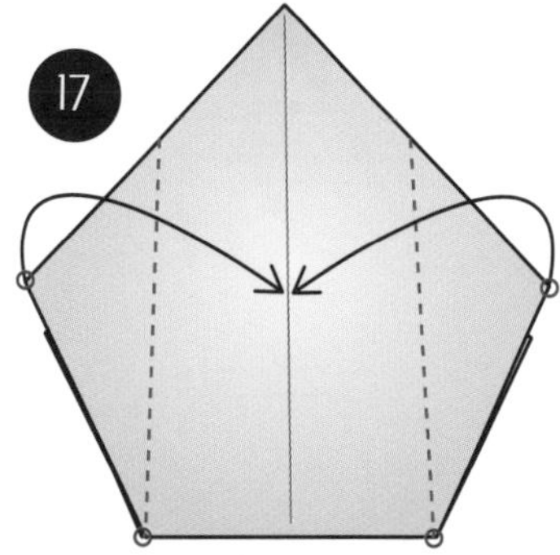

Fold the side corners into the center, using the circled points as a reference. Start your fold from the bottom corner and make the side corners touch and meet in the center.

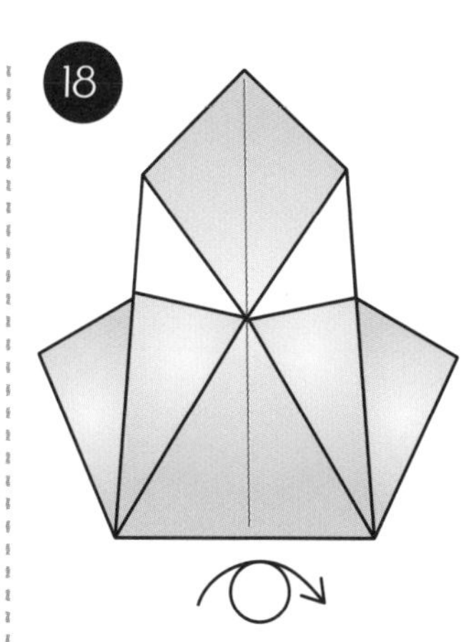

Turn the paper over.

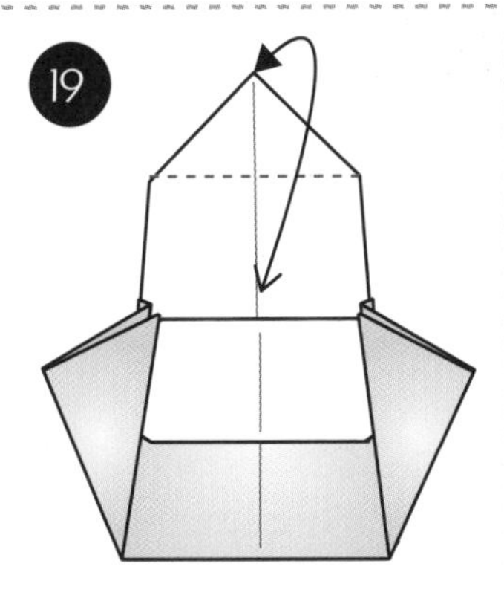

Fold the top triangle down and then unfold.

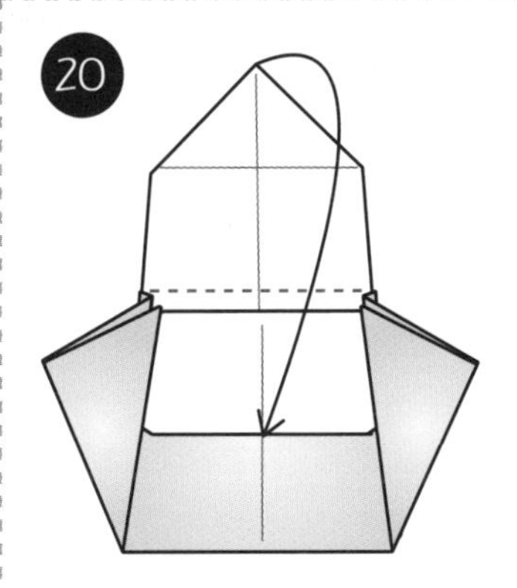

Fold the entire top flap down and over the front of the clutch.

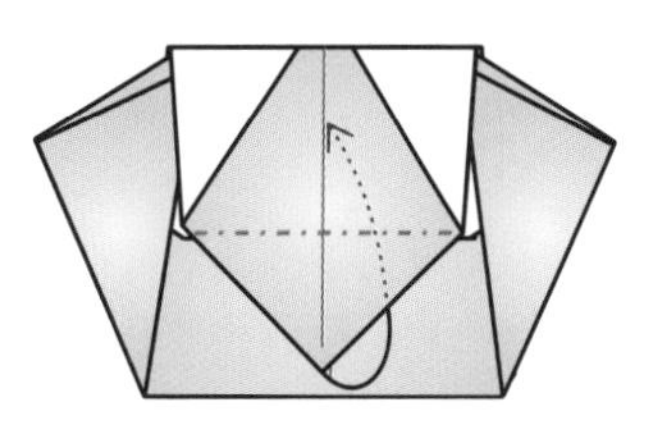

Mountain fold and tuck the small triangle under on the existing pre-crease to lock it in place. (You can also valley fold this triangle up and over the back to create a completely contrasting top pocket.)

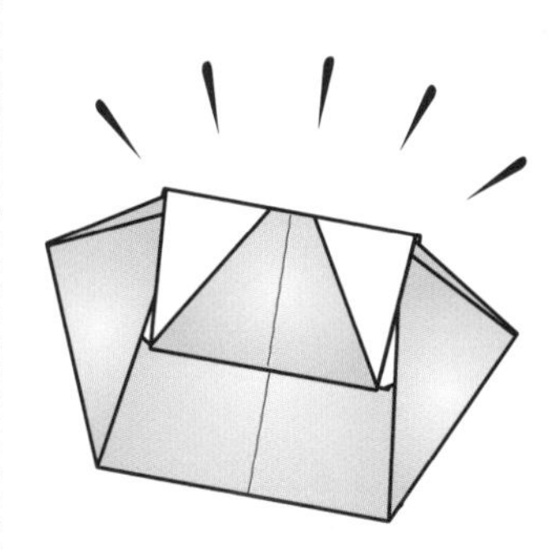

Enjoy your finished clutch!

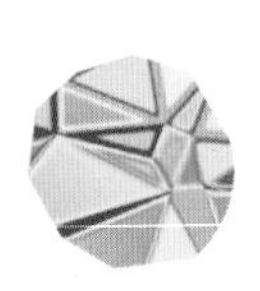

Brooch

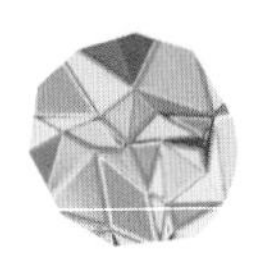

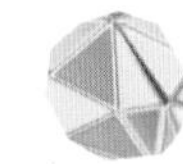

Brooches and pins are decorative accessories that can change an outfit dramatically, whether it's adding a hint of color or an unexpected element. You can find pin backs and fasteners at your local craft store or online and use these paper versions as part of your everyday outfits. You can also stick them on with double-sided tape or pre-adhesive glue dots or foam squares.

HOW TO USE

- Fold this brooch in various sizes and colors and add to jackets, scarves, and dresses.
- Make multiples and add brooches to a headband or a hairpin!

HOW TO FOLD

1

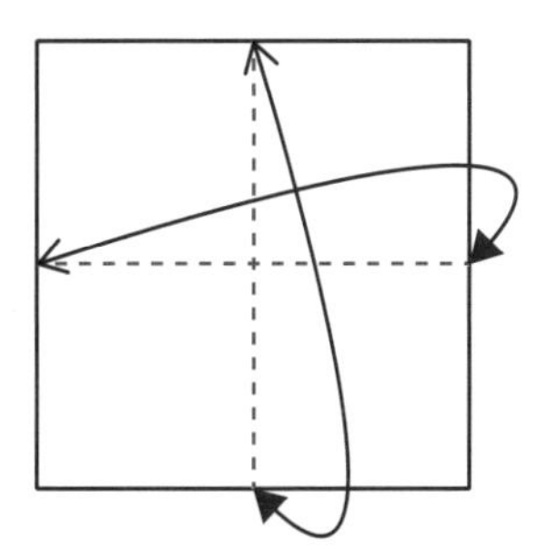

Fold the paper in half in both directions and then unfold. (Note: The side facing down will become the visible part of your brooch.)

2

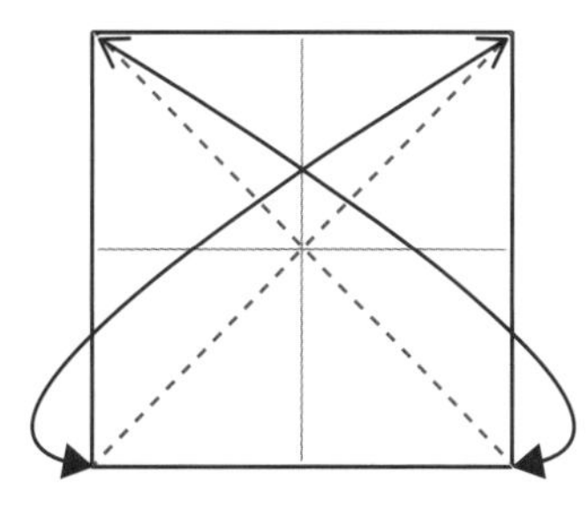

Fold the paper in half diagonally in both directions and then unfold.

3

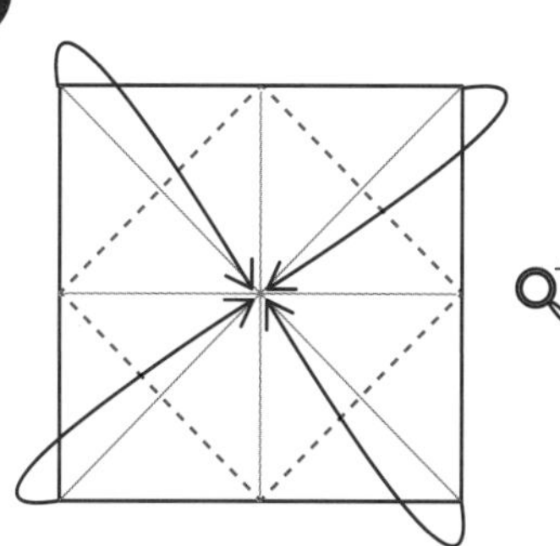

Fold all four corners into the center. (Note: The next step is a magnified view.)

4

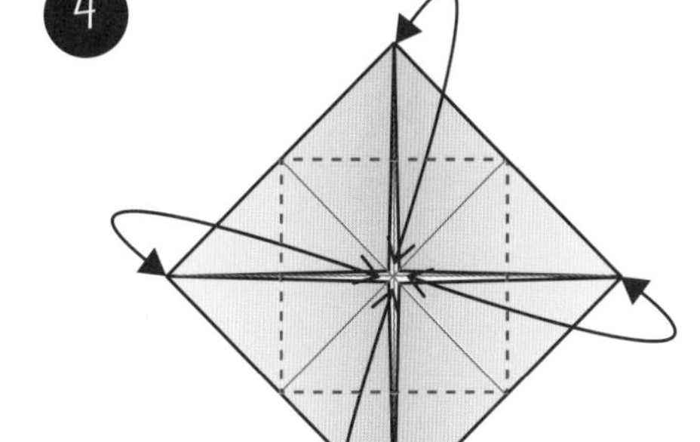

Fold all four corners into the center again and then unfold.

5

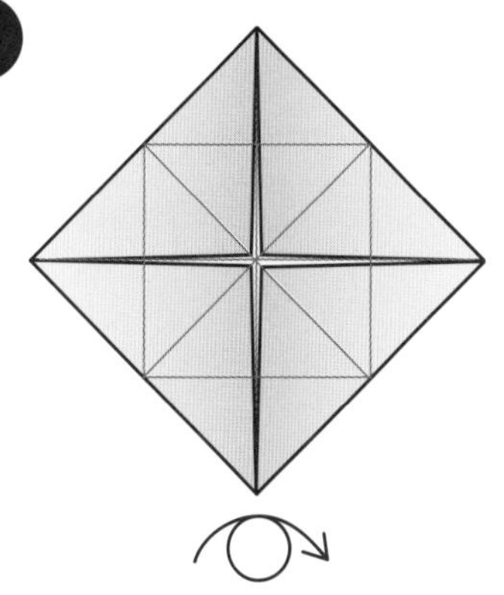

Turn the paper over.

6

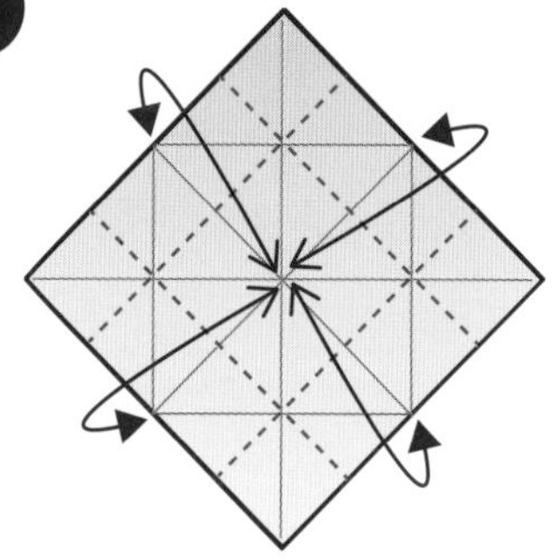

Fold the sides into the center crease, first horizontally, then vertically, and then unfold. (Note: Make sure to keep both the top and bottom layers in place.)

7

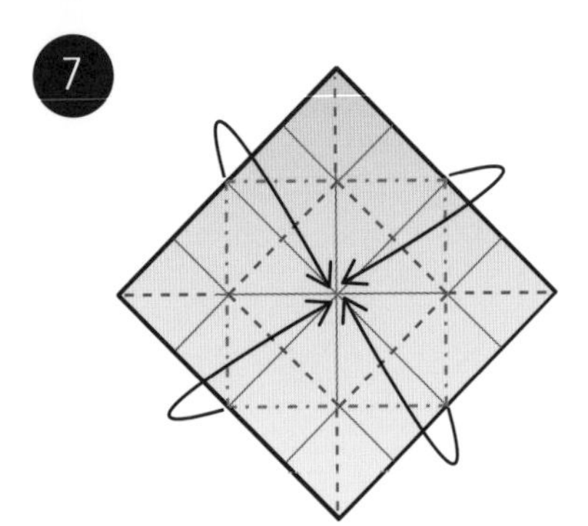

Fold all four sides of the square into the center while pinching the corners. (See the next steps for reference.)

8

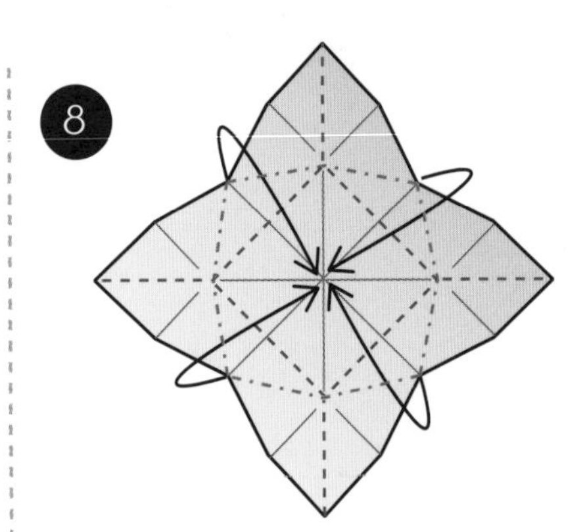

(Collapse in progress.) The pre-creases will help everything come together in the center. (See the next steps for reference.)

9

Fold the corners into the center using the existing pre-creases. (See the next step for reference.)

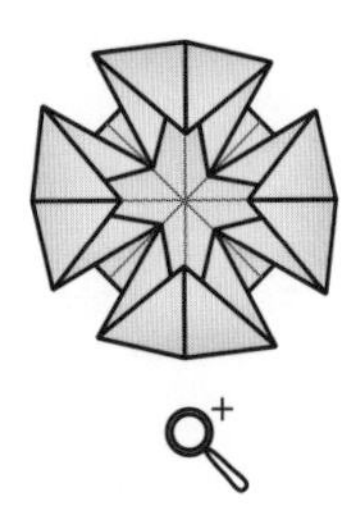

Flatten the model. This will create four squares on the top of the model. (Note: The next step is a magnified view.)

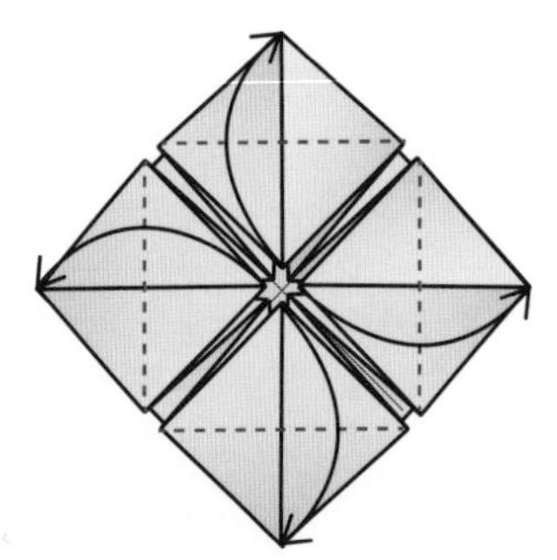

Valley fold the top corners to the back.

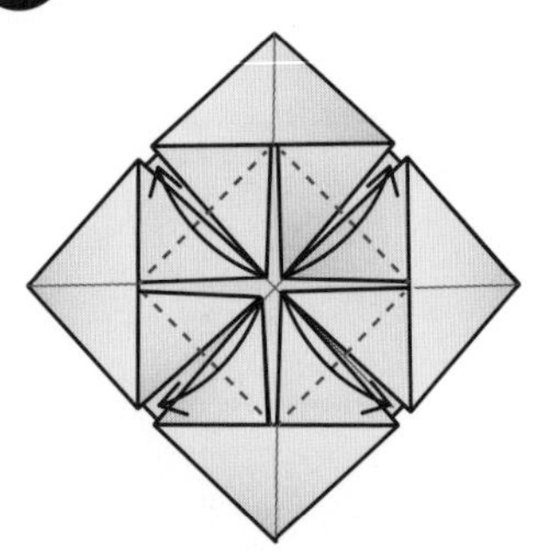

Valley fold the inner center corners out as well.

13

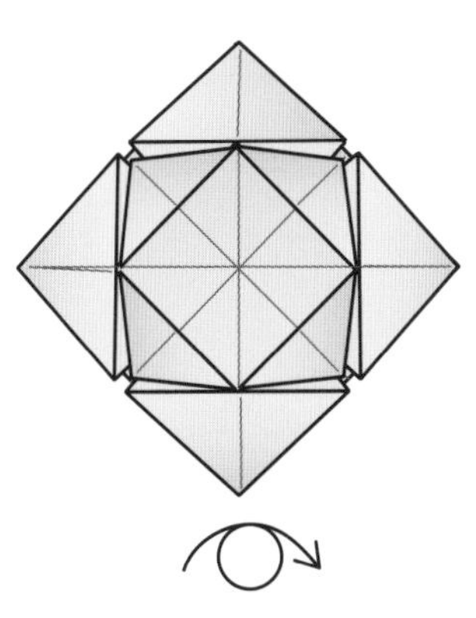

Turn the paper over.

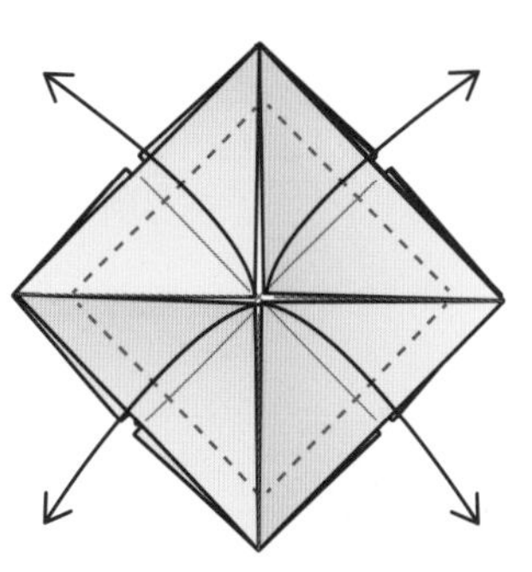

Fold the center corners out so they are slightly shorter than the full length. (See the next step for reference.)

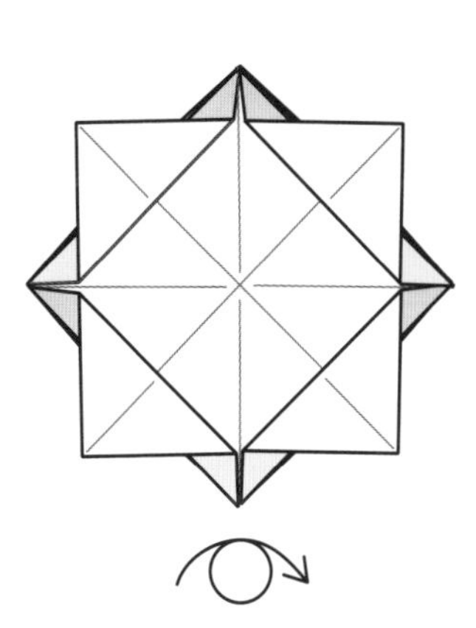

Turn the paper over.

Enjoy your finished brooch!

Flip-flops are easy to wear and carry, which makes them an essential accessory during the warm summer months. Just throw them in your bag and go! Try folding this paper version with large newspaper to make a life-sized pair of flip-flops.

STYLE TIPS

- Flip-flops are a must with a swimsuit at the beach in the summer.
- Pair your flip-flops with shorts and a T-shirt, or with a romper for an easy summer look.

HOW TO FOLD

1

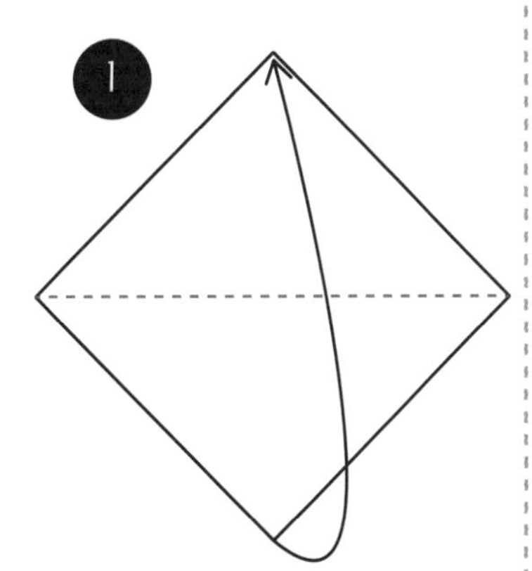

Fold paper in half diagonally. (Note: The side facing down will become the color/ pattern of your flip-flop.)

2

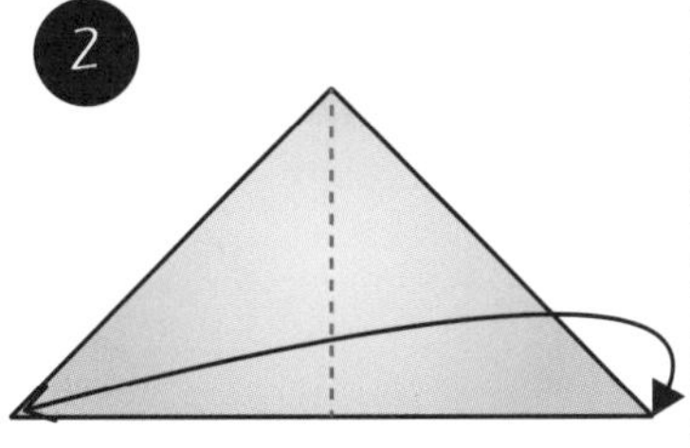

Fold the paper in half horizontally and then unfold.

3

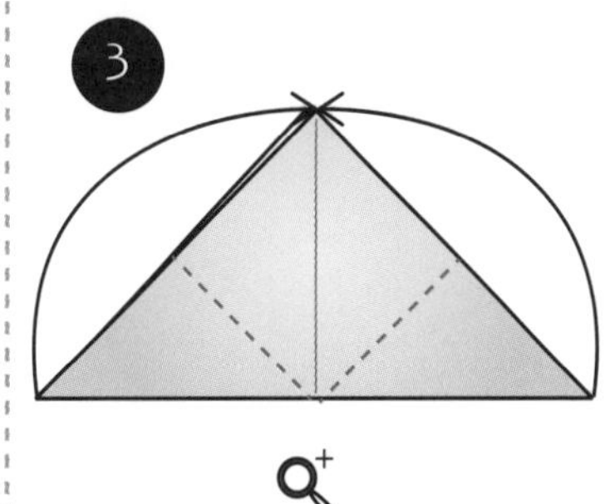

Fold the bottom corners up to the top. (Note: The next step is a magnified view.)

4

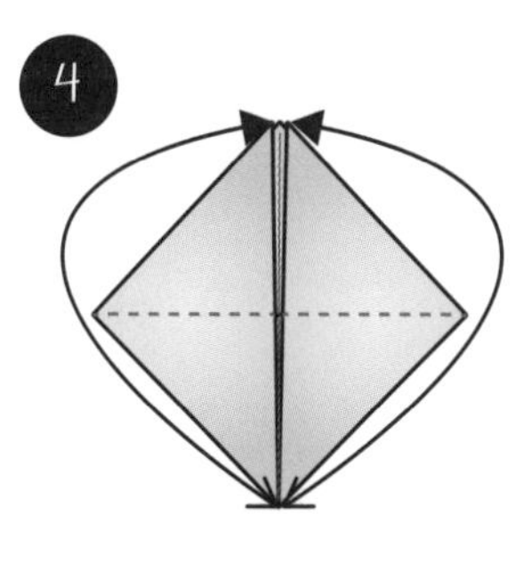

Fold the top corners down to the bottom and then unfold.

5

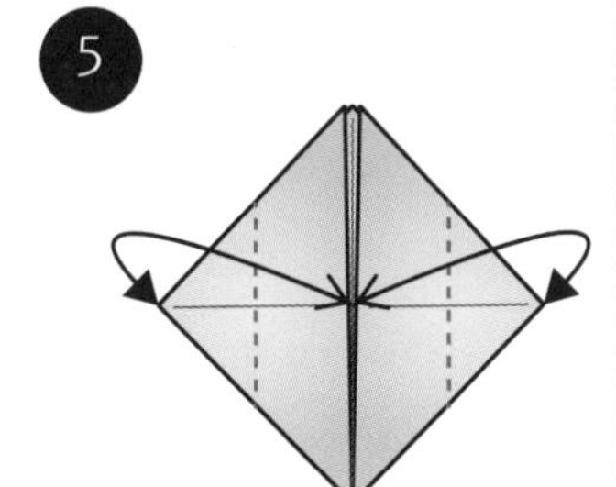

Fold the side corners into the center and then unfold.

6

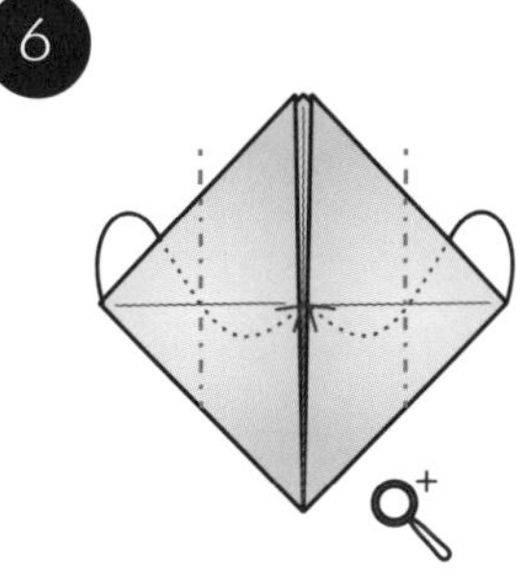

Inside reverse the corners on the crease created in the previous step. (Note: The next step is a magnified view.)

7

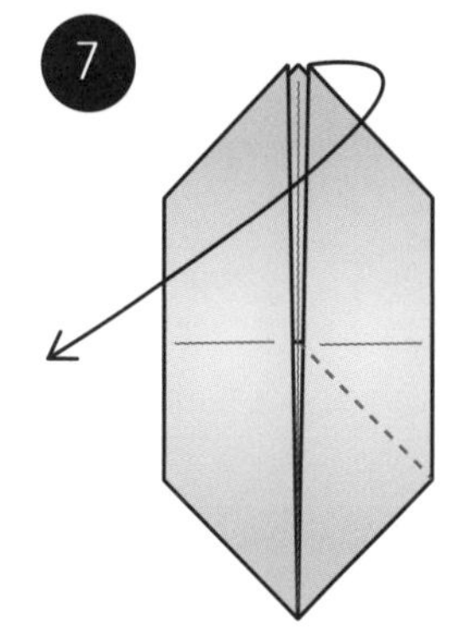

Fold the right corner flap down and across.

8

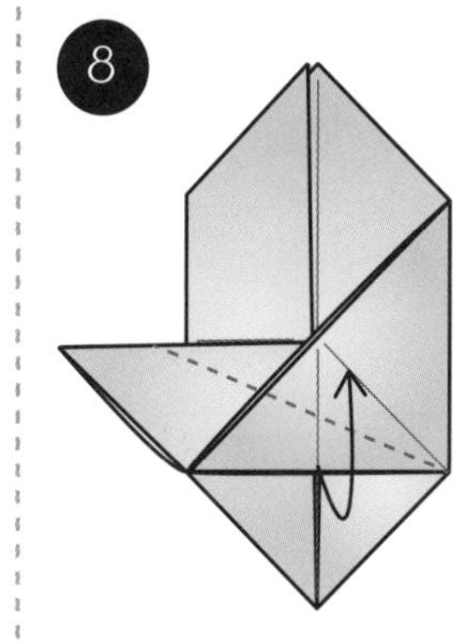

Fold the bottom edge of the flap up to the pre-existing diagonal crease. (See the next step for reference.)

9

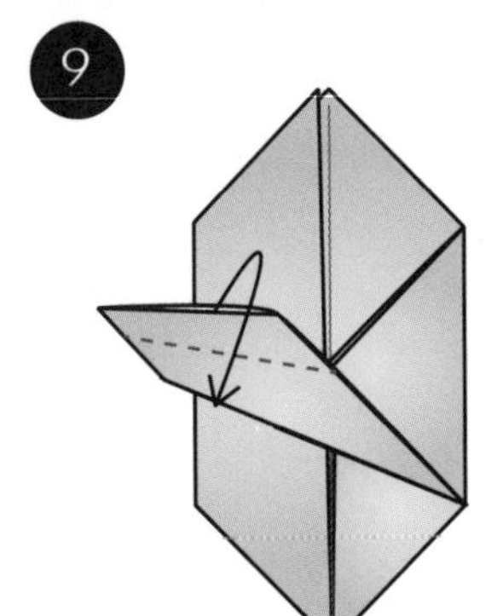

Fold the top edge of the flap down to line up with the folded diagonal edge. (See the next step for reference.)

10

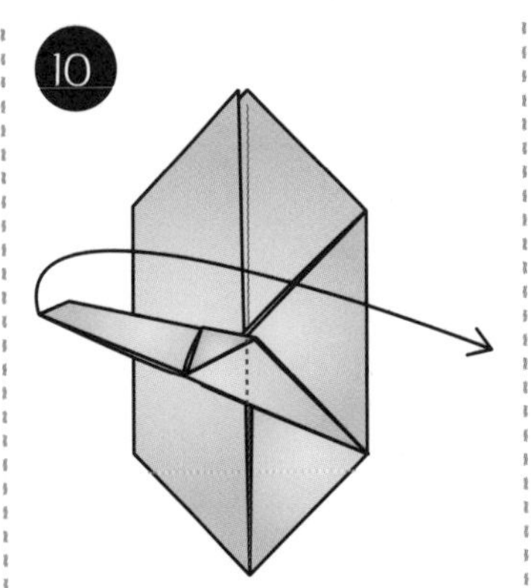

Fold the flap back out to the side along the center crease. (See the next step for reference.)

11

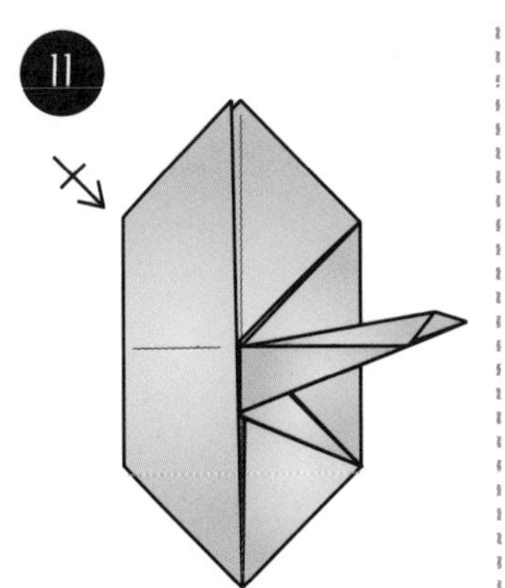

Repeat steps #7–10 on the opposite side.

12

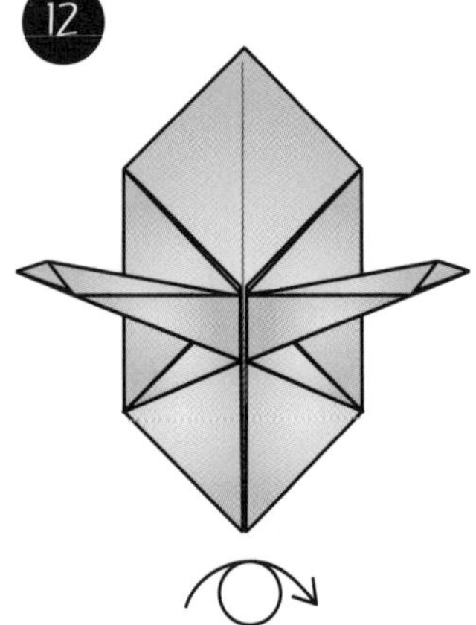

Turn the paper over.

13

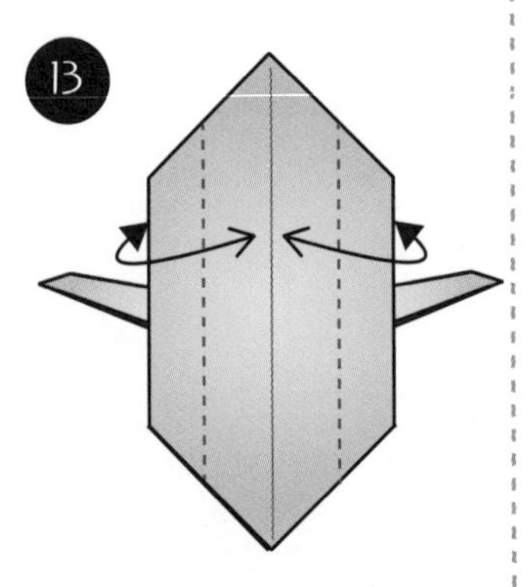

Fold the sides in so they don't quite meet in the center and then unfold. This will determine the width of the flip-flop.

14

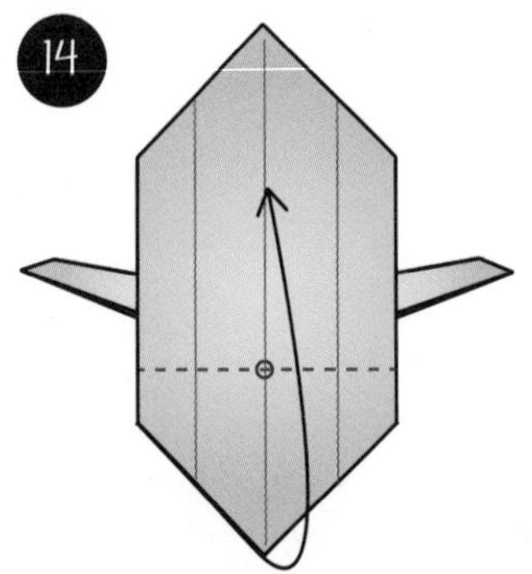

Fold the bottom edge up. Use the point where the side flaps meet in the center on the opposite side as a reference.

15

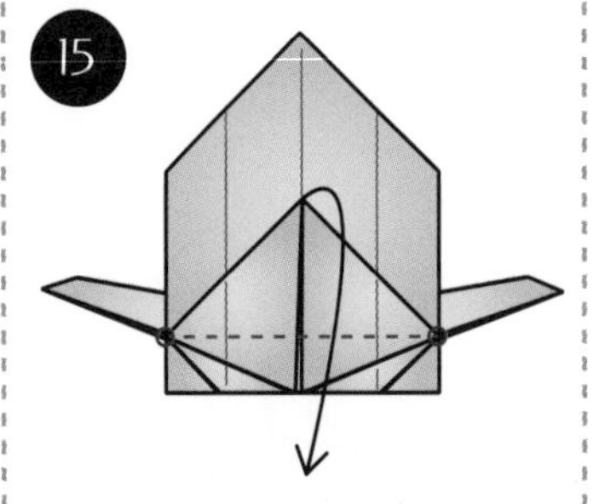

Fold the top corner back down at the indicated points.

16

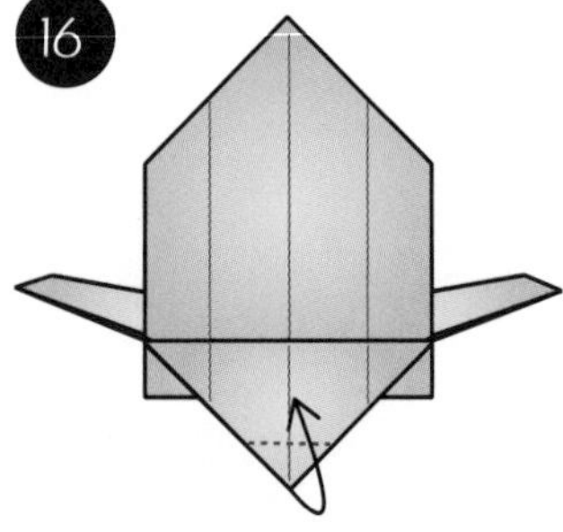

Fold the bottom corner up to blunt and shape the front of the flip-flop.

17

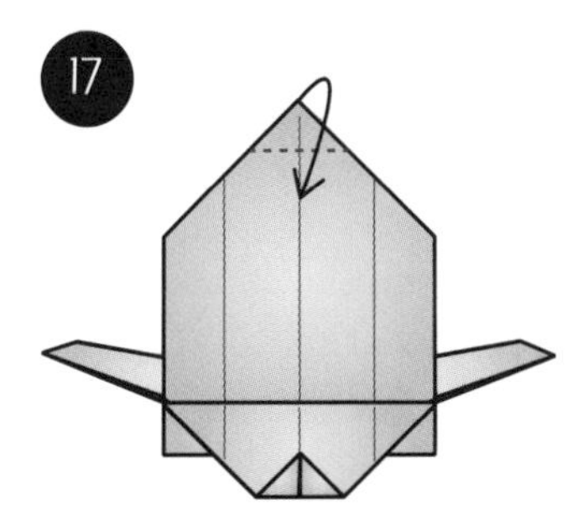

Fold the top corner down as well to blunt and shape the back of the flip-flops

18

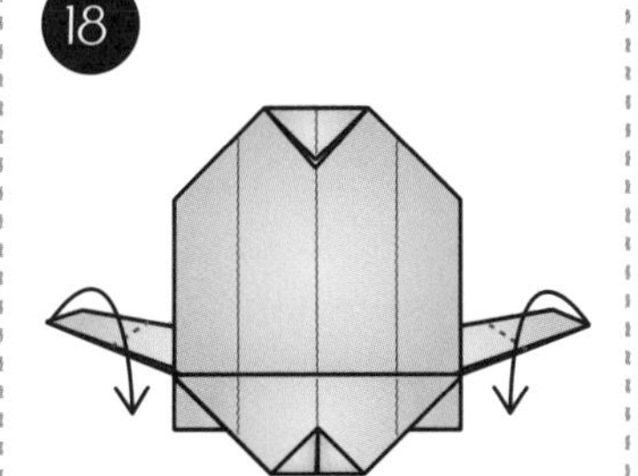

Fold the side flaps down at about the halfway point at an approximately 90° angle. (See the next step for reference.)

19

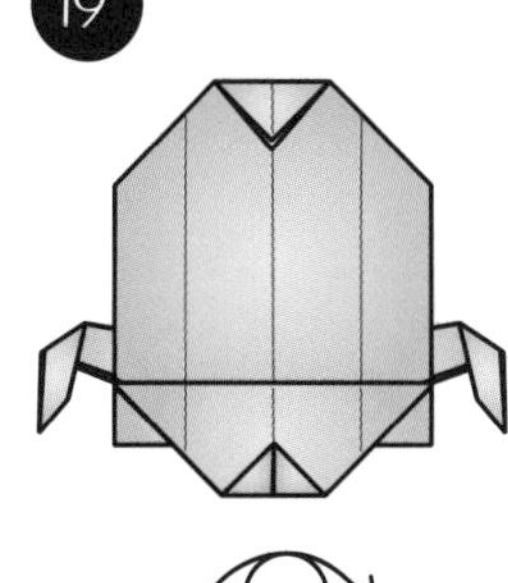

Turn the paper over.

20

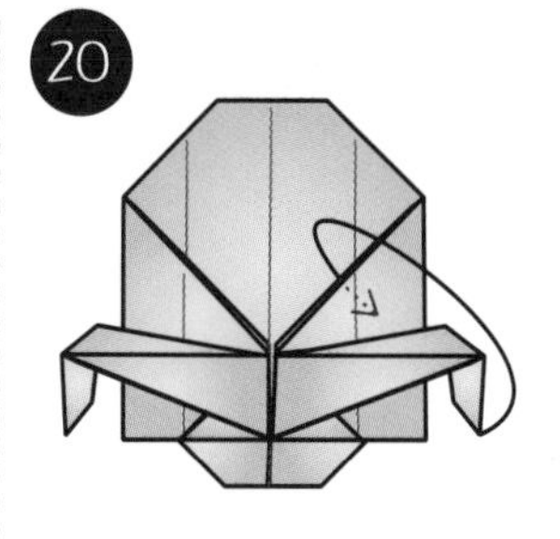

Lift one side flap and slide it underneath the diagonal edge. The tip you folded in step #18 will slide under but needs to line up with the vertical pre-crease from step #13. (Note: The model will become 3-D at this point as you create the straps.)

21

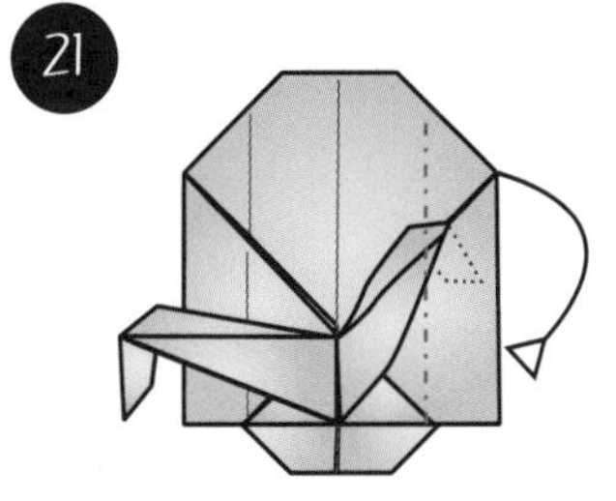

Mountain fold the side edge to the back, locking the tip of the flap in place and creating one of the flip-flop straps.

22

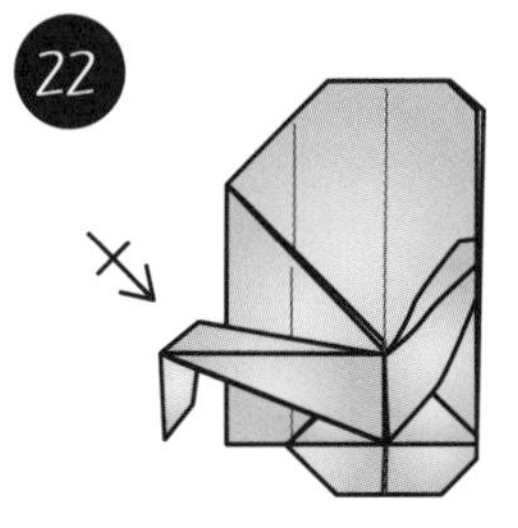

Repeat steps #20–21 on the opposite side. (Note: There are several layers to fold to the back. Push hard and flatten before you gently round and shape the straps.)

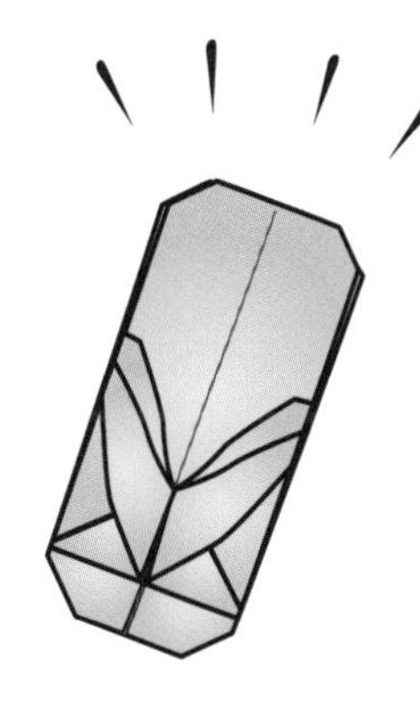

Enjoy your finished flip-flop!

*These instructions will make one finished flip-flop. Fold another to make a pair.

ABOUT THE AUTHOR

Sok Song's passion for folding paper bloomed from a hobby he taught himself during his childhood into an award-winning origami-design business called Creased, Inc. He later attended Parsons with the intention of incorporating his origami skills into garment construction and fashion design.

Sok's book *Crease + Fold* was published by Random House and has been translated into three languages, and his origami work has been featured on numerous TV shows, including *America's Next Top Model* and *Extreme Home Makeover*. His work has also been included in magazines such as *Cosmopolitan*, *Elle*, *GQ*, *Harper's Bazaar*, *Icon*, *InStyle*, *L'Uomo*, *Marie Claire*, *Pop*, *Self*, *Vanity Fair*, and *Vogue*. Other notable clients include Condé Nast Publications Ltd., Harrods, Kenzo, Imitation of Christ, MOMA, Macy's, Paul Smith, Saks Fifth Avenue, The Museum of Art and Design, The American Museum of Natural History, and *The New Yorker*.

Sok currently lives in New York City, although his folding work takes him all over the world.

ACKNOWLEDGEMENTS

Special thanks to Alison Deering, editor, and Aruna Rangarajan, graphic designer, for their ideas, contributions, and encouragement! This book would not have been possible without them. Also thanks for the help, support, and inspiration from Rick Burkhardt, Alan Clark, Caitlin Decker, Oliver Ernhofer, Paul Frasco, Martha Glenn, Kally Han, Judy Heiblum, Ben Heisler, Alex Horwitz, Anna Ishida, Shrikant Iyer, Judes Kapner, Mark Kapner, Gary Lambert, Scott Marrone, Adrienne Sack, Daniel Schnorbus, Thomas Sirgedas, Justin Spring, Jenny Stephens, Kathryn Wagner, Petra Wehle, Jill Wendorff, Mark Wilson, and Alan Wise. Thanks to the meticulous diagram testers for their time and input: Linda Bogan, Ryan Dong, Judy Kapner, Matthew LaBoone, Heike Schröder, Kathleen Sheridan, Paula Versnick, Kathryn Wagner, and John Weiss. Finally, thanks to the Vermont Studio Center, where much of the planning and initial design for this book was done.

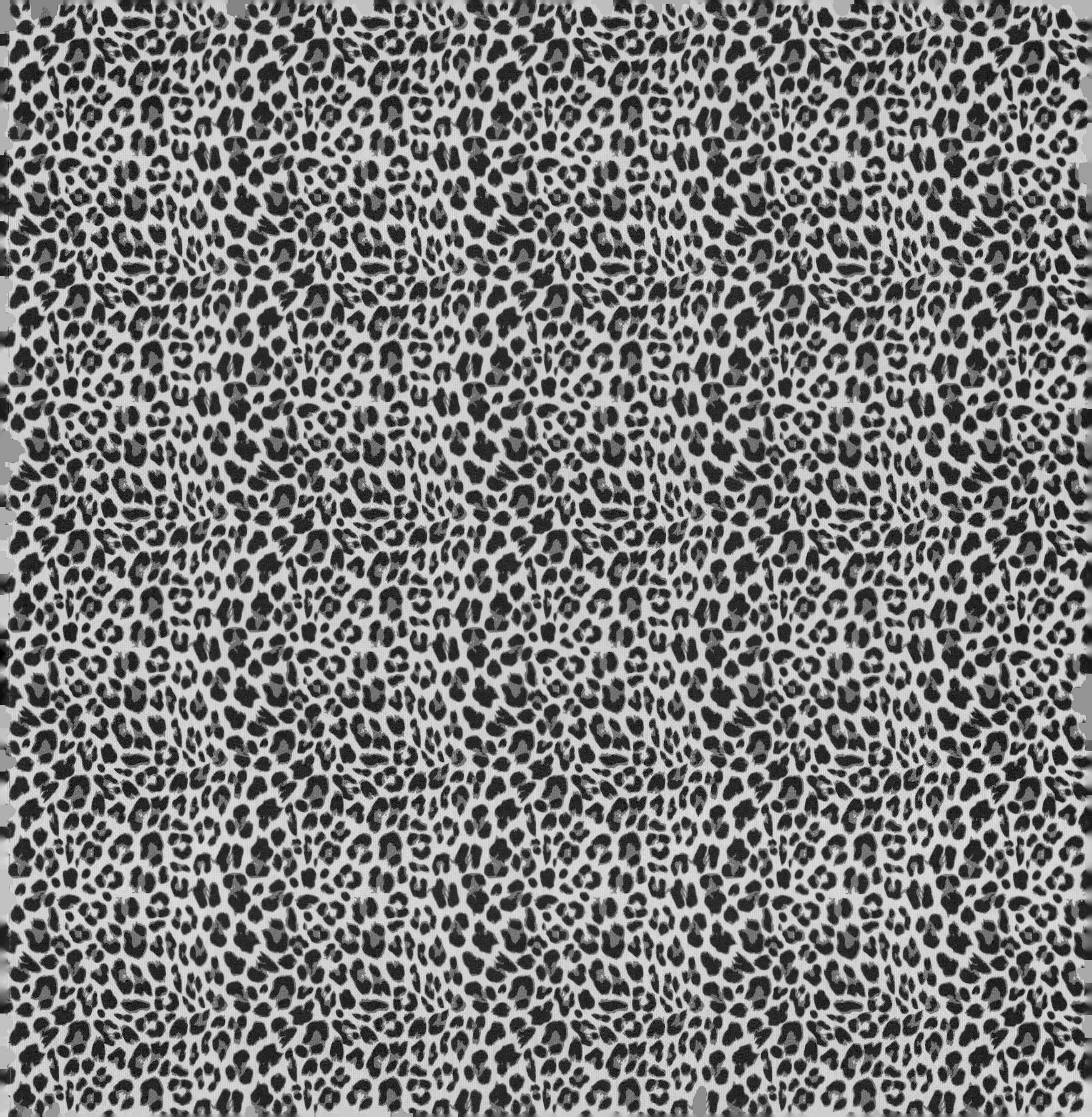

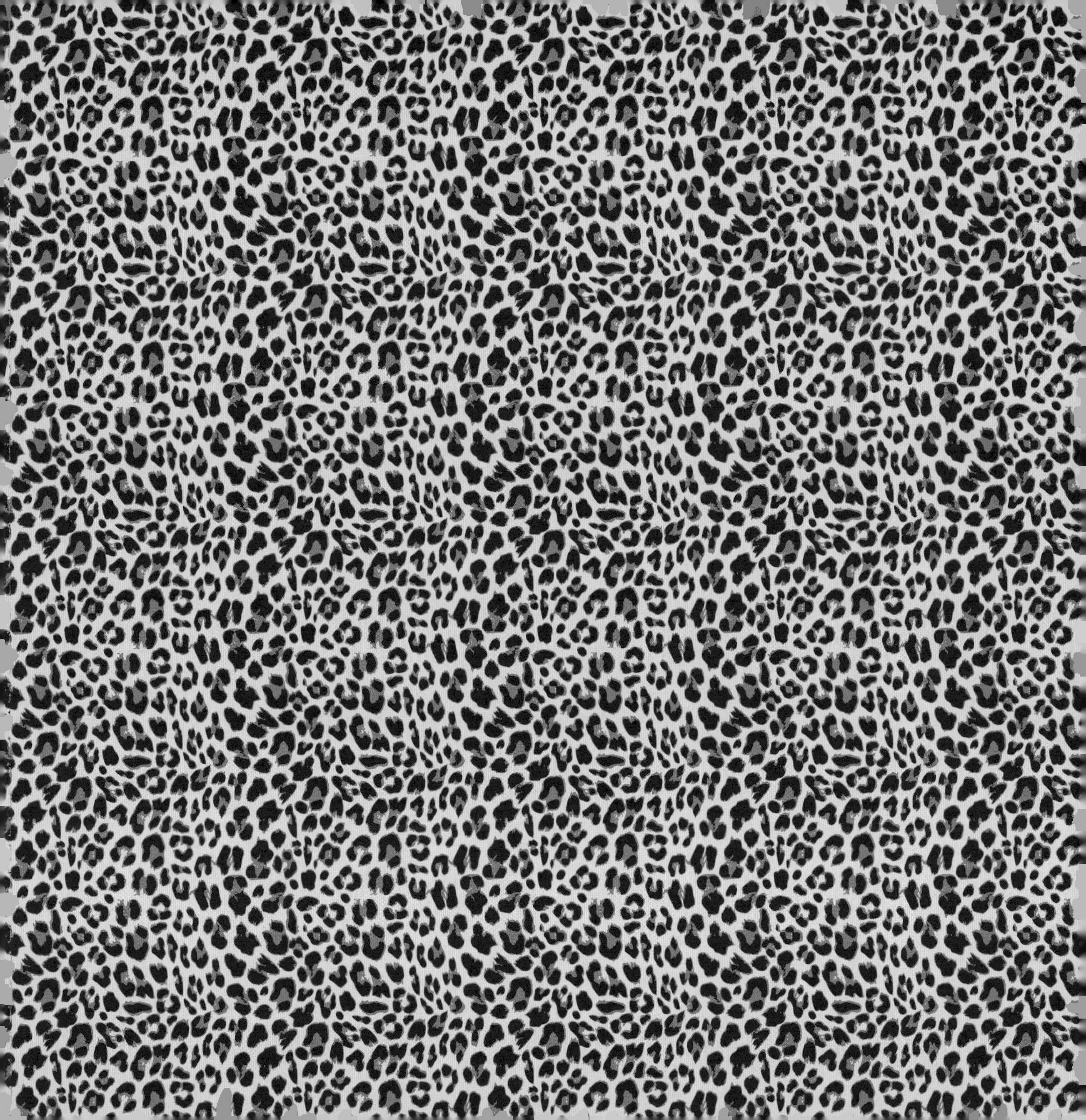

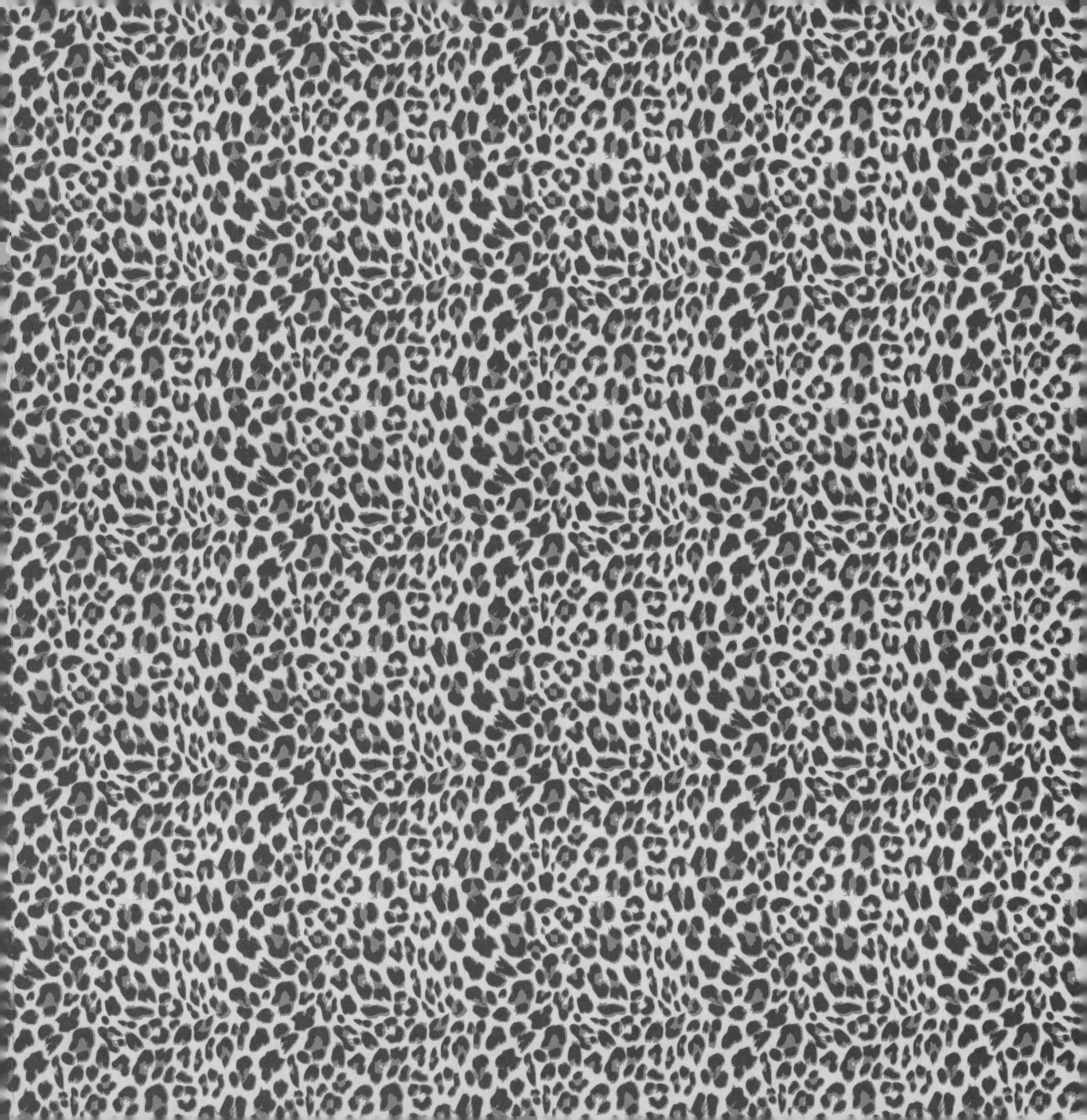

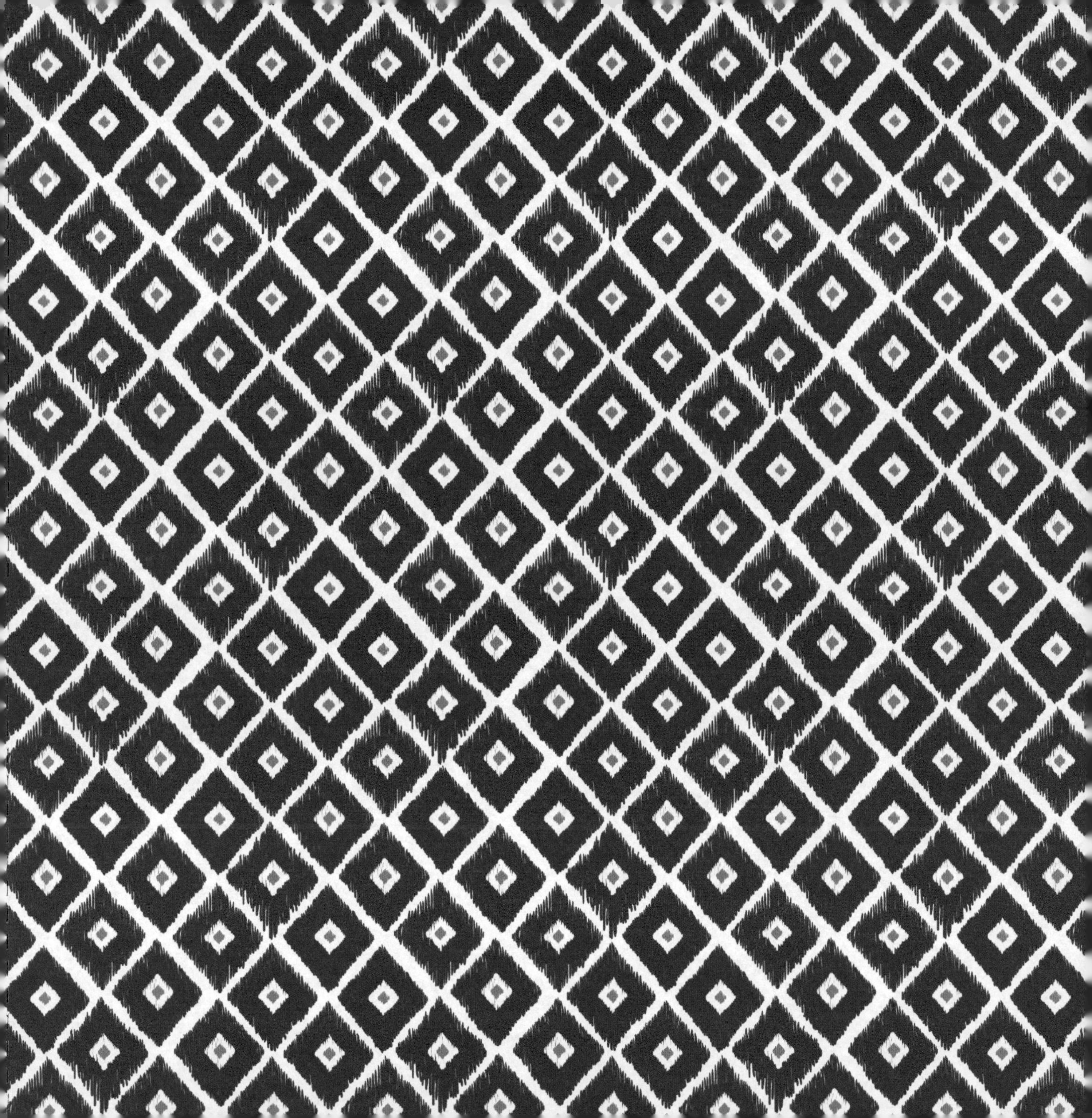

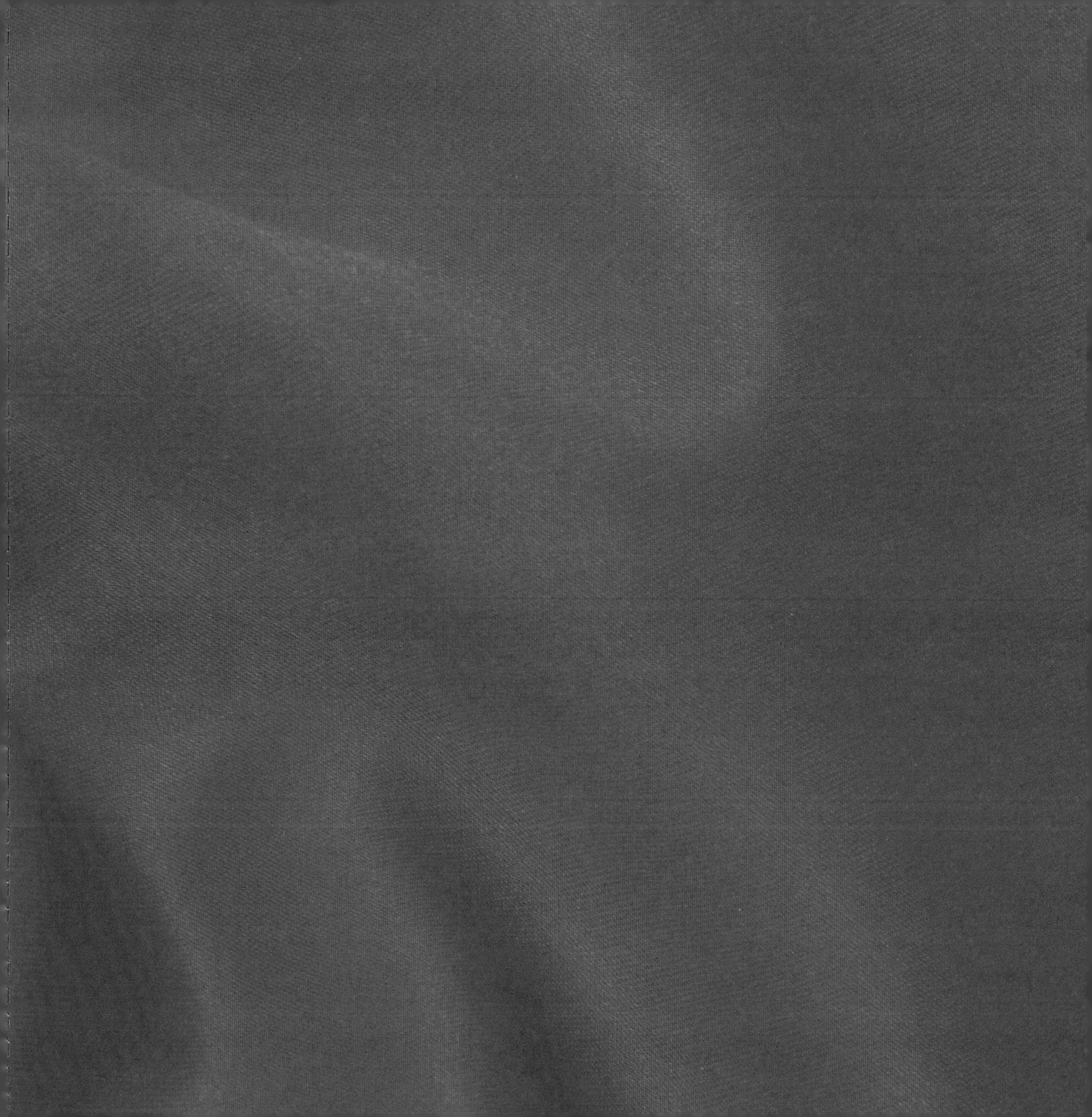

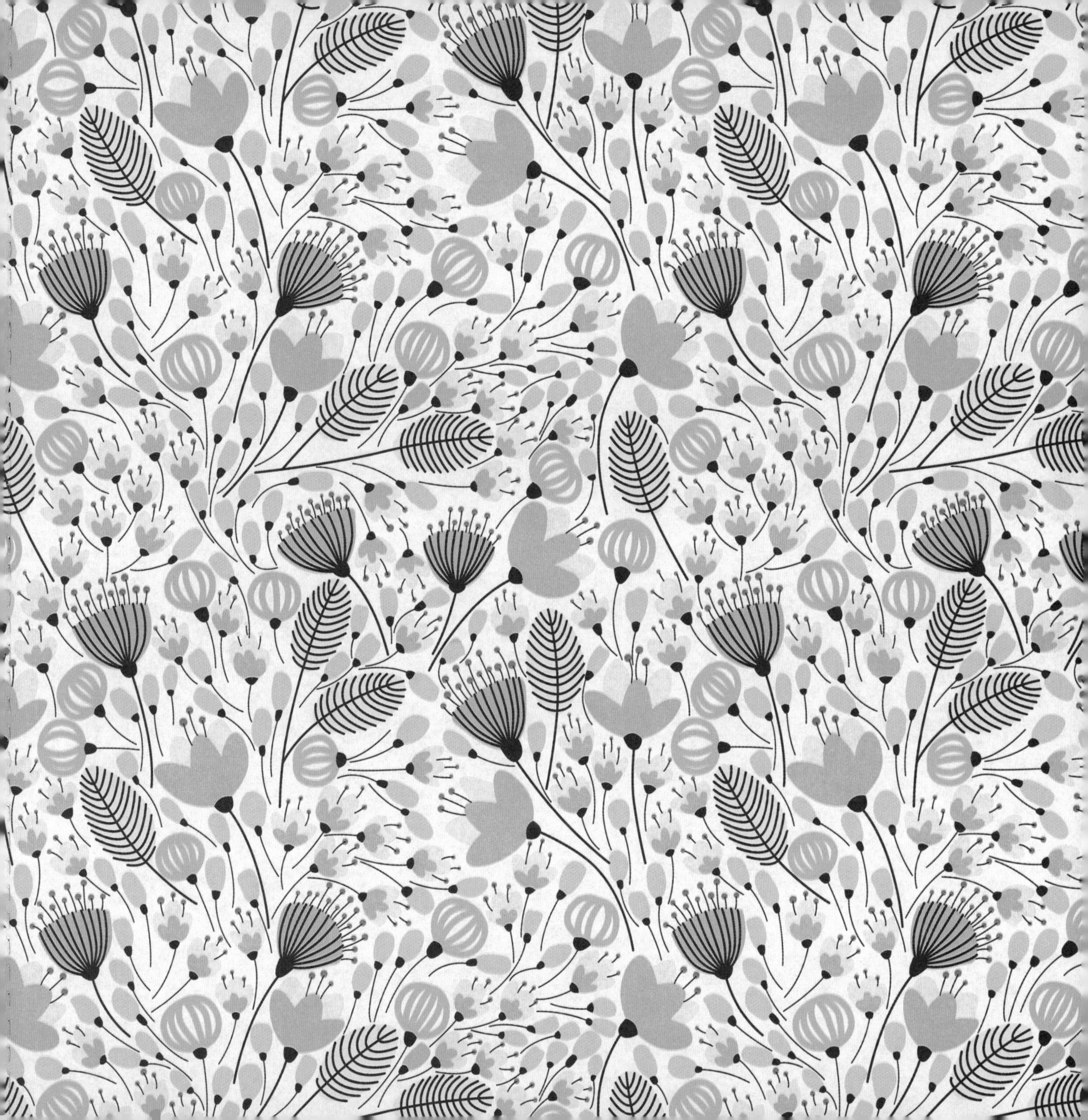

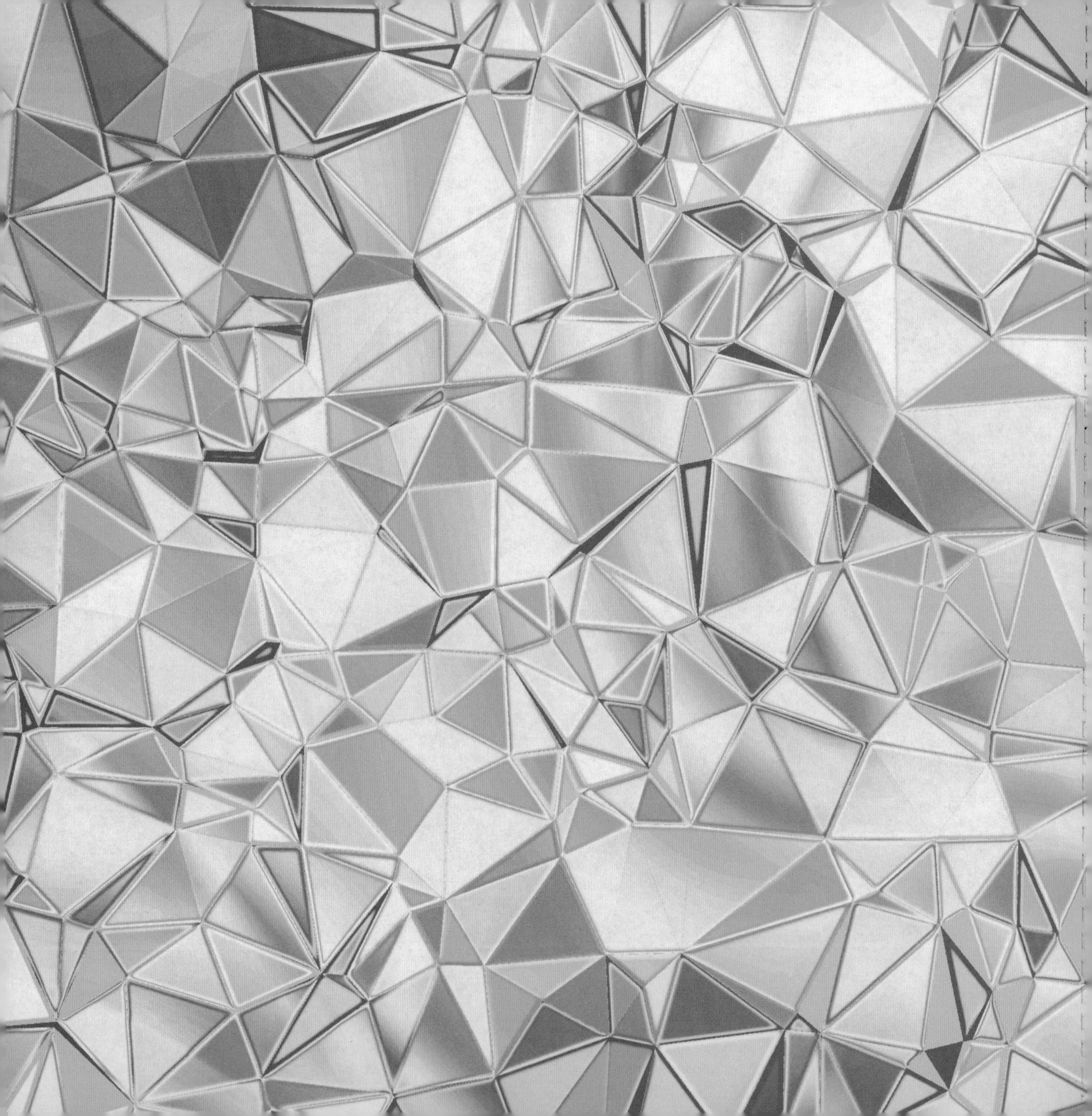

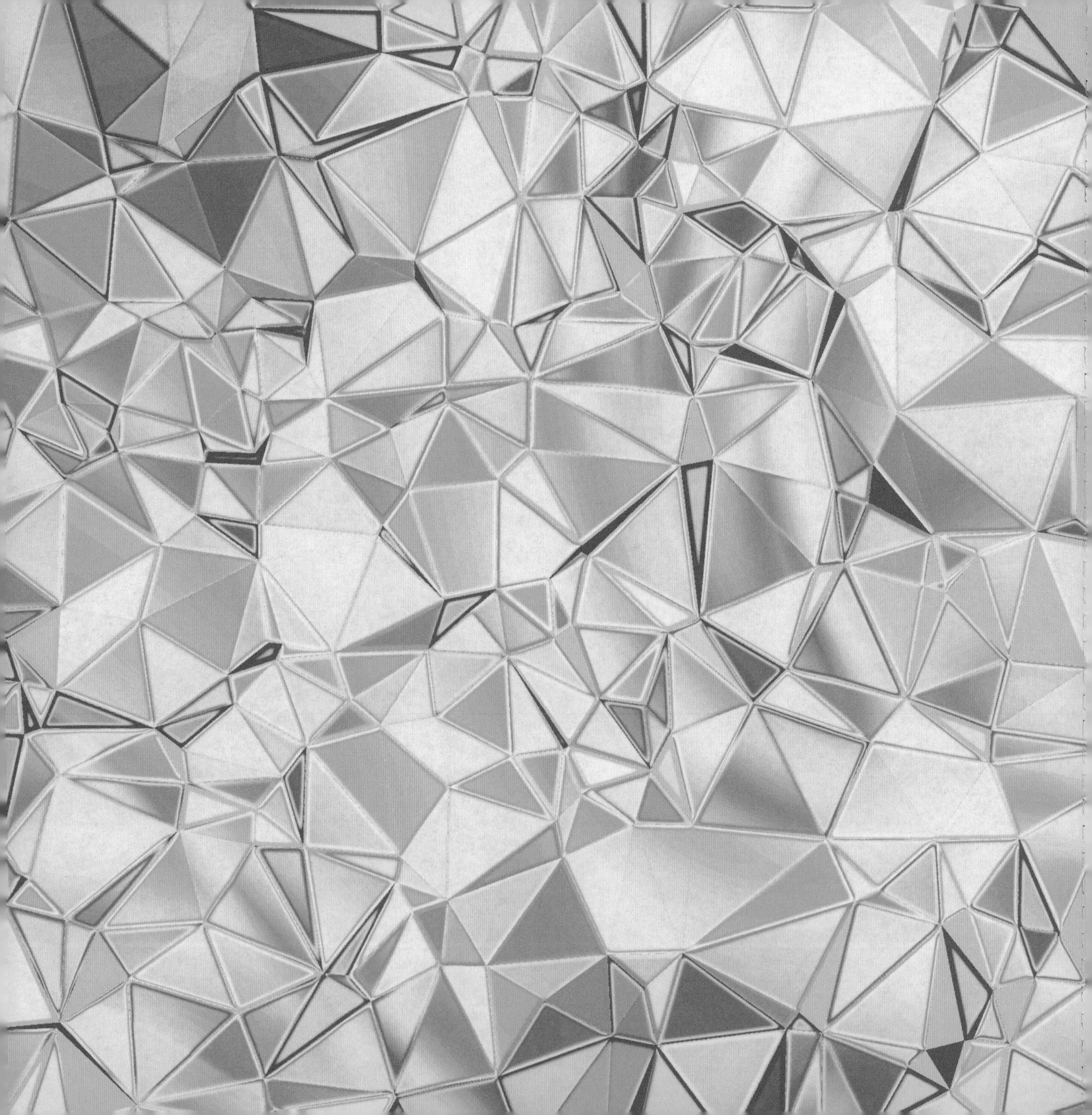